FIRESIDE

PARKSIDE

FIRESIDE ⚓ PARKSIDE BOOKS

Note to Readers

The case studies in this book come from many different sources. In all instances I have changed names and altered certain non-essential facts to protect the confidentiality of the individuals involved. When faced with several similar cases, I chose to present a single study combining elements of each case.

Compassionate Touch

THE ROLE OF HUMAN TOUCH
IN HEALING AND RECOVERY

by

Dr. Clyde W. Ford

A FIRESIDE/PARKSIDE BOOK
Published by Simon & Schuster
New York   London   Toronto   Sydney   Tokyo   Singapore

FIRESIDE/PARKSIDE
Simon & Schuster Building
Rockefeller Center
1230 Avenue of the Americas
New York, New York 10020

Designed by Crowded House Design
Manufactured in the United States of America

10   9   8   7   6   5   4   3   2   1

Library of Congress Cataloging-in-Publication Data

Ford, Clyde W.
    Compassionate touch: the role of human touch in healing and
recovery/by Clyde Ford.
        p.   cm.
    "A Fireside/Parkside recovery book."
    1. Touch—Therapeutic use. 2. Adult child abuse victims—
Rehabilitation. 3. Touch—Psychological aspects. 4. Emotions—
Physiological aspects. I. Title.
RC489.T69F67   1993
615.8'51—dc20   93–18287
                                                            CIP
ISBN: 0-671-75607-9

Parkside Medical Services Corporation is a full-service provider of
treatment for alcoholism, other drug addiction, eating disorders, and
psychiatric illness.

Parkside Medical Services Corporation
205 West Touhy Avenue
Park Ridge, IL 60068
1-800-PARKSIDE

*To my parents, Vivian and John,
who gave me my first experience
of compassionate touch.*

Contents

ACKNOWLEDGMENTS

For allowing me to participate in their journeys of healing and recovery I wish to thank the many men and women I have been privileged to work with over the years. They have truly been my greatest teachers.

I also acknowledge and thank: Terry Spohn, former editor at Parkside Press, who first encouraged this book and helped to bring it forth; Sara Skye Tucker, director of the Brigid Collins House, for reading and commenting on the sections of this book dealing with sexual abuse; John Small, publisher at Parkside, and Sheila Curry, the editor at Simon & Schuster.

I.

The Embodiment of
Healing and Recovery

*Our body is not limited to what lies inside the boundary of our skin . . .
There is no phenomenon in the universe that does not intimately concern us,
from a pebble resting at the bottom of the ocean, to the movement of a galaxy
millions of light years away.*
— Thich Nhat Hanh

Charlene was a forty-two-year-old successful business-woman with a charming smile and outgoing personality. She had come into my clinic complaining of lower back pain after a day of intense gardening. Seven years of practice had brought many similar cases. I anticipated a typical course of recovery lasting at most three to four weeks, but I was pleasantly surprised. After a week Charlene's pain had diminished substantially. She was able to walk comfortably and work a full day. After two weeks she was symptom-free.

But then a troubling pattern began to emerge. Every two weeks Charlene's lower back pain would reappear. She would return to my office puzzled, unable to pin her discomfort on any specific event. Physical examination never revealed any significant problems. While one or two treatment sessions would relieve her discomfort, it would return again in two weeks.

After several months of cycling through periods of pain and remission, both Charlene and I were frustrated. I questioned her about other stress in her life. She spoke of having marital problems but said she and her husband were in therapy. While this was an important source of stress, it was difficult to relate her marital discord to her lower back pain.

At our next session, I suggested a different approach. "Let's not try to get rid of the pain," I offered, "perhaps we can discover some meaning in it."

I began gently touching her lower back. I asked Charlene to focus on her awareness there and describe her sensations.

"I feel as if my lower back is a dark room," she replied. "I'm a little scared. There seems to be someone hiding in the corner of the room. She's afraid to come out."

I encouraged her to remain with the images and impressions emerging from her lower back. Charlene continued her story.

"There's a little girl in that room and she is afraid someone will hurt her," Charlene said in the voice of a small child. "Someone might come into the room and hurt her."

Charlene told the painful tale of sexual abuse perpetrated by a trusted uncle that lasted from her childhood through her early teenage years. She was very upset and surprised to find herself telling this story.

"It's as if a part of me knew this all along," she said sorrowfully. "But I didn't dare bring it into my awareness. Even in our marital therapy this has never come to light. The lower back pain was like a messenger who kept knocking at my door until I finally had to let her in."

Unlocking the Body's Messages

Charlene's body was the key to unlocking and opening that door. By doing so, she began a healing journey of recovery from sexual abuse. For the next three years I had the privilege of working with Charlene. At times her body offered vivid scenes of her abused childhood. Like a film library, various areas of Charlene's body appeared to store footage of her past. When touched, or when she became aware of these areas, a film clip might be replayed on the screen of her conscious mind.

At other times it appeared her body had recorded audio messages about her abuse, healing, and recovery. Often, touch would elicit these communiqués as though the replay button had been pressed on a tape recorder. Some were simple and direct pronouncements of the emotions—fear, anger, and powerlessness—that accompanied Charlene's abuse. Others told her what was needed to effect her healing and recovery: loving herself, realizing the abuse was not her fault, and eventually forgiving and getting on with her life.

Charlene's body led her through the cycle of healing and recovery. By revealing the story of abuse, Charlene's body moved her from denial to acceptance—a critical first step in the healing journey. Her body also assisted her in discovering the physical and emotional residue of the abuse—the many detrimental ways this trauma had affected her life. And her body gave her guidance in resolving the issues created by this trauma. Ultimately Charlene's body led her to forgiveness. In this final step of healing, Charlene did not simply absolve her uncle from responsibility for his actions, more important, she also released from her body and mind the anger, fear, guilt, and shame associated with his actions. This led to healthful physical and emotional changes for Charlene.

USING THE BODY TO HEAL

Initially some areas of Charlene's body were unavailable to her. For example, I once asked her to close her eyes and visualize her body from within. She could visualize her torso from her neck to her waist. However, try as she might she had little awareness of her body below the waist and above the neck. "It's like a black hole," she offered.

Charlene recalled times when she literally "turned off" areas of her body. Since she felt she could not physically protect herself from the abuse, vacating an area of her body was a mechanism she used to cope with the abuse. Many survivors of abuse report similar feelings of numbness or vacancy.

At the beginning of one session Charlene was aware of lower back pain. It felt like a knot or a ball of energy in the middle of her back, she said. Lower back pain often radiates into the legs.

I asked Charlene to close her eyes and become aware of the sensation in her legs. "I can't get to them," she informed me with alarm, "I can't find my legs inside of me."

She was quiet for several moments. The stress of not being able to connect with this area of her body seemed to push Charlene deeper within herself. Suddenly she emerged and blurted out, "I remember, I remember."

"I remember when I was about twelve years old," she recounted, "I couldn't protect myself with my legs, so I told them [her legs] to go away. It's as if my mind turned off my legs because they couldn't protect me anymore."

I asked Charlene to talk with her legs. She tried to discover the feelings they had held all these years. "They're feeling very guilty," she reported, "they're feeling they should have been able to protect me. They're feeling they don't deserve to belong to me because they failed me." She cried upon realizing why her legs were unavailable to her. She also realized the source of the feelings she had about her legs. "I've never liked them," she stated, "particularly my thighs. I've always felt angry at this area of my body."

Eventually there came a time for healing and forgiveness. "I know it wasn't your fault," Charlene said directly to her legs, "you're not to blame. You did your best, and by turning off, you even helped me survive. Now you need to know that I can protect all of us and I want you to be a part of me again."

Charlene was ready to reclaim this area of her body. I asked her to lightly place her hands on top of her legs and just observe what happened. Her awareness was immediately drawn to the small of her back. "The pain in my back is getting worse," she declared, "the ball of energy is throbbing. I don't know what to do with it." I reassured her to simply keep her hands where they were and continue to observe. It was not too long before this ball of energy broke open and released its contents. "I feel warmth flowing down my back," Charlene reported, "and from there into my legs." "Oh," she exclaimed, "they feel alive."

In ways like this we touched and helped to heal the wounded child within Charlene. Sexual abuse is devastating at any age. For a young child emerging into her own sense of individuality, sexual abuse is particularly destructive. One message of abuse is that normal boundaries of body and mind are not sacred. They can be violated at will. The world is no longer a safe place. Physical and psychological growth are often arrested. The child within is frozen by this trauma. Working with the body is a way to help this inner child grow and heal.

At one point in her therapy Charlene realized that she had walked around crouched for years. "I have been walking around trying to be invisible," she observed. "I was afraid someone might see me and that posed too great a threat." So she explored new ways of walking, moving, and using her body. Ultimately, Charlene came to feel comfortable about reinhabiting her body. This allowed her to take huge strides in recovering those parts of the psyche and soul given up to the abuse. Abuse survivors have been dispossessed of their bodies and must repossess them to heal and recover. This is not a process that occurs intellectually. Survivors often *feel* the consequences of their abuse. These feelings are not abstract concepts, they are experienced through the body. Likewise, healing from abuse must also occur at this feeling level of the body.

THE WISDOM OF THE BODY

From journeys like Charlene's I have come to respect the tremendous wisdom and compassion that reside within our body—useful and powerful tools for healing and recovery. The body is a road map for the journey of healing and recovery. It can tell us where we have been, where we are, where we need to go, and how best to get there. I have been on many similar journeys with courageous men and women like Charlene. Although each traveler's journey was unique there were many common threads. My intent in these pages is to weave these common threads into a tapestry enabling us to understand and work with the human body in healing and recovery from physical, emotional, and spiritual trauma.

I was first trained as a chiropractor, a practitioner who works with his hands. The human body and human touch have been central to my work in the healing arts. When I began my career I often saw people with chronic physical problems. Some of these individuals responded only marginally to my care. I tended to write them off and concentrate on those I could help.

But on many occasions those who failed to respond to my care told me of other sensations from being touched. They would report strange alterations in perception: "It felt as if time stood still, and this hour-long visit lasted only twenty minutes"; "Funny, I knew exactly where you were about to touch me, before I felt you there"; "The dividing line between your hand and my skin became blurred, I couldn't tell where one stopped and the other began"; "I wasn't asleep but I didn't feel awake either, I was in a halfway state somewhere in between"; or "I felt as if I was floating, hovering above the table watching everything take place."

Others described rich visual or auditory images while being touched: "As you touched that painful area I saw myself walking on a dry desert looking for water"; "The pain felt as if someone was holding a knife in me"; "I could hear that part of my body asking to be set free"; "I felt there was a straitjacket around my rib cage"; "My arm said let go, let go"; or "When that area is touched I see a wolf about to devour me."

Often, emotions simply surfaced during touch: "There is so much sadness connected with that area"; "How happy this part is to be cared for"; "This tension is a way of holding back my anger"; "I'm scared and this area reflects that"; or "My chest aches with the pain of my loss and grief."

While I accepted these experiences reported by my clients, I had no idea what to do with them. More than just reflections on the body, these were messages from some deeper place of heart and soul. Somehow, touch had opened a doorway beyond normal awareness. And beneath their chronic pain were chronic unresolved feelings. These feelings could emerge through the body in unexpected and novel ways. Our body remembers without censoring. Our conscious mind often edits, filters, and selects what we retain.

After several years of additional training in psychotherapy I actively sought ways of combining my experience with body and mind. I asked myself, "How do you help people work with emotions through their body?" My particular interest lay in discovering ways of using touch rather than talk to accomplish this. After all touch is the language of the body.

THE BODY'S ROLE IN EMOTIONAL HEALING

Much of my clinical experience comes from working with adult survivors of childhood sexual abuse. But the lessons learned about the body's role in healing and recovery are applicable well beyond this specific issue. I have applied what I have learned from working with these individuals with equal success to a wide range of circumstances. Whether it is treating a chronic muscle strain, recovery from addictions, healing from dysfunctional relationships, or attempting to find greater meaning and purpose in one's life or death, the body should not be ignored. Our bodies can be our greatest ally or toughest adversary in the process of healing and recovery. There are effective ways to enlist the body's aid through touch, movement, and awareness.

Too often, however, we pursue half solutions to healing and recovery. While the body is both the instrument and object of sexual and physical abuse, we primarily treat abusers and survivors with various forms of talk therapy. This is a half solution because the body does not have a central role in the recovery process.

On numerous occasions I have reminded therapists that sexual abuse frequently begins before a child has the mental and muscular skills needed to speak. At this age we primarily relate to the world through our bodies—touch is the principal mode of communication, talk is secondary. A child's reaction to abuse at this age has a definite bodily component. Unable to defend itself verbally or physically, the child's body absorbs the physical and emotional insult of abuse. Unable to integrate or make any sense of the experience mentally, the child's body attempts to come to terms with the abuse and help the child survive the trauma.

Years later, when evidence of the abuse surfaces, how can we ignore the body's role in the healing process? After all, the body was intimately involved in the original trauma. I believe these feelings and memories can be best accessed through the body, and that talking is often the least effective or meaningful way of reaching these stored experiences. Touch and movement—the body's native language—can be powerful therapeutic tools in recovery and healing.

MOVING BEYOND VERBAL THERAPY

I suspect that many people seek out hands-on practitioners—chiropractors, physical therapists, massage therapists, and other bodyworkers—in response to unconscious forces impelling their bodies into the healing and recovery process. Their initial complaint may be strictly physical: an ache or pain, a sprain, or a strain. They may have no conscious awareness of any deeper emotional or psychological trauma in their lives. But they are eventually touched by the practitioner in a way that brings these deeper issues to the surface.

What happens next? Standard procedure would have the hands-on practitioner refer this person to a competent psychotherapist, which is often exactly the right thing to do. But standard procedure isn't always possible or desirable. Sometimes a competent psychotherapist is already involved. The client may experience such a deep emotional catharsis that waiting to see a psychotherapist is inappropriate. Often the client's point of discovery cannot be recreated through talking.

Fortunately there are ways of bypassing talk and speaking directly to the body in a language it understands. Touch, like talk, can be a therapeutic language. Body therapists do not have to become psychotherapists to help people with emotions expressed through the body. But body therapists and psychotherapists do need to understand the importance of the body in working with emotional and psychological experience.

HEALING BODY AND MIND

At a certain point I discovered I could no longer fragment my approach to treatment. If I just treated physical symptoms without attending to related emotional and psychological issues, then the unresolved emotions had every potential to recreate additional physical symptoms. Likewise, just talking about emotional issues without attending to the expression of those emotions in the body allowed unresolved physical conditions to recreate further emotional unrest. Both body and mind had to be brought together in treatment.

Psychosomatic medicine, mind-body healing, is taken seriously today, though this was not always the case. Many approaches to healing and recovery utilize techniques like meditation, guided imagery, visualization, hypnosis, self-hypnosis, autosuggestion, and affirmation. Fortunately even scientific researchers have now come to some preliminary understanding of how such psychosomatic techniques work. Mind-body healing is just what it says: the mind's role in healing the body. Hence, mind-body healing techniques focus on the mind's relationship to the body. But there is another way to look at the coming together of body and mind, and that is to study the body's role in healing and recovery. The approaches to healing and recovery presented in this book focus on the body first.

Instead of asking how a particular thought, feeling, or image affects the body, we'll explore how a particular body sensation helps us understand a deeper emotional or psychological issue. Instead of considering anger or grief abstractly, for example, we'll investigate our body awareness of these emotions. Instead of talking about the creation of boundaries, we'll embody the creation of boundaries through touch and movement. The idea behind this type of work is straightforward: To heal and recover we need to ground emotional experience in the body, and we need to unearth the emotional and psychological issues beneath physical sensation. In either case the body is the focus of the therapeutic work.

THE BODY: AN EMOTIONAL CRUCIBLE

Perhaps the most important reason for focusing on the body in healing and recovery is that our body is the crucible of our emotional experience. Early emotional life is physical, not verbal. We learn by being handled. Bonding, separating, feelings, and needs and their fulfillment are first experienced through the body. How, when, and why we are picked up, put down, held close, or pushed away determine the quality of our early emotional existence.

What we learn then, for better or worse, forms the template of our subsequent emotional life. What we learn then governs the functional and dysfunctional patterns of our relationships as children, adults, and parents. What we learn then provides us the personal resources to lead a meaningful life and the personal challenges we face in that life. And what we learn then, we learn through our body.

Later in life, when we are faced with healing and recovery from emotional trauma, we can return to this earliest classroom. Here is an opportunity to rediscover what was taught well, and to relearn the lessons given poorly. This rediscovery and relearning need to take place through the body. Touch, movement, and body awareness are the teaching tools we can use.

There are other reasons for assigning the body a central role in healing and recovery. We each use different sensory channels to process our life's experiences. Some people are more verbal and auditory, others primarily visual, and still others tactile or kinesthetic. When we confine emotional experience to only one channel we limit ourselves.

If we deal with emotions through talk, then language becomes a limitation. It becomes essential that everyone we talk to speaks the same language with all the subtleties, nuances, and idioms commonly understood. Touch and movement, on the other hand, are more universal. A hug or smile requires no verbal translation. They have a similar meaning whether given in New York, New Delhi, or New Guinea. And we could dance equally well to music in Paris, Rome, or Soweto even if we do not understand the lyrics. The rhythm and movement of our bodies are a kinesthetic way of experiencing the music.

Dealing with emotions through mental images is also limiting. Try to translate an abstract feeling like anger into a concrete mental image. Most people simply end up "seeing" the events—the people, situations, interactions—that caused the anger. While that may reinforce why the anger exists, it is certainly not an image of the anger itself. It doesn't necessarily help us understand how we are affected by the anger. But something very different happens when we focus on the body first. When we become aware of anger we could stop and first ask ourselves, "What sensations am I experiencing in my body right now?" After tuning in to our feelings we might notice tightness, tingling, or pain in some area of the body. That is a concrete representation of how we are being affected by the anger.

BODY AWARENESS AND EMOTIONS

Simply being aware of the physical manifestations of emotional experience is sometimes enough to change the quality of that experience. Just watching physical pain rise and fall, for example, can help us deal with the anger behind that pain. We needn't say a word. At other times there may be a way of touching or moving the affected area of the body to alter the physical sensation and thereby shift the related emotional experience.

Jane's case is an example of using simple movement to work with emotional experience. She was a thirty-six-year-old elementary school teacher who first saw me for treatment of her anxiety attacks. This day she was obviously agitated. She couldn't sit still and her conversation raced from topic to topic. I asked her to take a few slow breaths but that helped only temporarily.

"OK," I said, "then really let yourself be with the anger. Stand up with your eyes closed. Once you really feel the anger throughout your body, start to walk around like that."

She stood up and paused long enough to get in touch with her anger. Then she began to pace around the room with long strides, wearing an evil look and displaying a "don't mess with me" attitude. I let her go on like this for several minutes and then asked her to stop. "What did it feel like to move in your anger?" I asked.

She didn't say a word. But she began laughing, so hard and

so long it became contagious and I started to laugh as well. We both laughed so hard that we couldn't speak for several minutes. Finally Jane composed herself and broke the silence.

"I get it," she exclaimed. "I get it. Here I am angry because I've done so much personal growth work yet I still can't find a suitable partner. But I'm walking around with a posture that would back off any sane person."

"OK," I suggested, still smiling, "now walk around in a way that doesn't back people off." Jane took a moment to envision that and then began walking with a much lighter cadence.

"My body feels different when I walk that way," she remarked. "I feel lighter and happy, more the person I know myself to be. I also feel more like a person I'd like to attract into my life."

AN INTEGRATED APPROACH TO HEALING AND RECOVERY

Many different names have been given to therapy done with the body and emotions. In my book *Where Healing Waters Meet*, I coined the term *somatosynthesis* to describe this type of therapy. I envisioned the body (soma) as a vehicle to integrate (synthesize) the physical, psychological, and spiritual dimensions of our journey of healing and recovery. Others have used names like bioenergetics, core energetics, body-centered psychotherapy, somatic psychology, somatoemotional release, emotional-kinesthetic psychotherapy, and synergy. This book extends the ideas presented in *Where Healing Waters Meet*. In addition to somatosynthesis I will often use the term *somatoemotional therapy* to describe this integrated approach to physical and emotional healing. Either term—somatosynthesis or somatoemotional therapy—refers to body-based therapy that simultaneously addresses emotional and psychological issues. The main idea is that this therapy is principally somatic—centered on the body through touch, movement, or body awareness.

Most approaches to healing and recovery emphasize the need to "feel feelings" and these oft-spoken words point directly to the body. Feeling has two meanings: (1) to be aware of emotional experience and (2) to sense through the skin and body. So "feeling our feelings" means more than just "expressing our emotions." It also means sensing emotions through our body. In somatoemotional therapy we use the body as a doorway to feelings. This can be a surprisingly direct route. What might take many sessions of traditional talk therapy can be accomplished in only a few sessions of somatoemotional therapy.

Somatosynthesis is not just for survivors of abuse. It can play a role in healing and recovery for us all. None of us came through childhood unscathed. Most of us have some wounds and scars from growing up in dysfunctional families. The same observation made earlier about survivors of abuse applies to us all: Our earliest emotional experiences, both good and bad, occurred first through our bodies. Only later did we process emotions mentally. What we learned through our bodies as children became the foundation of our emotional life beyond childhood. The stuff of life—personal relationships, family, work, health, life transitions—is laden with emotions. How do we cope? Normally, we manage our emotions mentally. Very rarely do we incorporate the body into this process. Somatosynthesis seeks to correct this. Although this book places special emphasis on abuse and more severe dysfunction, it is really about the benefits for all of us when we welcome our bodies into our life's journey of healing and recovery.

CONTROVERSY IN RECOVERY: THE ROLE OF TOUCH AND THE BODY

Somatoemotional therapy is controversial. Some would dispute the body's role in healing and recovery, particularly with survivors of physical and sexual abuse. I remember the account of one woman who participated in a workshop for sexual abuse survivors. She informed me that throughout the workshop chairs were kept a required eighteen inches apart. This supposedly emphasized the need for participants to avoid being touched inadvertently by each other. It was meant to underscore the necessity of creating safe physical boundaries.

Similar distance is maintained between therapists and clients in traditional psychotherapy where there has long been a touch taboo. It is believed that touch enhances feelings of sexual attraction between therapist and client, thereby derailing successful therapy. This belief is voiced even more loudly with abuse survivors in therapy. Here the notion is that touch reenacts the original abusive trauma and this damages the course of successful therapy. There is a measure of truth in all this, although I feel that excluding the body and touch from therapy is wrong. Since this book deals so directly with the body and with touch we'll examine this controversy further.

BOUNDARIES AND THE BODY

A major tragedy of sexual and physical abuse is that it strips away the body's boundaries. Many survivors of abuse, and many other people struggling with dysfunction, have difficulty creating and maintaining physical and psychological boundaries. Touching an abuse survivor might seem to reinforce this lack of boundaries and the powerlessness resulting from the original trauma. But boundaries are created through interaction, not isolation. Touch can be as effective in creating boundaries as it is in removing them. As we'll see in later chapters, we first learn to create boundaries through our bodies and through touch. When we need to relearn these skills, we can and should return to the body again.

Touching an abuse survivor does have every possibility of bringing to the surface the emotional forces related to that abuse. This can be a very important part of the healing process when safety has been built into a therapeutic relationship, when appropriate boundaries between therapist and client have been established, and when an atmosphere of concern and compassion is present.

I began *Where Healing Waters Meet* with the story of a woman I saw for a routine physical examination. During the course of the examination I needed to touch her legs, and upon doing so she painfully began to recall an incest experience at the hands of her father. She had not come to see me for this, nor had

I planned to embark on such a course of discovery with her. To her great surprise she became aware that this issue was still very much alive and unresolved, even though she had been in therapy for more than fifteen years. Of course, I was surprised that touch could evoke so much so quickly. It was this incident that caused me to explore further the role of touch and emotional recall.

TOUCH AND EMOTIONAL RECALL

Emotional recall is a normal part of healing and recovery. Touch is a very useful tool because touch can recall past emotional experience. The issue is how to work with emotions through touch, rather than avoiding touch because it elicits emotions. One fascinating aspect of human touch is that it is our only reciprocal sense. You can see without being seen, hear without being heard, taste without being tasted, and smell without being smelled. But you cannot touch without being touched. It is this very reciprocity that makes touch so controversial in psychotherapy.

We are taught as psychotherapists about two important forces driving the therapeutic interchange between us and our clients. One force has to do with the client's issues that are projected onto the therapist. For example, when the woman I touched during an examination recalled her incest experience she was, in effect, projecting onto me some aspect of her father who abused her. In psychological terms we call this *transference*. A second force deals with the therapist's issues that are stimulated by, and then projected back onto the client. A client might say to me, "Doctor, I don't know what to do will you help me?" If I believe myself to be the client's rescuer I might step into that situation and take over from my client. I might tell him exactly what I feel he should do. Being a rescuer, however, is my issue and not the client's. The psychological term for this second force is *countertransference*.

Neither of these two forces are bad, and both are expected to emerge during therapy. In fact, good therapists know how to use them to further the process of healing and recovery. Touch, by virtue of being reciprocal, enhances these projections between client and therapist. Touching a client will evoke certain emotional responses. But by touching my clients, I'm also being touched by them. Therefore, I, too, am subject to experiencing emotional issues arising through my body. This is unavoidably true not just between therapist and client but whenever we touch another human being.

Can touch evoke sexual attraction between therapist and client? Yes, but that's not the point. Touch can evoke a range of emotional issues between therapist and client, and sexuality is just one. Once again the real concern should be the skillful use of the issues elicited through touch, and not the avoidance of touch because it elicits such issues.

In my workshops and seminars I often pose the following question: Is a hug good for everyone? It is a way of focusing attention on the idea that we often go to extremes with touching: Either we feel touch should be strictly avoided, or that everyone should be touched. With an abuse survivor, for example, even a hug isn't always good. When least expected, a hug can be the most healing gesture in the world. At other times it can be the worst thing possible for those with a history of being touched when they least expect or desire it. Skillfully using touch means knowing when to touch and when not to touch as well.

Using touch to bring the body into healing and recovery requires care, concern, and compassion on the part of professional and nonprofessional caregivers. Later I'll describe a protocol called Safe Touch, which lays out the steps for safely introducing touch into healing and recovery. The concerns raised by those who caution against touch can be honored even when touch is used to further the healing process.

We do not always need to touch to work with the body. Movement and body-awareness are two other important methods of bringing the body into healing and recovery. One benefit is that neither body-awareness nor movement requires another person—we can do them on our own. This alleviates many of the concerns raised by touching. Movement and body-awareness can also be enhanced by incorporating self-touch. Many of the exercises in this book can be done alone, if needed, using self-touch, body-awareness, and movement.

These three methods are useful but they alone are not sufficient. Healing and recovery require that we move beyond dysfunctional relationships and learn to develop and sustain healthy relationships with ourselves and with others. Being in relationships with others requires that we are in contact with them physically, emotionally, and spiritually. We first learned about being in relationships through our bodies and through touch. And we can return to human touch when we need to rediscover and relearn the meaning of being in a relationship. For these reasons touch is an important therapeutic tool in the healing and recovery process. We needn't be afraid when traumatic emotional issues are raised through touch. We simply need to learn what to do when they surface.

TOUCHING MIND AND EMOTION THROUGH THE BODY

Under the right circumstances, touch can send a message that it is all right to recall and release long-held physical and emotional pain. Consider the stories of Adele and Elizabeth, two women I met in one of my workshops. Adele was a woman in her midfifties. She stood out from the other sixty workshop participants because of her brash style. Throughout the beginning of the workshop it seemed that nothing I could do or say was satisfactory for Adele, and she glared at me when I walked among the group during supervised practice sessions.

At the end of the second day I walked past a table where Adele lay on her back during her partner's temporary absence from the classroom. In a strident tone she said, "My lower back is hurting! Can you help?" Since the class was practicing how to release tension in the lower back and pelvis I suggested using those techniques to help with her pain. Normally I would have asked her partner to do this but she had no partner at that moment. I decided to step in feeling it also might be a way to lessen the tension I felt between us. With one hand placed just below the small of her back, I gently rested my other hand over her lower abdomen. Using a barely perceptible amount of compression, I waited to feel Adele's muscles and other soft tissue relax and let go. This was the technique the rest of the class was practicing as well.

After a few minutes her body began to move between my hands, slowly at first and then much more vigorously. Her legs, which had been stretched out together along the table, raised quickly so that her feet were flat on the table, close into her body and spread apart. Adele started breathing erratically, sweating profusely, contracting her abdomen hard against my hands and sounding loud gasps of pain. It was pretty obvious that she was reenacting the experience of giving birth.

In the meantime Adele's partner had returned. I dispatched her to Adele's head and shoulders for support while I continued to hold Adele and instructed her to breathe regularly and push. In effect we conducted a Lamaze birth without a real child being born. What was born, however, was the real cause of Adele's deep-seated anger. In gasps of air between contractions Adele narrated a story of the actual birth of her daughter twenty years earlier.

"My contractions had started," she said, "but things weren't moving fast enough for the doctor. He told me he didn't feel he could wait. He had something else to do that day and had to leave shortly. He wanted to induce labor and give me anesthesia."

Adele had joyfully awaited the natural birth of her child, so the doctor's suggestions came as a blow. "I was in so much pain," she remembered, "that I didn't have the strength to argue with him. I agreed and they began injecting me with anesthesia. But something went wrong and the needle punctured my spinal cord. I went into a coma and the last words I remember hearing from the doctor were 'Oops, I think we're losing her.'" With that Adele lost consciousness for nearly twenty-four hours and awoke to find herself in a different hospital bed unaware of what had been done with her baby.

"I didn't know where my baby was," she continued, "I didn't know what had happened. I had almost died. I was scared and angry. Even though my baby was eventually returned to me I felt as though I had missed her birth, missed bonding with her immediately. From all the trauma I was also never able to nurse her. I felt abused by that doctor and I think I've hated most men ever since!" While most of the class was now looking in our direction, another saga unfolded across the room.

A woman named Elizabeth heard Adele's birthing sounds, and her body also assumed a birthing position. She too began to breathe, push against her partner, and cry out. Adele was far enough along so I could leave her in the hands of her partner and rush over to this second simulated birth. Again I had Elizabeth's partner hold her shoulders while I coached her along. Finally both Adele and Elizabeth completed the birth, and the entire class gave a collective sigh of relief. We sat around as a group for fifteen or twenty minutes, unable to say anything, amazed, humbled, and awed by what we had just witnessed.

While the actual birthing experience of both women was different, they shared the common fact of being placed under anesthesia. They were denied the physical experience of the birth. Even twenty years later, their bodies could recall the physical sensations and emotions unavailable to them while their children were being born. The reenactment helped them recapture what was missed during the birth, and release the hurtful feelings held onto over the years.

THE BIRTH OF EMOTIONS

Why and how are emotions experienced so profoundly through touching the body? One answer to this question begins even prior to birth, barely two weeks into life, at a time when the human embryo resembles a tiny plate, two millimeters long, with a groove down the middle. This plate is poised on the verge of great change. On either side of the central groove, ridges are about to push up as though a volcanic eruption were causing a new mountain range to form along a river canyon.

These ridges, called the neural crest and the valley between them, the neural groove, are part of a layer of the embryo called the ectoderm (see Figure 1.1).

Neural crest cells eventually give rise to the skin and a majority of the brain and nervous system. In other words, the structures that allow us to feel sensation (the skin and receptors for touch) and the structures that allow us to experience emotions arise from the same group of cells. Feeling, as in sensation, and feeling, as in emotional experience, share a common heritage in the body. This relationship between body and emotion continues after birth.

When we're experiencing emotions we usually speak about what we're feeling. Therein lies the reason for the double meaning of the word feeling. All emotional experience is tied to changes taking place in our body, and our awareness of these bodily changes informs us about the emotions that are present. We actually do feel physical sensation as we experience the feelings we call emotion.

Look at the physical changes that accompany anger. We might first notice our breathing becoming rapid and more shallow. Muscles in our throat, neck, back, and face stiffen. Changes in circulation take place as some blood vessels dilate and others constrict. The small muscles that control our body hair will contract and cause our hair to stand on end. More subtle changes take place as well. The production and secretion of certain hormones and chemicals changes. These hormones affect the function of our organs and influence the activity of the nervous system, which in turn causes many of the other changes noted previously.

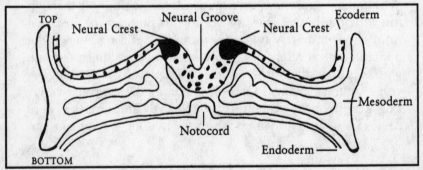

Figure 1.1
Section through an embryo showing neural groove and neural crest

The Bodily Basis of Emotions

Emotional experience is built upon the awareness of changes taking place in our body. Figure 1.2 is a schematic representation of how this occurs. Bodily events are all the changes taking place at the onset of an emotional experience—neurological changes, muscular changes, circulatory changes, and biochemical changes.

Individual events may happen beneath our threshold of awareness, but together these events mount until we can feel change within our bodies. One way of describing our feelings then is our awareness of bodily change. Over time each of us accumulates a backlog of life experiences associated with our awareness of particular feelings, and this forms our unique emotional nature.

It is impossible to separate body and emotions. "A disembodied human emotion," observed William James, father of modern psychology, "is a sheer nonentity." Although we normally think our mind stores and recalls emotional experience, our body may have a more important role in this process. "Our natural way of thinking about these emotions," James continued, "is that the mental perception . . . gives rise to bodily expression. My theory, on the contrary, is that the bodily changes follow directly the perception . . . and that our feeling of the same changes as they occur is the emotion. . . . We feel sorry because we cry, angry because we strike, afraid because we tremble."

A century ago James correctly predicted his theory of emotions would not be accepted by the medical and scientific

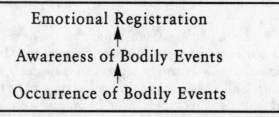

Figure 1.2 Hierarchy of emotional experience

establishment. Now scientific evidence supports James's conclusion—bodily changes do precede emotional experience. An exciting new field called psychoneuroimmunology is based in part on this assumption.

Our bodies are both a source of and storage site for our emotions. This is frequently the case after trauma—not just the trauma of abuse but even less psychologically damaging trauma like an automobile accident. Perhaps it is winter and we're driving on an icy stretch of road. The car skids, and now a number of events transpire rapidly.

First, we're aware of losing control of the car. As it begins to skid we instinctively grip the steering wheel tighter attempting to control the vehicle. We might notice a tree or a ditch or oncoming traffic. There is heightened anxiety about an impending collision. Our fear rises instantly and our entire body braces for the impact of the collision. Fortunately we miss the tree and the traffic, but head into the ditch pretty hard. The impact causes our head to be whiplashed back and forth several times. We're alive, not hurt seriously, but very shaken after the impact.

We would walk away from such an accident with more than just a sore neck. Most accident victims report emotional upset as well—nervousness, inability to sleep, anger, fear, and anxiety. These emotions are locked into the body along with the muscle spasm from the whiplash. The physical condition (muscle spasm) and the psychological condition (fear and anxiety) occurred simultaneously, and they each reinforce the existence of the other. Both conditions need to be treated. Tending to one and ignoring the other creates the possibility that the unattended condition, physical or psychological, may cause the treated condition to return.

We could, of course, substitute physical or sexual abuse or some other trauma for the automobile accident with equivalent results: Emotional damage occurs simultaneously with physical damage. Still, the effects of the trauma need to be treated physically and psychologically. The body can store and recreate emotional trauma in much the same way the mind can store and recreate physical trauma.

STORING AND RECALLING EMOTIONS
THROUGH THE BODY

This remarkable ability of the human body to store and recall emotional experience was recounted by author–physician Oliver Sacks in his book *The Man Who Mistook His Wife for a Hat.* Here Sacks tells the story of a New York City "street woman" with a peculiar neurological disorder called Tourette's syndrome.

In those afflicted with this syndrome the boundary separating conscious and unconscious forces is ill-defined. Sufferers seem driven by excessive nervous energy to produce strange motions and bizarre compulsive behavior—tics, jerks, abnormal contortions, exaggerated mannerisms, noises, profanity, and involuntary imitation of others. Sacks described seeing a woman who, in the course of one city block, imitated the forty or fifty persons who passed her by. In slower than normal motions she grotesquely pantomimed their facial expressions, body language, and attitude. She was a perfect mirror—reflecting back what their posture and body language communicated about how they felt, and who they felt they were. "The woman not only took on, and took in, the features of countless people," Sacks observed, "she also took them off."

The tension mounted as these encounters continued and Sacks wondered how she would handle the emotional energy accumulated from her caricaturizations. He followed her a short way down the block where she turned into an alley. There, to his amazement, she recreated each of the forty or fifty caricatures once again. Only this time instead of taking two or three minutes for the entire series, she went through them all in a matter of seconds! She erased from her body's recorder all that she had stored.

CLUES WITHIN THE BODY

Tourette's syndrome may simply lay bare a process that takes place in us all, for I have witnessed similar displays in the clients

I see. My first clue to a history of abuse is often how a person's body reacts to simple touch.

Nancy was an attractive woman in her early forties, head librarian at a local community college who had recently married for the second time. I had seen her periodically over a four-year period for complaints of lower back or neck pain. On one occasion she came to see me complaining of lower back and stomach pain.

I asked her to lie on her back and I rested my hand very gently on top of her stomach. The moment I asked Nancy to bring her awareness to the area I was touching she started coughing violently as though trying to dislodge an object that she was choking on. Then she turned over on the table, grabbed a tissue, and continued to cough uncontrollably. She also started repeating the phrase, "I've got to cough it out," which soon became "I've got to get him out."

Eventually she could not contain what was inside her. A story she tried so hard to keep in spewed out. "Him," she told me in a hesitating manner, was a stepfather who had sexually abused her from her childhood through her teenage years. Nancy was very embarrassed by what had emerged. "I've not told this to anyone," she confessed, "not my first or second husband. I thought I had put this behind me," she continued. "I can't believe this is coming out now."

Intellectually she may have distanced herself from these years of abuse, but time and distance do not fool the body. Human touch, like Tourette's syndrome, helps us cross the bridge between our conscious and unconscious selves and access information our bodies have recorded and stored away.

Personal experience can dramatically bring home the realities of observations. I, too, know what it means to cross over that boundary and retrieve information long buried in my unconscious self. The following happened when I was simply sitting, relaxing, and observing my breath. I wasn't trying to change or control my breathing, I was simply noting my inhalations and exhalations. Suddenly, I had the impression of hearing a voice say, "Get ready, we're going deep."

Then I had the sensation of diving like a submarine releasing its ballast. I plummeted deeper and deeper into dark, unknown waters. With a jarring motion, this diving sensation stopped abruptly and I found myself a young child standing next to a much older relative. From her mouth came a spate of negative messages about men—how they were not to be counted on, how untrustworthy they were, how men were unprotecting, unproviding, and uncaring. In that moment I understood I had been struggling against many of these dysfunctional messages in my life and in my relationships. For the first time I felt their origin within my family. It was strange feeling these messages that had been embedded into some deep, cellular level of my being—and I wanted them out!

My body bent over and I started to vomit, cough, and cry. Though nothing was expelled, I felt I was finally purging these unwanted recordings. The experience left me shaky and bewildered, but also feeling much lighter. When we give our bodies a chance they can guide our healing with tremendous purpose and power.

JOURNEYS, TRAVELERS, AND GUIDES

Journey is an appropriate metaphor for our process of healing and recovery. It evokes the many shared aspects of an actual journey and a therapeutic journey. With this metaphor come terms more suggestive of the actual healing process than the sterile clinical terms frequently used. For this reason I use *Traveler* and *Guide*, rather than doctor and patient, when referring to the participants in somatoemotional therapy. These terms more closely match the actual roles enacted on a healing journey.

Travelers who venture into unknown areas often employ the services of a Guide. It is understood that the Guide will take the journey with the Traveler. No Guide would simply sit at a base camp writing out instructions for the Traveler to climb a mountain, then say, "Follow these instructions and call me in the morning on the radio to let me know how you're doing." Yet this scenario is often played out between a patient and a doctor dispensing medication from behind a desk.

No Guide would tell an inexperienced Traveler, "Why don't

you climb the mountain. When you're finished come down and we'll sit around and talk about it." Yet sometimes this scenario is played out in psychotherapy when therapist and client speak only in intellectual terms about emotional issues.

And no Guide would outfit a beginning Traveler with the best gear, believing that equipment alone would allow the Traveler to make the journey. Yet this is often the case when a body-oriented therapist focuses exclusively on fixing physical symptoms without considering the deeper emotional and psychological issues related to those symptoms.

Instead, Traveler and Guide journey together, sharing hardships, obstacles, joys, and excitement. The Guide may have more experience, but he or she cannot be removed from or unaffected by the journey. The Guide may possess greater knowledge of the journey's course, but the Traveler cannot be carried by the Guide—the Traveler must walk the entire journey from beginning to end. Traveler and Guide are companions on a journey seeking truth in support of healing and recovery.

For some journeys it is important to engage the services of an expert Guide—one who has taken the journey many times before; one who knows the tricky spots and likely obstacles. In the therapeutic journey many expert Guides can be found. But we may spend at most only a few hours each week with these Guides. Most of our journey occurs in their absence. We needn't always rely on professional Guides. In fact, we cannot always rely on them. All of us have the potential to be healer/helpers for each other. We should not try to take over the role of professional Guides with superior training and skills. We can simply discover how to bring our care, concern, and compassion to bear with others. The body—through touch, movement, and awareness—provides ways of doing this. Many of the exercises I describe in this book, for example, can be used by nonprofessional healer/helpers for themselves and others. Of course none of the exercises should ever be undertaken in lieu of seeking help from a trained therapist.

Some of the most important therapeutic breakthroughs occur outside of a professional's office. Shortly after my first book was published, a Traveler whom I'd been seeing for several years told me an exciting story. She'd just been to visit her father and stepmother in California. She'd sent them a copy of my book several weeks before she arrived. Unknown to my client, her stepmother had urged her father and younger sister to try several of the exercises suggested in the book. None of them were trained therapists, but what emerged surprised them. Through their bodies, they began to unravel a family pattern of abandonment and neglect. When my client arrived home the family sat down to talk about the experience. My client had the opportunity of speaking to her father, as she said, "in a direct way I never dreamed was possible." The episode was unsettling and led her parents into further counseling with a local therapist. When I next saw my client she was ecstatic, because this experience validated so much of what she had uncovered on her own. The journey begins with our first steps toward healing and recovery. And our bodies can show us what steps we can take.

COMPASSIONATE TOUCH

Compassionate touch is essential for bringing the body into healing and recovery. It is as much an attitude as a skill, which creates a climate for healing and recovery. It is a way of introducing compassion into the healing and recovery process. It represents a belief that healing and recovery are the gifts of living in compassion toward one's self and toward others. However, this is very different from the ordinary meaning of compassion. Compassion is often defined as empathy and sympathy for another's suffering—having a wishful desire for their healing.

Compassion actually comes from two Latin words: *com* meaning together and *passion* meaning to suffer. So one way of interpreting compassion is "to suffer together." It is from this interpretation that we get the ordinary meaning of the word. But *together* also means *at one with*, and, therefore, we could interpret compassion to mean "at one with suffering." What a strange idea, to be at one with suffering!

Yet this is exactly what is asked of us on our journey of healing and recovery. To be at one with suffering is the opposite of being in denial. You don't ignore suffering, you don't try to resist it. You go deeper until you reach a point where that suffering opens into a much larger experience. Then it becomes suffering no more, it is simply an awareness of your experience. Have you ever driven on a narrow inland mountain road toward the ocean? Your vision is initially restricted by hills and curves. You might feel confined by the dense forest on either side. This is like the initial experience of suffering—pain, restriction, and confinement. But you stay with the road, and over the last hill you finally see the ocean. Your restricted vision now opens to a vast horizon. Your confinement now turns to unlimited space. What do you feel about the narrow road now? Perhaps you're simply aware that you had to stay on it in order to reach the sea. This also happens with pain and suffering.

Going Deep with Pain

Being at one with suffering is not just an abstract idea. It actually happens, as I have described in several cases so far. When someone comes to see me with physical or emotional pain I don't plan ways of alleviating or erasing the pain. Instead I ask the patient to be with the pain, going deeper into it to discover what really is there. As a very simple example of this process, suppose you have lower back pain. Maybe it feels like a knifing pain, and you stay with that feeling to discover that you really do feel knifed, or betrayed, by someone you trusted. Your body was trying to defend against that betrayal by tightening the muscles of your lower back to the point of pain. Now you recognize the betrayal you're dealing with. With this awareness you no longer need to hold onto the pain in your body—you can let it go. In this way healing becomes the gift of compassion; the gift of being at one with suffering.

Of course the pain may involve more than the lower back, and the issues may be more complex than simple betrayal. But regardless of the nature of the pain or the complexity of the emotional issues the process of healing and recovery is the same: You stay present with the pain as it changes from substantial to insubstantial. Various layers of related physical and psychological experience may be revealed and peeled away during the process. Ultimately this pain is disarmed and enfolded into your continuing life experience. The pain that once hurt you now enriches your life with greater meaning, purpose, and insight. You have followed a raging river until it emptied into a serene sea. You have developed compassion toward your suffering by being at one with it.

COMPASSION AND HEALING

Healing and recovery ask for such compassion not only toward oneself but also toward others. Compassion is not empathy, nor is it wishfully hoping for relief from suffering. Compassion is the active process of being at one with suffering and following suffering wherever it leads. The gift of compassion, the gift of being at one with suffering, is healing. Often it is not even necessary to know specifically what the suffering is related to. David, a young man who volunteered for a demonstration at one of my workshops, illustrated this in a wonderful way.

I first asked David to lie down and relax. Then I invited him to be aware of some problem or issue he was dealing with in his life. "Don't tell me what it is," I requested, "just be aware of it." David informed me when he was so aware, and I then asked him to locate an area of his body that seemed related to that issue. "It's between my shoulder blades," he informed me, "there's a steel rod between my shoulder blades." David also gave me permission to lightly touch the area where he experienced this steel rod. I asked him to remain aware of this area and whatever changes took place there.

Occasionally David's attention would wander to other areas of his body. When this happened I would gently ask him to once again become aware of the area I was touching. It took about ten minutes before a series of dramatic changes began to occur. "The steel bar is starting to break up," he said, "I feel a lot of smaller pieces now." Several moments later he added, "And now these fragments are breaking up into even smaller pieces." But the process continued. "The fragments are breaking up even further and I feel aware of the molecules that formed those fragments of steel!" he exclaimed.

"Just stay with it," I offered, and I continued a constant, firm, light pressure between his shoulder blades. David was very excited now as he reported the continuing changes. "The molecules aren't solid either, I'm experiencing the atoms beneath those molecules. And now," he burst out, "the atoms are dispersing and blending into the rest of my body."

It took about twenty minutes to complete this process. Before opening his eyes, I asked David to bring his awareness back to his shoulder blades and also back to the issue he first began with. "Well, the steel bar isn't there anymore," he said, "and while the issue hasn't vanished it's not nearly as intense, it's not affecting me in the same way." I never found out what issue David was working with, and quite frankly I never really needed to know.

THE PATH OF COMPASSION

Through compassion, suffering ultimately gives way to healing. And compassionate touch is used to help a Traveler like David stay present with suffering—both physical and psychological—until that suffering can be released and reintegrated. This is probably the belief behind the reminder we hear to "stay with your feelings." It is another way of saying, "stay with your suffering," which in turn leads to compassion and healing.

Compassion seeks the wholeness beneath suffering. The Travelers I have described stayed with their feelings until those feelings were transformed from the initial arena of pain to a much larger arena where that pain could be released and absorbed—like a river meeting an ocean. This larger arena is the ground of wholeness beneath suffering and pain. Sometimes this ground of wholeness can be reached very quickly, and sometimes it takes days, or weeks, or months, or years of staying with feelings, staying with suffering.

COMPASSION: ANCIENT WISDOM OR MODERN THOUGHT?

There is a belief in Buddhism that if you stay with a feeling long enough you will reach the bodily sensation beneath that feeling. If you stay with bodily sensation long enough you will reach the biochemical reactions that produce the bodily sensation. If you stay with the biochemical reactions long enough you will reach the molecular constituents that give rise to the biochemical reactions. And if you stay with the molecular constituents long enough you will reach the most fundamental particles, which cannot be further subdivided—called _kalāpas_ in the _Pāli_ language.

These _kalāpas_, it is said, only appear to be solid particles; actually they are vibratory waves. The fundamental reality beneath sensation and feeling, according to Buddhist thought, is one of vibratory energy. Out of this fundamental wholeness, sensation and feeling arise. Into this fundamental wholeness, sensation and feeling dissolve. When we identify with sensation and feeling we identify with our suffering. When we follow sensation and feeling back to this ground of wholeness we move through suffering to healing. This certainly parallels my experiences with Travelers on the journey of healing and recovery.

In a more surprising way this system of thought parallels modern physics, although it was discovered nearly 2,500 years earlier without the use of sophisticated scientific equipment. Until the time of Einstein, Western science thought the material universe was composed of fundamental building blocks—little particles that fit inside larger particles, that fit inside still larger particles, and so forth. After penning one equation, $E = mc^2$, Einstein began a revolution in science. It changed previous scientific thought forever by demonstrating that these fundamental particles were not so solid after all, actually they were vibratory waves.

Take either view—ancient wisdom or modern thought—and the same conclusion is reached: Fundamental reality is not a mass of separate entities, it is a ground of vibratory wholeness. Our ordinary experience—thoughts, feelings, sensations—emerges from this ground of wholeness, and can be dissolved back into this wholeness. Healing is wholeness—the two words come from a common ancestor, *hael*, in Old English. And compassion seeks this ground of wholeness and healing beneath our ordinary experience of life. From *hael* we also get the words *holy* and *hallowed*. Thus, compassion, is also about our sacredness and spirituality. On the healing journey we seek the hallowed ground of compassion.

healing

THE ATTITUDE OF COMPASSION

Compassionate touch is also closely related to "unconditional positive regard"—an idea originating in the client-centered approach to psychotherapy pioneered by Carl Rogers. Both phrases, *compassionate touch* and *unconditional positive regard,* reflect an attitude of acceptance toward the Traveler. There is willingness to allow the Traveler to embody whatever feelings are present in the moment—anger, pain, love, fear, courage, joy, and resentment. There is little attempt to edit or color the Traveler's experience.

I am reminded of how an actual Traveler and Guide might interact when, on an arduous wilderness journey, they come upon a beautiful sunrise. I can't imagine the Guide saying, "Come on, friend, we've no time to watch this sunrise, we'd best be on our way." This would deny the Traveler the experience of the sunrise. Likewise I can hardly envision the Guide saying, "Notice how the sun comes up, the colors that are present at the horizon, the clouds moving slowly by to either side, the shimmering effect of the light on the water," and so on. Such remarks would intrude on the Traveler's experience of the sunrise.

I can picture both Traveler and Guide pausing for a quiet moment to watch this sight; enjoying this shared beauty in the silence of their innermost thoughts and reflections. On the journey of healing and recovery not all of the Traveler's experiences will be as beautiful as a sunrise, but they can all be honored in the same way. In Rogers's words, the Guide—whether a professional or a friend in the role of healer/

helper—can have an attitude of "nonpossessive caring" toward the Traveler.

The importance of this aspect of compassionate touch cannot be underestimated. In a study by the National Institutes of Mental Health on the effectiveness of psychotherapy, an experimental group of professional therapists and a group of nonprofessionals were compared. Clients, unaware of who were trained therapists and who were nonprofessionals, were randomly assigned to members of both groups. The only instructions given the nonprofessionals were to hold their clients in the highest positive regard—to listen empathetically without offering additional analysis or commentary.

Periodically, both groups of clients were evaluated for progress. Through the first six months there was no appreciable difference between clients who saw professionals and those who saw nonprofessionals. It was only after six months that the training of the professional therapists began to make a difference. This study concluded that the attitude of the therapist toward the client is an essential ingredient in effective psychotherapy. To initiate a positive outcome, unconditional positive regard was more important than specific therapeutic technique. Compassion is the attitude needed by both Traveler and Guide on the journey of healing and recovery.

PARTICIPANT OR OBSERVER?

I offer participants in my workshops two ways of taking part in the demonstrations I conduct: they can observe as spectators or partake as equals. Usually these are "fish bowl" demonstrations where I and a volunteer are in front of as many as several hundred individuals. It's easy to see how the group could simply observe the process taking place in front of them. But how could they be equals?

One simple suggestion usually helps to clarify how this is possible. I ask participants to view the demonstration with the attitude, "How am I affected by what is taking place before me?" This is very different from a spectator concerned only with "What is taking place before me?" This difference, however, is crucial in allowing participants to be part of the demonstration. Asking "How am I affected . . . ?" suggests a realm of experience that unites the two of us directly involved in the demonstration with the rest of the workshop participants.

This linkage is rather straightforward. "There are but a few human themes that will emerge from this demonstration," I tell the group, not knowing beforehand exactly what will happen. I then enumerate some of the possible themes—love, loss, betrayal, abandonment, sadness, anger, fear, shame, triumph. "Each of you already has some relationship to, or experience with these themes," I continue. "In that sense whatever emerges is not separate from you but really a part of your own life experience presented now through the words and actions of two other people."

At the end of the demonstration I ask for comments not on what was observed but on what was felt and experienced by everyone. Many individuals speak about the fear or anger or joy they experienced when those same emotions emerged during the demonstration. This is a meaningful exercise in developing that compassionate view of self and others so necessary on the journey of healing and recovery.

Like these workshop participants, you, the reader, also have a choice. As you read through case studies you can observe how interesting they are, or you can ask yourself how you are affected by them. You can read the scientific and factual material as a technical report, or you can consider the impact of such findings on your own experience of body and emotions. You can approach the exercises in this book as a spectator or a participant, considering what it might be like to try them or actually taking the time to get involved.

One choice is not better than the other. But in each case the latter choice adds another dimension to this material—developing compassion toward self and others. Regardless of the particular issues you face on your own journey of healing and recovery, it is this compassionate view of self and others that touches and unites us all.

2.

THE NEUROBIOLOGY OF COMPASSIONATE TOUCH

Our whole cubic capacity is sensibly alive, and each morsel of it contributes to its pulsations of feeling, dim or sharp, pleasant, painful or dubious, to our sense of personality.

— WILLIAM JAMES

Nature is often frugal, adapting designs that work in one domain for others, implementing successful functions from one species to the next. Attributes found across species and domains are testaments of natural success. Touch is one such attribute. From the smallest single-celled organism to the largest living mammal, touch—physical contact and mechanical stimulation—occupies a central role in life. *Thigmotaxis,* movement in response to touch, and *thigmotropism,* growth in response to touch, are the biological terms for this ubiquitous presence of touch in nature.

Plants are thigmotropic. Bind a tree that would normally grow to a height of sixty feet and it will barely grow six inches —a Japanese art called bonsai. Animals are also thigmotropic. Bind a foot that would normally grow to be ten inches and it only grows to be three—a former Chinese practice of keeping women in bondage. Even an amoeba, the smallest form of animal life, is thigmotactic. Touch an amoeba with a bacterium and it creates artificial limbs, called pseudopods, from its protoplasm. As these arms engulf the bacterium, digestive juices squirt out. The bacterium is dissolved and devoured by the amoeba. But touch an amoeba with a fine needle and pseudo-pods form on the opposite side to help it scurry away. Approach and avoidance, bonding and separating, yearning for and turn-ing from, are the basic behaviors of life—the building blocks for more complex behaviors and emotions. Even simple life forms possess these behaviors and they are aroused through a simple act, the act of touching.

TOUCH AND HEALING: AN INSTINCTUAL HUMAN CAPACITY

Touching is no less important for more complex life forms, like human beings. In *Where Healing Waters Meet,* I proposed that the need to touch for healing and recovery was instinctual—built in to our nervous system. This suggestion comes from watching humans when they are injured or hurt. A pin prick, or the touch of a hot object, initiates a well-known, prewired, neu-rological reflex called the *nociceptive reflex*. Nociceptive comes from the Latin *nocere* meaning pain. This reflex causes a sharp contraction of muscles to move our body away from the source of pain. But immediately afterward we touch the affected area. We suck our finger, press deeply near a cut, or wrap our arms tightly around our bruised midsection.

These instinctual actions are beneficial. Moistening a burned area promotes healing, pressing an open wound acts as a tourniquet, and binding an injury is a means of immobiliza-tion. I coined the term *curaceptive* (from the Latin *cura,* to cure) to describe this healing reflex based on touch. Chances are that early humans observed this curaceptive reflex and determined that what worked for self might also work for others. With this observation, the practice of using touch to promote physical healing emerged.

Touch plays a similar role in emotional injury and recovery. When a situation offends us, we say, "I'm repulsed." When a situation pleases us, we say, "I'm attracted" or "I'm drawn to that." We place our hand out, fingers pointing straight up to say, "Stop, no more!" When a situation touches us we often touch ourselves—clutching gently near our heart, for example, as if to draw in the event or feeling. These actions are evolutionary revisions of an amoeba's simple avoidance/approach behavior. Deep within these instinctive actions lies a common thread linking us across space and time with all life.

BODY, MIND AND EMOTIONS

In 1642 Frenchman René Descartes published a book destined to become a cornerstone of modern philosophy and science. Simply entitled *Meditations,* in it Descartes laid out a comprehensive world view based on the separation of body and mind. Descartes is best known for his statement, "I think, therefore I am." With this starting point, Cartesian logic divided the world into the *realm of thoughts* and the *realm of things.* Mental phenomena like thoughts, ideas, images, will, and emotions occupied the first realm. Physical objects like trees, rocks, planets, clouds, and houses occupied the latter realm. These two realms, according to Descartes, were separate and unequal. The most a person could do, he claimed, was to *think* about *things.* Thoughts, Descartes reasoned, could not affect things, and things, in turn, could not affect thoughts.

The human body was relegated to the realm of things by Descartes. "I consider the body of man as being a sort of machine so built up and composed of nerves, muscles, veins, blood and skin," he stated. The human mind was, of course, assigned to the realm of thought. On the question of emotions and the body, Descartes was unequivocal. In *Meditations* he wrote:

> There is certainly no affinity (that I at least can understand) between the craving of the stomach and the desire to eat, any more than between the perception of whatever causes pain and the thought of sadness which arises from this perception.

THE SPLIT BETWEEN BODY AND MIND

Three hundred fifty years of science and philosophy have been built on this Cartesian split between body and mind. It is so deeply rooted in Western thought that most of us simply take this separation for granted. "Do you feel you are a body, or do you feel you have a body?" asks Ken Wilber. Most of us would answer that we have a body in the same sense that we have a car, a house, or a job. Our body becomes just one other thing in our already cluttered world of things.

"Biologically there is not the least foundation for this dissociation or split between the mind and the body," Wilber continues, "but psychologically it is epidemic. Indeed the mind-body split . . . is a fundamental perspective of Western civilization."

Such a fundamental perspective is not easy to change. The notion that mind could affect body has yielded somewhat in recent years. Research findings in various fields have clearly shown the effects of mental states on physical states. John Basmajian, for example, showed that people could be trained to control the activity of one individual cell in their body. Small electrodes were implanted in a motor unit at the fleshy base of the thumb and connected to a speaker. (A motor unit is the smallest division of a muscle. It has a single nerve cell and the muscle fibers controlled by that cell.) Basmajian's experimental subjects became so adept at controlling motor unit activity that 99 percent could produce special effects over the speaker on command. "Various gallop rhythms, drumbeat rhythms, doublets, and roll effects were produced and recorded," notes Basmajian. Basmajian's research is part of a large body of evidence in the field of biofeedback. Other studies have shown that heart rate, blood pressure, brain wave activity, muscle activity, and other apparently involuntary body functions can be brought under voluntary control.

THE NEUROBIOLOGY OF EMOTIONS

Equally important findings about the mind's influence on the body come from the exciting, new field of psychoneuroimmunology (PNI). The word literally means studying the mind's (psyche) influence through the nervous system (neuro) on the body's defense system (immunology).

Medical researchers previously assumed the immune system and the nervous system were separate and unrelated. In the late 1960s, however, George Solomon demonstrated that stress could suppress the immune response of laboratory animals, while healthy, supportive early life experience could enhance immune response. Solomon's findings were initially ignored by the scientific mainstream. Scientific orthodoxy held that the immune system was self-contained. It responded only to foreign agents—bacteria and viruses, for example—and it could not be affected by the psychological state of the individual.

Researchers like Jeanne Achterberg and Carl Simonton found equally provocative evidence that people with life-threatening diseases like cancer could heal themselves using visual imagery. Almost all the imagery focused on the immune system: legions of good cells attacking invading bad cells; good sharks gobbling up weaker prey; saintly cells purifying diseased cells in the fire. The statistically significant findings of researchers like Solomon, Achterberg, and Simonton were often dismissed simply because other researchers had no way of explaining their results. Unpopular results, no matter how valid, are not readily accepted by the scientific mainstream.

A breakthrough in understanding the mind's effect on the body came when research demonstrated that the immune response in rats could be conditioned. We're all familiar with Pavlov's dogs. Ivan Pavlov was the Russian Nobel prize recipient who, at the turn of the century, simultaneously rang a bell and presented dogs with meat. Naturally the dogs salivated when they saw the meat. After a few trials through, the bell alone was enough to cause salivation. This is considered a classically conditioned response.

In 1970 Robert Ader performed a similar experiment with rats. Only he replaced Pavlov's bell with sweetened water, substituted cyclophosphamide for meat, and measured immune response not salivation. An animal's immune response, measured by the number of white blood cells, normally drops after ingesting cyclophosphamide. Ader mixed the cyclophosphamide with sweetened water. Rats liked the sweetened water, which normally produces no ill effects on the immune system. After drinking the mixture of sweet water and cyclophosphamide, as predicted, the immune system response of the rats was depressed. To complete the experiment, Ader gave the rats sweetened water without cyclophosphamide. The result was surprising: Once again the rats' immune system dropped. Such conditioning could occur only through the brain and nervous system. Scientific orthodoxy had to give way. Ader's experiments were an elegant way of showing the mind's effect on the body: A state of mind (the association between the two normally unrelated events of ingesting sweetened water and cyclophosphamide) could change the body (immune system response).

Ader's work paved the way for an explosion of research in PNI. The race was to find out just how the mind could so profoundly affect the body. By the middle of the 1980s the first leg of this race had ended. The winners were not just the researchers participating in the trials, but Western civilization as it began to reclaim and heal the split between body and mind.

MOLECULAR BIOLOGY AND EMOTIONS

Molecular biologists contributed to PNI with the discovery of endorphins and enkephalins—brain chemicals with narcotic effects thousands of times more powerful than morphine. In discerning how these neurochemicals worked, receptor sites were discovered on the surface of brain cells that coveted these substances. These receptor sites accepted only matching molecules, in much the same way that a lock accepts only a matching key. Once seated in its receptor site, these molecules changed the function of the cell. For endorphins this change resulted in powerful pain-killing effects. The discovery of endorphins and enkephalins (both names for the same substance) led to the discovery of an entirely new class of brain chemicals called *neuropeptides*—endorphins were just one of some sixty to one hundred neuropeptides found in the brain. This discovery brought neuroscientists into PNI because it turned out that chemicals previously thought to facilitate transmission of nerve impulses were nothing but neuropeptides.

A number of surprising events then happened. Ed Blalock, a

medical researcher, discovered a neuropeptide in a test tube filled with white blood cells. Called adrenocorticotrophic hormone (ACTH), this substance is supposed to be found only in the brain. Not only could the white blood cells receive neuropeptides but they could also make them.

Candace Pert and her colleagues at the National Institutes of Mental Health (NIMH) in Maryland were pivotal in the convergence of molecular biology and emotions. As a graduate student, Pert isolated the first endorphins. With her colleagues at NIMH she began to map out where neuropeptide receptor sites were located in the brain. Using radioactively tagged molecules, she located receptor sites in the limbic system, an area of the brain that regulates organ function and emotions.

The first pieces of the PNI puzzle were slipping into place. Areas of the brain associated with emotions and organ function had high concentrations of neuropeptide receptors. These same neuropeptides controlled the transmission of impulses over the nervous system—nerve cells had neuropeptide receptor sites. And these same neuropeptides programmed the activity of the immune system—white blood cells also had neuropeptide receptor sites. The system was actually multidirectional, because all parts made and received neuropeptides. Pert and others began to call neuropeptides "information messengers." They communicated back and forth among systems previously thought to be separate and distinct.

NEUROPEPTIDES AND THE BODY

The story did not end there. Pert asked the next logical question: If receptor sites for neuropeptides are found in the brain, nervous system, and immune system, where else are they? The answer was yet another surprise. Neuropeptide production and receptor sites are located throughout the body. Pert found them in the spinal cord, around organs, and in muscle tissue. So widespread was this system of messenger chemicals that substances formerly thought to be digestive enzymes actually turned out to be neuropeptides.

For years cholecystokinin (CCK) was thought to be just an

enzyme our intestines secreted to digest fats. Then CCK was discovered to be an endorphinlike neuropeptide. It causes a pain-killing effect in the brain that puts us in an emotional state of well-being. CCK also affects our desire to eat by shutting down the brain's appetite center. Finally, CCK receptors exist on cells of the immune system. So separating the digestive system from the nervous system, from the immune system, and from our emotions is more a matter of scientific convenience than a fact of body function. It is impossible to separate the body from emotional experience. "Emotions," concluded Candace Pert, "are not just in the brain, they're in the body!"

Neuropeptides that regulate moods in the brain maintain tissue integrity in the body. These chemicals control the movement of monocytes—key cells of the immune system. Monocytes are formed in the bone marrow before finding their way into the bloodstream. Like an ever-vigilant emergency response team they circulate waiting for trouble. Injury calls monocytes into action. Neuropeptides released at the site of injury broadcast a chemical distress signal causing monocytes to migrate out of the bloodstream into body tissue. Once outside the blood, monocytes—now called macrophages—are essential for wound healing. They synthesize collagen, the main ingredient of all forms of body tissue. Macrophages also rid body tissue of foreign substances like bacteria and work with helper and killer cells of the immune system to fight disease. Macrophages also produce neuropeptides, such as pain-killing endorphins, and they have receptors for every neuropeptide discovered so far. In other words, the same neuropeptides that promote emotional well-being cause bodily changes that result in physical well-being.

Some monocytes reside in the body where they become part of our flesh and organs. Other monocytes, proposes molecular biologist Michael Ruff, cross the blood-brain barrier, entering our brain to become glial cells. (Ruff's suggestion even raises the eyebrows of psychoneuroimmunologists, but then most of the early findings in this field have been equally outrageous. Most also have been shown later to be true.) Glial cells are essential to brain function. They produce myelin, the protective covering around nerves, and provide nutrient support for nerve cells.

They also direct the growth of nerve fibers through the production and reception of neuropeptides. This function is critical to nerve regeneration after injury or damage. When glial cells are not present, nerve fibers regrow in useless entangled mats.

Nerve fiber growth is also related to memory. Unlike many cells in the body, adult brain cells do not divide. Instead they grow and branch out much like the roots of a plant or tree. Experience increases the growth and branching of nerve fibers in the brain. This process is guided by glial cells and regulated by neuropeptides. So the same chemicals that regulate emotions guide the growth and branching of brain cells related to experience and memory. Pert has even suggested that glial cells can be programmed in the brain then migrate back out through the bloodstream into the body.

BODY, SENSATION, AND EMOTIONS

The location of neuropeptide receptors points to the intimate relationship between emotions and the body. Another hot spot of neuropeptides is an area of the spinal cord called the dorsal horn. Dorsal horn cells are the first to receive sensory impulses emanating from the skin and from our internal organs. Pain, temperature, and light touch travel through these cells toward higher brain centers. These dorsal horn cells, notes Pert, are "enriched with virtually all the neuropeptide receptors." The presence of neuropeptides modifies how these cells receive and pass along sensory information. Thus the same neuropeptides that regulate emotion in the brain regulate our perception of sensory stimuli through the skin. Feeling has always had two meanings: one related to emotional experience, the other related to sensation through the skin. In reality these two meanings are nothing more than different aspects of the same process.

This relationship between body and emotions continues to follow the course of sensory perception toward the brain. Right after the spinal cord passes through the skull is an area called the *midbrain*. Sensory impulses traveling toward the brain contact cells of a midbrain region known as the *periaqueductal gray (PAG)*. The PAG is a fascinating region of the brain. Pert has described this area as "blazing" with neuropeptide receptors. Previous research proved the PAG to contain nerve centers that regulate internal body functions like respiration, food intake, and blood sugar. The PAG is also the only area of the brain that responds to touch.

Ordinarily, brain tissue is insensitive to mechanical handling. For this reason brain surgery requires anesthesia only in the scalp. After penetration of the scalp and skull, touching the brain usually produces no response—except in the PAG. Karl Pribram, a neuroscientist and neurosurgeon, recalls discovering this peculiar attribute of the PAG by accident. During routine brain surgery he pushed and pulled lightly on this area causing the patient severe head pain, nausea, retching, and vomiting. I think of the PAG as the skin of the brain. It is a model-in-miniature of the relationship between touch and emotions. The same brain areas that process somatosensory information (information obtained through the skin) control bodily function. These areas are, in turn, regulated by the neurochemicals of emotional experience.

BRAIN, BODY, AND EMOTIONS

We find a similar relationship between body and emotions at the next higher stage of sensation in the brain. Here body and mind converge in a brain area known as the *limbic system*. The limbic system lies deep within the temporal lobes of the brain. It's not too hard to locate. Place both thumbs above the top of your ears and bring your index fingers around over the top of your head to touch each other. Next imagine where a line between both thumbs intersects a line dropped straight down from the tip of your index fingers. That's the approximate location of the limbic system.

The limbic system is called the "emotional brain" because electrical stimulation of this area produces classic emotional responses—sadness, laughter, crying, elation, etc. This area also regulates our primary instinctual drives—fighting, fleeing, feeding, and sexual behavior. The limbic system receives sensory information from the skin and other sensory receptors. Not surprisingly, brain cells in the limbic system are also blazing with neuropeptide receptors. The amygdala, a small area of the limbic system, is a chief site of this convergence between body, emotions, and behavior. Surgical removal of the amygdala in monkeys severely disrupts these instinctual drives. Feeding and sexual behavior increase dramatically, and radical changes in interpersonal relationships (fighting and fleeing behavior) result as well.

Karl Pribram successfully performed amygdalectomies (surgical removal of the amygdala) in three out of eight monkeys living in a family group (Figures 2.1A–D). The results of these surgeries show the connection between the limbic system, emotions, and the functional and dysfunctional relationships in family groups. At first, Dave was the dominant, self-assured, and feared ruler of the group. Zeke was the aggressive, attacking pretender to the throne, and Riva was an aggressive family member in the number three position of the social hierarchy. Larry, in the number eight position, was submissive, cowering, and beat upon by everyone else.

DAVE 1
(Dominant, self-assured, feared)
 ZEKE 2
 (Aggressive, attacker)
  RIVA 3
  (Aggressive, active)
   HERBY 4
   (Placid, unaggressive)
    BENNY 5
    (Alert, active food getter)
     ARNIE 6
     (Noisy, eager)
      SHORTY 7
      (Submissive to others, aggressive towards Larry)
       LARRY 8
       (Submissive, cowering, frequently attacked)

ZEKE 1
(Dominant, aggressive)
 RIVA 2
 (Daring, competes with Zeke)
  HERBY 3
  (Nonaggresive)
   BENNY 4
    ARNIE 5
     SHORTY 6
     (Submissive to others, aggressive towards Larry
      LARRY 7
      (Dominates and attacks Dave)
       DAVE 8
       (Completely submissive, fearful)

Figure 2.1(a) Dominance hierarchy in colony of preadolescent male rhesus monkeys before surgery. Drawn after Pribram, 1962.

Figure 2.1(b) Dominance hierarchy after bilateral amygdalectomy performed on Dave. Drawn after Pribram, 1962.

RIVA 1
(Dominant, not threatened by others)
  HERBY 2
  (Nonaggressive)
    BENNY 3
      ARNIE 4
        SHORTY 5
          LARRY 6
            ZEKE 7
            (Submissive to others, intermittently aggressive towards Dave)
              DAVE 8
              (Cringer, avoids interaction)

Figure 2.1(c) Dominance hierarchy after bilateral amygdalectomies performed on Dave and Zeke. Drawn after Pribram, 1962.

RIVA 1
(More dominant, unpredictably aggressive and vicious)
  HERBY 2
  (Nonaggressive)
    BENNY 3
      ARNIE 4
        SHORTY 5
        (Aggressive towards Larry)
          LARRY 6
            ZEKE 7
            (Continues intermittently aggressive towards Dave)
              DAVE 8
              (Outcast, flees from all)

Figure 2.1(d) Dominance hierarchy after bilateral amygdalectomies performed on Dave, Zeke, and Riva. Drawn after Pribram, 1962.

With each operation the dominant individual dropped to the bottom of the hierarchy and the second in line took over. After Dave's operation, Zeke took over as king and Larry began attacking a fearful, cowering, submissive Dave. Zeke fared a little better than Dave. After Zeke's operation, Riva became the leader and Zeke dropped to the number seven spot. Zeke was frequently attacked by and submissive to others including Larry, but he was aggressive toward Dave. The interpersonal relationships took an interesting turn after Riva's operation. Herby, who was next in line to succeed, had never been very aggressive from the beginning—Pribram characterized him as the "laid back" artist of the group. Without a credible challenge from below Riva remained on top but he was more dominant, unpredictably aggressive, and vicious. Dave, by this time, had become an outcast who fled from contact with anyone else. These experiments point to the amygdala's importance in regulating normal and dysfunctional interpersonal behavior.

Not only did the removal of the amygdala alter the fighting/fleeing behavior of animals but it also increased feeding and sexual behavior. Essentially, surgical removal of the amygdala left animals unable to register critical emotional states—safety, threat, and satisfaction—and then take appropriate actions. A similar inability to connect mind and body appeared in human subjects who underwent amygdalectomies to remove tumors. They gained tremendous amounts of weight but were unable to distinguish an internal state of being hungry or full. Surgical removal of the amygdala resembles the dissociation seen in survivors of such severe trauma as repeated sexual abuse—an idea we'll examine more fully in a later chapter.

SPHINCTERS AND EMOTIONS

There is yet another body area where research points to the abiding unity of body and mind. Pert and her colleagues found rich endowments of neuropeptide receptors in specific muscles of the body. These were sphincter muscles.

The word *sphincter* comes from a Greek word meaning that which binds tight. Sphincters are ringlike bands of muscles that restrict passages or close natural openings in the body. Except for the ear canal, every natural opening in the body has an associated sphincter:

- anal sphincter
- urethral sphincter
- vaginal sphincter
- esophageal sphincter (muscles encircling the top of the stomach)
- oral sphincter (muscles encircling the mouth)
- palatopharyngeal sphincter (try to swallow and breathe simultaneously to feel this sphincter encircling the nasal passage as it enters the throat)
- ocular sphincter (muscles encircling the eyes)

At birth sphincters function involuntarily. They are among the last muscles we learn to control. Surprisingly, control of these muscles parallels our psychological birth, the subject of the next chapter. Therefore sphincters are intimately related to emotional experience. Newborns are often described as living in a world with few physical or psychological boundaries: a state of unbounded fullness in which everything is Mother and Mother is everything, a state of self-absorption, a state of physical and psychological fusion with Mother.

Physically, newborns' bodies are literally in this unbounded state because sphincters are uncontrolled. Like an undammed river, everything in the infant's body flows. This fact has not escaped parents. It is why there are diapers and bibs for babies, and burping cloths for the shoulders of adults. Everything flows from unstoppered orifices. This flow of physical material in the infant's body can be likened to the flow of unconscious material in the infant's mind—unregulated and uncontrolled. Psychological birth fashions a unique, separate, individual self out of this undifferentiated flow in the mind. Sphincter control fashions a unique, separate, physical self from this unregulated flow in the body.

Sphincter control is yet another way the child disengages from Mother. Sphincters, and the body flows they regulate, are the first body areas the child reclaims from Mother. Once sphincters come under the child's control, Mother's authority no longer intrudes into the child's body. Sphincter control is also important for locomotion. Once the child is upright and walking, gravity makes controlling the flow that much more imperative. Sphincter control is a yardstick of readiness for interpersonal relationships. Toilet training, for example, is one way society gauges a child's fitness for extended periods away from Mother with other children.

CONTROLLING PHYSICAL AND PSYCHOLOGICAL BOUNDARIES

To grow psychologically and interact socially we must develop normal repressive mechanisms. Otherwise uncontrolled anger might always lead to antisocial behavior, like hurting or harming someone. Sphincter control is the body's counterpart to normal psychological repression. Sphincters are among the first physical boundaries the child controls—sentinels of the deepest parts of self. Tragically, they are often the first boundaries violated by others. Sexual abuse is a violation of sphincters. In less severe trauma, sphincters are often still involved. Under stress, for example, many people lose control of their sphincters with embarrassing consequences. With such an important physical and emotional burden placed upon sphincters it is not at all surprising that they are neuropeptide hot spots.

PERCEPTION AND EMOTIONS

From the periphery of the skin to the core of the brain, neuropeptides seem to appear where body, mind, and emotions converge. Neuropeptides, however, are just one key to this convergence. Another lies in how we feel, that is, how we perceive through our body, especially through our skin. We perceive by creating images. Though vision is important, not all these images are visual. You can listen to a symphony to experience an auditory image, smell something fragrant to experience an olfactory image, taste something sweet to experience a gustatory image, and touch something soft to experience a somatic image. Images are the way we make sense of and organize impulses from the external world that impinge on our senses.

Images are also the way we make sense of our internal world—physically and emotionally. If I ask you to describe how you're experiencing your body right now, you'd use images. Some of your images would translate from the somatic to the visual mode. For example you might say, "I have a burning pain in my right leg." There's not really a fire in your leg, the heat of an inflammation causes you to feel that way. Fire then is both a somatic and visual image. You also might say: "I have a knot in my neck," "a catch in my back," "a knifing pain," "I'm stiff as a board," or "I threw out my back." A high degree of visual imagery is implicit in these statements. Some images derived from our body are even auditory, as in the phrase "I had a screaming pain."

Note how far away these statements are from the anatomical truth of how you're feeling. No one says, "I'm experiencing a localized protective response to the injury of my leg that is characterized by dolor, calor, rubor, and tumor," the medical definition of inflammation. Similarly, no one describes a stiff neck by saying, "the paraspinal muscles of my cervical spine are in a state of tetany." We use images to describe our internal physical experience.

We use similar images to describe our emotional experience. Emotionally descriptive phrases come from body-based images. Figure 2.2 is a partial list of such phrases. Imaging underlies our perception of external and internal events, and it is the basis for describing emotional experience. The human body is exceptionally good at somatic imagery—the ability to translate touch, pressure, and movement into meaningful information. Through somatic imagery our body can inform us about internal and external events, and it can also inform us about underlying emotional experience. Often the information available to us through the body is not available through our other senses.

Banged my head against the wall	Holding it in
Bearing a heavy burden	Ice in his veins
Blood boiling	Livid
Bound with shame	Makes me want to vomit
Breathless	No intestinal fortitude
Burdened with guilt	No room to breathe
Can't stomach that	No leg to stand on
Choked with feeling	Pain in the ...
Cold heart	Pisses me off
Cold shoulder	Saving face
Feeling choked up	Sent shivers up my spine
Galls me	Shouldering the world's problems
Got a lot of gall	So angry I can't see straight
Gut wrenching	Spineless
Hair standing on end	Suffocating
Hanging one's head in shame	Tears me up inside
Happy feet	Tight (jawed, assed, lipped)
Heart break	Turns me inside/out
Heart ache	Uptight
Heart felt	Vent my spleen

Figure 2.2 Body-based emotional descriptors

Seeing and Hearing Through the Skin

Several experiments with vision and hearing prove that touch can supply information unavailable to our other senses. In 1972 Paul Bach-y-Rita devised an apparatus called the Tactile Visual Substitution System. He translated the image from a television camera into a corresponding array of small plungers applied to the backs of blind individuals. Depending upon the brightness of the television image the plungers pressed either firmly (corresponding to a dark portion on the image) or gently (corresponding to a light portion of the image). Thus, a "pressure image" was created from a video image. Amazingly, when the camera was trained on a cup or a window, individuals who were blind from birth could correctly identify the object.

In 1977, researcher M.A. Clements reported a similar set of experiments with people who were deaf from birth. Clements translated sounds into an array of small vibrating plungers applied to the skin. These plungers vibrated depending upon how much bass, treble, alto, or soprano frequencies were present in the composite sound. As a symphony was played, for example, the amount of each frequency shifted continuously and rapidly, and the vibration of the plungers followed these shifts. Through the skin, the brain and nervous system was able to translate these vibrations into meaningful information enabling blind individuals to correctly identify a variety of sounds presented to them.

Communication Through the Skin

These experiments remind me that touch communicates far more than pressure or pain. Images related to physical sensation and emotional experience are available through the skin. Donna was a young woman in her midtwenties who volunteered to work with me during a workshop demonstration. I first asked her to lie down on a table and relax. After several minutes I invited her to scan her mind and become aware of a predominant emotional or psychological issue she was dealing with in her life. I really didn't want to know what the issue was, just that she was aware of it. Donna nodded her head to inform me she was aware of that issue. Next I asked her to scan her body and find an area related to that issue. She pointed to her upper abdomen on the right, slightly beneath her rib cage.

"What's it like there?" I queried. "It feels as if there's something lodged here," Donna replied. "Tell me how much pressure I need to mimic the sensation you have in that area," I continued. Donna then guided the pressure I applied to her abdomen with the flat surface of my right hand. "That's enough," she indicated. "I can feel it now. It's as if there is a rock or stone caught in there."

For the next several minutes I asked Donna just to observe the rock or stone she imaged in her abdomen. What was it like to feel as if there was a rock caught there? How was that rock related to the issue she was dealing with? For the demonstration, I didn't want her to talk about her experience. I simply wanted her to stay with her body awareness. After a while I asked her what she wanted to do with that rock. "My immediate response is to pulverize it," she answered quickly, "but I'm not sure that's what really needs to happen." "All right, Donna," I said, "take some time and consider what we could do with this rock. When you're ready, let me know."

A few minutes passed before Donna informed me what she wanted done. "Let's just take it out," she said. With her help we excavated the rock in her abdomen. First she guided my pressure deep enough to get under the rock. Then she directed me to lift up the rock, "slowly," she said, "so we don't lose it and have it slip back." Finally the rock was out and Donna became aware of a gaping hole in her side. "Perhaps there's something you want to fill that hole with," I suggested, "a feeling, a thought, a color, or something of your choosing." "I want to fill it with love for myself," she said softly. "Take however long you need to fill that area," I reassured her, "and let me know when you're through."

Donna took several minutes to fill that area with the love she sensed was needed. Afterward she took some deep breaths, opened her eyes and sat up. "I feel light," she noticed, "light and a little giddy." At the end of the demonstration she made these comments:

I've been dealing with the residue of my divorce. Although it happened nearly five years ago, I still have a lot of emotional pain from that experience. The rock was a good image for that pain. I've done a lot of therapy around my divorce. I was a little angry that these issues were still present in my body. That's why I wanted to pulverize the rock, to get rid of it quickly. I thought about it for a while and that didn't feel right. I decided it would be better just to experience the rock being lifted from my body. The closer it got to the surface of my skin, the happier I felt. When you finally removed it, I felt a tremendous burden had been lifted from me.

Touch helped Donna create an image to her emotional experience. By mimicking Donna's initial sensation in her abdomen a clearer image of that sensation emerged—a rock or stone. Then touch worked with that image and the related emotional issues—slowly removing the rock. Touch instead of talk was the primary means of communication, and Donna's ability to image somatically allowed the process to work. There are many ways that somatic imagery unfolds. It may be as simple as identifying a somatic image with related physical sensation and emotional experience as in Donna's case. Or somatic imagery may reveal itself through movement. Merely asking a person to "move as if you experienced that feeling throughout your body," can initiate ten or fifteen minutes of continuous somatic imagery. Through the succeeding chapters you'll see somatic imagery at work in a variety of forms. You might keep in mind that beneath all forms of somatic imagery is the body's potential for organizing sensory and emotional experience in meaningful, often novel ways.

THE BODY BEYOND THE SKIN

We can sense ourselves beyond the bounds of our body. There is a spatial boundary or personal space that extends beyond our skin. This body beyond the skin is intimately connected with our physical body, as the research of Nobel laureate Georg von Békésy showed. From his early work with the Hungarian telephone system, Békésy became fascinated with human hearing. Unfortunately hearing is difficult to study. The ear drum and ear ossicles—the membrane and bones involved in hearing—are located deep inside the skull. These structures are also fragile and very minute. Békésy devised ingenious methods to overcome these limitations. But his greatest ingenuity may have been demonstrated when he recognized that human skin could substitute for the human ear.

Both the skin and the ear are essentially vibrating membranes connected by nerves to the brain. The huge surface area of the skin allowed Békésy to perform hundreds of experiments on the skin and interpret them in terms of hearing. Békésy paved the way for the tactile visual and auditory substitution systems we described earlier. Because of Békésy's research we not only know more about hearing but we know more about touching as well.

Békésy first placed a pair of vibrators on both arms of experimental subjects. As long as the vibrators moved at different speeds or with different strengths Békésy's blindfolded subjects could determine the presence of two vibrators. When moving at the same speed and with the same strength the vibrators produced a surprising result. Subjects reported feeling only one spot vibrating and that spot was "out there" in the space between both arms where no skin existed. Whether placed on the knees or two adjacent fingers of the same hand, two equal vibrators gave the same result. Subjects identified one vibrating spot on their skin "out there" in the space between the vibrators where there was no skin.

Békésy went on to show that sensory projection is a normal function of the human brain and nervous system. We routinely project our sense of touch when we write. To convince yourself try a simple experiment. Begin writing, but focus on the pressure you're using to grasp your pen or pencil. Next try varying that pressure as you write—it can't be done! Then write normally, and be aware of where you're feeling sensation. Is it where your pencil meets the paper, or where your skin meets the pencil? Surprisingly, it is where your pencil meets the paper.

Your grasp needs to be constant to project your sense of touch beyond your skin surface to the end of the writing implement. Next time you eat, use a tool, or paint, notice how you project your sense of touch to the end of the instrument you're using.

Of course we're more familiar with sensory projection in sight and hearing. When we see a car a quarter of a mile away we experience it being far away. The actual light waves impinge on sensory receptors in our eyes but we don't experience perception at the surface of these receptors. Similarly, sitting between two well-balanced stereo speakers gives us the perception of sound coming from the space between the speakers. This is the same phenomenon that Békésy recreated through the skin.

Békésy's work shows that somatic therapy need not end at the skin. I extend somatic therapy to the body boundary formed at the skin and projected away from its surface. What takes place within this spatial boundary is significant physically and psychologically. I have worked with sexual abuse survivors for whom direct touch is not advisable. We can often still work somatically within the spatial boundary projected away from their skin surface.

Dolores Krieger, a nursing professor at New York University, documented the physiological changes that took place when nurses "touched" patients away from the skin. She called her method Therapeutic Touch, an apparent misnomer because there was no direct touch. Krieger showed significant changes in the red blood cell count of patients receiving Therapeutic Touch. Other researchers documented beneficial changes in stress levels and personality traits from this method.

John Zimmerman, a physicist at the University of Colorado, studied the parties giving and receiving Therapeutic Touch. He used an extremely sensitive device, called a SQUID magnetometer, to measure the magnetic field changes between the practitioner's hand and the client's skin. While the practitioner applied Therapeutic Touch, the magnetometer recorded a significant increase in magnetic field strength. Ordinarily we would be unaware of small magnetic fields, although they are sufficient to affect ongoing events in our body. Neuropeptide reception, for example, is governed in part by small electromagnetic forces. The interaction between a neuropeptide and its receptor could be affected by such a weak magnetic field. We have already seen how a single neuropeptide can produce widespread physical and emotional changes throughout the body. The pathways exist for a small change in our personal space to induce profound change in our physical and emotional experience.

Feel Globally, Act Locally

Buckminster Fuller made popular the environmentally conscious phrase, "Think Globally, Act Locally." Its message was simple. We need to consider that every action taken affects the world as a whole. To create change, according to Fuller, we cannot act on the world as a whole but only within our local sphere of power and ability. I'm often asked questions like, "Where does fear reside in the body?" or "What does this pain in my left leg represent?" or "What's the significance of this throbbing in my toe?" My usual answer is to say, "I don't know." This response frequently bewilders my questioners so I'm quick to add, "but I'm sure we can find out." I always think of Bucky Fuller's simple message when answering such questions. What Fuller said about actions and the world also applies to emotions and the body: Emotions are global not local.

I doubt specific emotions find homes in specific areas of the body. Some do maintain such a belief, but my clinical experience has never shown this to be true. Scientific understanding of the brain and nervous system argues against a pigeonhole theory of emotions and the body. One difficulty with the idea of "a place for each emotion and each emotion for a place" is that it limits a person's useful insight into emotional experience. For example, the first time I saw Roberta, a forty-three-year-old divorced mother of three, she complained of lower back pain. She informed me it was related to the lack of support she experienced in her life since her divorce. Surprised at the confidence she expressed regarding the origin of this pain, I asked, "Why do you say that?" "Oh, I read it in a book," she responded. "I looked up back pain and it said that back pain meant you lacked support in your life."

Contrast Roberta's case with that of Paul, also divorced, and also complaining of lower back pain. "I have no idea what this pain is related to," he said. "Let your awareness go to your lower back," I suggested. "When you're ready, describe the sensations you're experiencing there." First Paul described the tight twisted feeling of the muscles in his lower back. Eventually those sensations led him to his emotions. "This pain feels really angry," he noted. Suddenly a basis for that anger seemed to jump out at him. "My children," he blurted out. "The divorce left me with only weekend visitation rights and that really angers me." Paul's anger soon turned to sadness and grief as he began to weep, not only over the loss of his children, but the ending of his marriage as well. Paul's lower back pain was related to his need to grieve for personal losses, though neither Paul nor I knew this beforehand.

There is no cookbook for emotions and the body. Any emotion can be related to any area of the body, and any area of the body can be related to any emotion. Sometimes several emotions surface from one area of the body, as in Paul's case. At other times different threads of the same emotional experience emerge in different areas. This is why I describe emotions represented globally in the body. Consider the neuropeptide system as one reason for this global representation of emotions: The same neuropeptide that mediates mood in the brain, for example, can affect many different sites in the body. Global representation of emotions provides for unique therapeutic methods. The following exercise is based on this global representation of emotions.

TALKING HANDS

If you're attempting this exercise alone then read each step several times and commit the steps to memory before beginning. Otherwise have someone else take you through each step of the exercise.

1. Begin by relaxing.

Either sit or lie down in a comfortable place: an easy chair, a carpeted floor, or your bed will work fine. Loosen your clothing.

2. Use your breath to help you relax.

Focus your awareness on your breathing and take deep full breaths. On the inhalation, silently repeat to yourself "I am." On the exhalation silently repeat "relaxed." Do this for several minutes.

3. Become aware of the affected part of your body.

Bring your awareness to whatever area of your body is in pain, under stress, or just needs your attention. Without trying to change, control, or analyze that area, notice what this area of your body is like.

4. Discover the related emotions.

What emotions surface as you are aware of this area of your body? Again, don't try to change, control, or analyze these emotions, just be aware of them.

5. Use your right hand.

Make your right hand into a shape that expresses how this affected area of your body feels. Perhaps you need to squeeze your right hand into a tight fist, or stretch your fingers out beyond their normal reach. Do whatever you need to do to let your right hand represent how your body feels to you. Once you've done that, hold your right hand in that position and just observe it for several minutes.

6. Use your left hand.

Keep your right hand in position, but now let your left hand take on the shape of how you'd like your body to feel if it were not affected. Perhaps the fingers are loose and limber, maybe your wrist is limp and your hand is just dangling. Again, do what feels right to you.

7. Move your awareness between both hands.

Slowly switch your attention between your left and right hands. Move back and forth between the representation of how you're experiencing this area of your body now, and how you'd like to experience it.

8. Now transform your right hand.

Slowly let your right hand take on the shape of your left hand. After your right hand has completely changed into the shape assumed by your left hand, notice how your body feels, and notice how you now experience the related emotions. Repeat steps five to eight several times.

9. Disengage from the exercise.

When you're ready to conclude, close your eyes and bring your awareness back to your breathing. Take several deep breaths and then open your eyes.

ACTING LOCALLY, HEALING GLOBALLY

I am always amazed by the response to this exercise. Ninety percent who try this simple process report feeling physical and emotional changes afterward. A typical response comes from a workshop participant who noted, "The pain has lessened in my arm and something has shifted about the anger I felt. I can't say what, but something has changed and I feel different." The exercise is based on the body's ability to represent physical and emotional experience globally. Chances are your hands were pretty far from the affected area of your body. Yet changing your hands could change this area. How does something like this occur?

One answer is that a specific connection exists between your hand and the affected area of your body. That's similar to saying a specific emotion is connected with a specific area of your body. Of course the problem is that in a room of a hundred people the right hand might be connected to a hundred different areas of the body and a hundred different related emotions. A much better answer comes from what we know about how our body processes sensation and takes action.

Let's take an example even simpler than this exercise as an illustration. Do you remember in grade school when you practiced penmanship for hours and hours? You trained your dominant hand to write. Find a pen or pencil and write your first name on a piece of paper. Now, without practicing, switch the pen or pencil over to your other (nondominant) hand and write your name just below that. One signature is probably a little shaky, but I'll bet the construction of the letters is similar. OK, you say, over the years I've occasionally doodled on a piece of paper with my nondominant hand. Perhaps this hand has learned to write just a little bit. Anyway, you might reason that the same set of muscles exists on both sides of the body, so transferring the skill shouldn't be too difficult. Grip your pen or pencil between your teeth and lips and write your name again. Look closely, I'm sure it's a bit unsteady, but I'll bet it still looks similar to the other signatures. You never trained your neck and facial muscles to write, and yet they can do so without practice. Next time you're at the beach, write your name in the sand with your big toe. The signature will again be similar.

The skill of writing is not stored in the cells of your brain associated with your dominant hand. Rather the experience of learning to write was broadcast throughout cells in a wide area of your brain—all the cells went to school. You specifically practiced with one group of cells—those controlling your dominant hand—and they got much better at the task. But any of the cells can access this common experience. In the same way emotional experience and physical sensation are broadcast over wide areas of the brain and body. You can access that experience in many places, like your hands. And when you change your hands that new experience is again broadcast throughout your brain and body. In other words, you can act locally and be sure that you will affect body and mind globally.

The evidence supporting the body's role in healing and recovery is manifold. It comes from understanding the body's contribution to psychological growth and the neurobiological pathways by which body, mind, and emotions converge.

3.

THE BODY CRUCIBLE

The body is the temple of the soul.
—TRADITIONAL PROVERB

O ur body is a crucible for molding and shaping our psyche. Our sense of who we are as unique individuals comes first from sensing that we are physically separate from others—a self separated by body boundaries from other selves. Our sense of who we are in relationship to others comes first from our experience of bonding through touch and physical contact—a self connected to other selves through our body.

Ordinarily we think of our physical and psychological development as independent processes. Physical development comes first. We mature from a simple single-celled organism at conception to a complex, multicelled organism at birth. Psychological development, so this conventional wisdom goes, begins shortly after birth.

Actually, physical and psychological development, are not nearly as separate as they seem. The majority of physical development is completed by birth, but our body continues to change in more subtle ways that support the growth, development, and eventual birth of our psyche. In this chapter we want to explore the body as a crucible for the development of the human psyche—the mold out of which our personality and behavioral traits emerge.

Bonding and Separating: The Dance of Life

Human psychological development—the emergence of the personality traits and behaviors unique to each of us—occurs around two major issues: how we bond and how we separate. Bonding and separating are powerful life forces. From the moment of conception until the time of death we dance back and forth between our bonded and our separate selves. Our bonded self seeks connection and relationship with others, while our separate self seeks to establish and maintain a unique, independent identity and existence. Our success in this dance of life depends upon how well we learn its steps. One step drives the next. The moment we bond we seem to move toward separating. Once separate we seek bonding again.

So the dance begins. Driven by the force of creation, thousands and thousands of sperm struggle incessantly to bond with but a single egg cell. The urge to bond has emerged first. Eventually one sperm will succeed in making contact with the egg and establishing the first bond of life. However, no sooner has this powerful bond been established than the process of separation begins. The fertilized egg stays whole but for an instant. Within two days it has separated into two, then four, then eight, then many additional cells as the equally powerful force to separate and differentiate takes hold.

The dance goes on. With the continued separation of the egg a second powerful urge to bond emerges. By the fifth day after fertilization, when the developing embryo appears no more than a mulberry-shaped cluster of cells, it is well into its journey of bonding. The fertilized ovum undergoes a tortuous twisted journey through the fallopian tubes, searching for a home in the wall of the uterus, and a firmer bond with Mother.

But bonding gives rise to separating. As the tempo of the dance increases, intense cell division and differentiation take place. The fertilized egg is on its way to becoming a separate individual and already we are discovering the essence of the dance: how to bond yet stay separate and unique.

Eventually a great separation occurs through birth, but the dance goes on. For the moment after this great separation takes place an equally great bonding must happen. This bond between mother and child is as essential for our life outside the womb as our bond with the uterine wall was for our life inside the womb. Yet even as this life-sustaining bond flourishes, we are being swept along a new path toward individuation and separation. This is a journey the eyes cannot see, for it takes place deep within the human psyche. Just as the hidden development of the fetus results in the physical birth of the human infant, this hidden process taking place now results in the psychological birth of the human infant.

THE PSYCHOLOGICAL BIRTH OF THE HUMAN INFANT

Psychological birth, usually complete by about three years of age, is as monumental as physical birth. With our psychological birth we are left with the basic structures and behaviors that will define who we are as unique individuals. But the dance is not over. By the time of our psychological birth we have acquired most of the steps of this dance of bonding and separating. From this point we polish and refine our performance through years of bonding and separating with others. Mother is our first dancing partner, then family members, and finally we take up this dance of bonding and separating with the strangers we encounter throughout our life.

The dance of bonding and separating is the essence of human relationships. How, when, and why do we bond? What do we get and what do we give when we bond? How, when, and why do we separate? What do we get and what do we give when we separate? How successful are we in bonding with others yet maintaining our integrity as separate unique individuals? These are the questions we dance around. We each move to our own rhythm. How we learn to dance early on establishes the rhythm by which we dance later in life. And the earliest steps of this dance we learned through our bodies.

Learning the Dance

Let's go back and observe the beginnings of this dance again, now with an eye toward the body's crucial role in learning the steps. Our observation begins shortly after birth, at a time when there is little physical or psychological separation between mother and child. The infant's body and mind exist in a state often termed a *plenum*. This is the ultimate bond: a seamless, defenseless state in which few boundaries exist. Intense, close physical contact between mother and child are characteristic of this early state. The body of the child is contiguous, confluent, and continuous with the body of the mother. Equally intense psychologically merging is present. There is little to distinguish the child's sense of self from its mother. This bond between mother and child is all-important and all-encompassing—little exists outside of it.

Our body is the basis for this initial state of bonding. At birth touch is the infant's most well-developed sense. This initial bond between mother and child unfolds through the contact of their bodies. The progress of bonding can be followed by observing how the mother touches the child. Bonding is at first a tentative affair. Using fingertips only the mother explores the infant's body. The outline of a face is traced, the texture of hair is discovered, a head is gently nudged toward a breast. But a relationship is a mutual undertaking and the mother is awaiting the infant's response. Through cooing, cuddling, and nestling she learns how her infant responds to touch. Not all of her touching may feel pleasant so she hesitates, partly from the fear of being rejected by her child.

Gradually the bond deepens and the embrace between mother and child encompasses more of each other's body. Three to five days after birth, the infant's head will be supported by the mother's palm, its buttocks cupped by her whole hand. Mother no longer explores at fingertip distance but offers large parts of her body to support, nurture, and caress the infant. The infant, in turn, starts to learn a language of touch rich in emotional meaning and texture.

"It is the messages the infant picks up through its own [body]," notes Ashley Montagu, author of the classic book *Touching: The Human Significance of the Skin*, "that tell the infant what the holder 'feels' about it." Feeling, as we have noted earlier, has the double meaning of physical sensation through the body and expression of emotional experience.

In the first few months of life little exists for us apart from this intense bond with Mother. Much of our early time outside the womb is spent sleeping. When we do wake to take care of bodily needs, Mother is there to assist us through some form of physical contact—feeding, burping, diapering, bathing, or comforting us.

In this earliest relationship there is little distinction between self and other; between "I" and "not-I." There is no more a psychological boundary between ourself and our mother than there is a physical boundary. We have not yet formed a sense of our bodies apart from our mother, and we have not yet formed a sense of self apart from her. Our initial physical and psychological growth is, in essence, a struggle to emerge from this bonded state. It has been compared to the struggle of a chick pecking its way out of an egg. In fact, the emergence of a healthy individual from this initial bonding has been described as "hatching." Ultimately the body leads us out of this state of fusion, but this intensely bonded state must come first.

A Crack in the Egg

As newborns we mold ourselves to those who hold us. We curve our backs to the crook of an arm that cradles us. We sprawl ourselves over the surface of the stomach we are laid on. We crawl into the protective corner of a lap that supports us. Molding is one way we bond through our bodies. By six months, however, we also begin to distance ourselves when being held. Now we arch back against an arm that holds us too close. We push up against the surface of the stomach, and we crawl to the edge of a supporting lap. As our body develops greater physical strength we push away from the arms that enveloped us so tightly.

Our body signals our hatching from this state of fusion. Our first boundary is a body boundary. "I am not Mother," first means "my body is separate from hers." Margaret Mahler, the famed child psychologist, noted with surprise that children who were too "tightly enveloped" by their mothers often compensated by physically distancing themselves earlier and more vigorously. They either avoided physical contact with their mothers or contracted their back muscles so strongly when being held that their bodies resembled bows.

"Where are you," asks the children's rhyme I heard often while growing up. The answer my mother intoned and expected me to repeat was "I'm in my skin." But long before we can repeat this answer we have embodied its truth. The first boundary between "I" and "not-I" is a boundary formed at the skin. By the eighth month of life we have discovered the world of self. And it is a different place from the world of the other.

The world of self is a world "in here," a realm within my body bounded by my skin. I stop at my skin. People and objects from the world out there, the world of the other, can approach me but they cannot cross this skin boundary and become me. I can even possess a portion of the world out there. I can have my mommy, my bottle, and my teddy bear. They may be mine but they are not me. This skin boundary is a prototype of the other boundaries we will form throughout our lives.

CREATING BOUNDARIES THROUGH THE BODY

Not long ago I drove the short distance from my home to the Canadian border. Instead of crossing into Canada I decided to walk right on the line separating the two countries. First I straddled the border, one foot in the United States, the other in Canada. Then I jumped back and forth between the two countries. The ground was unchanged by the border. Canadian soil looked just like American soil. So did the grass, trees, and flowers growing on either side of the border.

I felt different, however. When I jumped over to the Canadian side I felt vulnerable and not quite as safe. There were different rules and laws here. I did not have the same rights here. My home wasn't here. Although this border was arbitrarily defined, it created a boundary within which I felt greater safety, outside of which I felt more vulnerable. That is one function of a boundary, it separates an area of familiarity and safety from one of unfamiliarity and danger.

We create similar boundaries with our bodies. A father bemusedly told me of a kissing game his eight-month-old daughter likes to play. "When I ask for a kiss," he said, "she reaches out and barely touches her lips to my cheek before quickly pulling away. She does this several times," he noted, "after each time she waits, laughs, and just observes me."

"She's learning to manipulate me," he lamented playfully, "just like her mother." I suggested that what she was really learning was how to manipulate her boundaries. Like jumping back and forth between Canada and America this little girl was dancing on the border where "Daddy ends and I begin." In effect, she was exploring the creation and dissolution of boundaries between herself and her daddy.

Mahler termed such behavior "practicing," and viewed it as the first step in the hatching process. A young child may crawl away from mother's feet. Then, realizing it has gone too far for comfort, the child quickly returns to grasp or clutch her leg. Children distance themselves from the safety of bodily contact, and then return when they need reassurance and emotional refueling.

While skin may define this all-important boundary between "I" and "not-I," there are other aspects of our young bodies that also contribute to our growing sense of self. Greater strength and muscular coordination give us the physical capability to move away from Mother and others. Greater weight eventually means we are picked up less often and spend more time without being touched. Greater control of internal functions like vomiting and elimination help us reclaim portions of our body once managed solely by Mother. Greater awareness of our bodies, and the bodies of others, brings discovery of sexual differences and realization of the body boundary between male and female.

DISCOVERING THE NEED FOR BONDING AND SEPARATION

We are fascinated with our separateness. Yet by the middle of our second year of life this fascination begins to fade as we seek bonding again. Mahler observed this in children who at first explored on their own with little concern for the whereabouts of their mothers. As they continued to mature, these children became increasingly more concerned about mother's presence. This was not regression to an earlier stage. We actively explore our needs to be separate first. At a certain point we then become aware of our needs for bonding as well, and actively seek to meet those needs. Here, too, the body plays a leading role.

"The 'refueling' type of bodily approach that had characterized the practicing infant," Mahler reports, "is replaced, during the period from 15 to 24 months and beyond by a deliberate search for, or avoidance of, intimate bodily contact."

We learn that we can dance away from the arms that hold us, and we can dance back into those arms as well. Of course, this implies that our dancing partners are willing to release and receive us as these needs arise. All things considered, by the end of our third year we have pretty well mastered the rudimentary steps of this dance. It is a simple process, but one we reenact time and time again throughout our life.

The basic steps of the dance are this: (1) we begin from a bond of trust and safety; (2) we explore the world beyond this safety zone; (3) we return to the safety zone for support and reassurance when needed; and (4) we go back out to explore beyond the safety zone again. It is a process reminiscent of the mythological journey of a hero or heroine. After all, it is the protagonist who travels beyond safe bounds for exploration and conquest. Physical and psychological birth, like all journeys of healing and recovery, mirror this mythological quest.

This dance, this give and take between bonding and separating, between merging and emerging, is the basis upon which we form a healthy sense of self. It is also the foundation for healthy relationships with others. This early dance of bonding and separating, notes Mahler, is "the primal soil from which all subsequent human relationships form." Most major life events are variations on this simple theme of dancing between bonding and separating. Here the body is our great teacher in learning the steps of the dance.

THE BODY IN TRAUMA

If all were perfect we would go through physical and psychological birth unscathed. The picture presented until now is certainly ideal: a physical birth with no complications; a wonderful, loving mother who is sensitive and responsive to the shifting needs of her growing child; a supportive family environment. Certainly this is a nontraumatic stage upon which to learn this dance of bonding and separating. In reality such a setting is rarely the case. The obstacles we encounter learning this dance of bonding and separating become the issues we face on our journey of healing and recovery. Sometimes these are minor obstacles and the related issues are easily addressed. At other times there may be major trauma, and the resulting issues remain with us throughout our lives.

Earlier I recounted the stories of children, observed by Margaret Mahler, who encountered such obstacles in separating from overly bonded mothers. The inability of these mothers to let go, literally and metaphorically, became an early issue of healing and recovery for these infants. Many children responded swiftly and decisively to this healing crisis: They arched their bodies away from their mothers while being held and otherwise sought ways of avoiding the excessive physical contact symptomatic of being held "too tight" in this bond.

However, the trauma may be too great for the young body and mind to overcome. Perhaps we are first beginning the process of separating when severe distress occurs: mother dies, we are accidentally injured, mother becomes psychologically impaired, or we become the victim of physical or sexual abuse. These traumatic events may be more difficult for us to surmount

than an overly bonded mother. Similarly, we may have proceeded partially through our separation from Mother when
trauma occurs. In either case a red flag is raised and our dance
is prematurely interrupted. Eventually the dance proceeds, but
our wounds remain.

Trauma can occur at any point, but we seem most sensitive
to it as we undergo life transitions. At such times we are often
moving from a period of bonding to one of separating, or vice
versa. Birth after months in the womb, bonding with, then separating from Mother, moving through puberty from childhood
to adulthood, being married after years of living alone, getting
divorced after years of being married, and our inevitable death
after years of living are but a few of the critical times in our
dance of bonding and separating. Entering a new phase of the
dance is stressful by itself. Added external trauma simply tele-
graphs the message that the phase we are about to enter is not
safe. There is no simple formula and many factors determine
the severity of the trauma: our age when it occurs, our experience up to that point, and the nature of the trauma itself.

THE WOUNDED INNER CHILD

The "wounded inner child" is a phrase frequently used to describe the effect of this trauma. Our inner child sought to learn
this dance of bonding and separating, then freely move between
these two endpoints. Instead, we are traumatized while taking a
step and this trauma becomes part of each similar step we take.
In this way we can carry a wound with us for many years. While
we usually speak of the wounded child within our heart and
mind, we also need to attend to the wounded child within our
body.

Our body is the original dancer in this ballet between bonding and separating, and touch its first instructor. Making skin
contact is the physical expression of bonding, while pulling
away from contact is expressive of separating. Our body is also
first to encounter the trauma. We are traumatized by omission
and commission. We may not have gotten what we needed
(omission), or we may have gotten what we did not need (com-

mission). For our body this usually means no physical contact when we needed it (omission), or physical contact when we did not need it (commission). In either case we are left with a wounded body, confused about the security of bonding or the safety of separating.

THE LOST SATELLITE AND THE SUBMERGED SELF

Trauma arrests growth, and stalled development halts our dance. Frequently, the more severe the trauma, the more indelibly it is recorded by our body and mind. Then, each time we reach a similar part of the dance we halt again, unsure of how to proceed, fearful of taking the next step. When called upon to bond we have difficulty, when it is time to separate we are stymied. There are two scenarios that capture the body's experience with arrested growth: the Lost Satellite and the Submerged Self. For the Lost Satellite the challenge is bonding. The Submerged Self struggles to separate.

The Lost Satellite

When I think of a lost satellite I envision a small craft launched from a mother ship to explore an unfamiliar part of the universe. As food and fuel diminish, the satellite returns to the last point of rendezvous only to find the mother ship has left. The satellite searches in vain for the mother ship, but this small vessel is destined to wander the universe alone. It refuels and re-supplies when and where it can, but the satellite is unable or unwilling to dock with other craft for more than brief periods of time.

In a similar way we may become lost and stranded. Birth is an obvious point of launching. Failing to bond immediately after birth puts us in the position of the Lost Satellite. We have important physical and psychological needs that must be met. We have nutritional needs that are normally met by bringing our body into intimate physical contact what our mothers. If we are not breastfed our body still needs physical contact to survive and thrive outside the womb. Premature babies who are handled by their mothers fare better than those who are not. Even in the absence of being handled, preemies who have a warm object to touch and cuddle develop faster and more normally than those placed in a sterile lifeless environment. As a result of this knowledge, placing stuffed animals in the cribs of hospitalized premature infants has become a more widespread practice.

Psychologically, this need to bond early through touch is equally profound. Mahler reported on the psychological development of autistic infants who failed to bond with a mothering parent. "These children are deficient in the capacity to use the mother as a beacon of orientation in the world of reality," she wrote. With few exceptions, the result was a form of psychosis in which the actual mothering person was treated as nonexistent, and adaptation to the world outside the child was severely distorted. Sadly, with these infants Mahler noted "essential human characteristics get blunted and distorted in their rudimentary stage or fall apart later on." These children become Lost Satellites.

Fortunately, after being born most of us are able to bond with a mothering person. But there are other times when we are vulnerable to being Lost Satellites. As young infants we may be successful at hatching from this early bond and exploring a new world of individuality. Then comes a point when separation ceases to be enough. The need to bond arises and we seek ways of reconnecting with a mothering person again. If this reconnection is not successful—due to trauma or the unavailability of a mothering person—we can find ourselves a Lost Satellite.

John, an adult client, recalled a message he heard over and over again from his mother. "From as early as I remember she'd tell my sister and me, 'you don't need anyone in your life.' " In part John felt his mother was trying to help him become more independent. But the message was unbalanced and he took on the characteristics of a Lost Satellite. "Later in life," he went on, "I had difficulty forming bonds in my relationships with women. I'd hear that message and say to myself, 'I don't really need this person!' "

John struggled for years with this message, and the loneliness and isolation it brought. "What I wish I'd heard," he mused, "is that there are times in your life when you don't need anyone. But," he added, "there are times when you do need other people and both times are OK." John's trauma was relatively minor in comparison to a child whose mother dies, or who is sexually abused during this time of reconnection.

As we grow we take on other partners to dance with us in bonding and separating—our father, siblings, friends, and mates. Regardless of our partner, when we bond, then separate, then need to rebond, there is the possibility of becoming a Lost Satellite. I recall a client named Alice whom I first saw for upper back pain. Alice was twenty-five years old, and a little taller than normal, yet she stood with the stooped posture of a woman thirty years older. I asked her when she first remembered holding her body this way. "It was around puberty," Alice recounted, "I developed sexually early and my breasts were much larger than other girls my age. My brothers made fun of me and my parents were dismayed."

Alice's body, beyond her control, was separating her from her family. Of course this is a normal occurrence for girls and boys in puberty. However, instead of receiving reassurance about what was happening to her body, Alice received ridicule and alarm. At a period when she needed to know that rebonding was all right, the message Alice received was that it wasn't safe.

Alice continued her story. "I just wanted to hide who I was becoming," she sobbed, "I felt so ashamed of being a woman. I wanted to hide my breasts." It was then she first rounded her shoulders and pulled in her chest to hide her budding femininity. Alice had taken the stance of a Lost Satellite. She illustrates the body posture of a Lost Satellite. Lost Satellites often have bodies that appear rigid, tight, in-drawn, and defended. Lost Satellites harbor a message that bonding is not safe—this is their original wound. Like turtles, they feel the only place of safety is within a well-defended emotional and physical shell. Tragically, this shell is protecting a soft, lonely inner core. But you would not know that from the outside, for often the Lost Satellite appears independent, self-sufficient, in control, aloof, and emotionally cool.

Lost Satellites are usually not in touch with their emotions because to feel means to reconnect with their original wound—separation without the ability to bond. Lost Satellites are often not in touch with their bodies because body awareness brings on the need for human contact and human touch—the very things the Lost Satellite did not receive before turning within. Lost Satellites rarely ask for, or seek out, the help of others because to do so would reopen their primal wound.

Somatic Therapy With Lost Satellites

Arthur was a forty-four-year old senior engineer for an international computer firm when I first saw him. I opened the door to my examination room and I was a little shocked to hear him say, "Hello doctor, please come in and have a seat." I wanted to laugh but I quickly realized he was dead serious. I sat, and he proceeded to list my credentials. He knew what schools I had attended, knew about my previous career as a computer systems engineer at IBM, accurately listed the seminars I had taught, and even knew I'd graduated cum laude from chiropractic college. After reporting on my educational and professional background Arthur concluded, "I think you're someone I can work with." I was stunned. He must have read my résumé I thought. But it didn't end there.

"I have a problem in my neck at the fifth cervical vertebra," he continued. "I believe it has rotated to the right and needs correction. That should take approximately ten treatment sessions and if you are ready to work with me, I'm ready to work with you," he finished. In all my years of clinical practice I have never experienced a client as controlled or controlling as Arthur. I agreed to work with him partly out of curiosity and partly out of sensing how much he needed connection with other people, and how difficult that was for him. He had a thin, tight, rigid body. I often felt his body tense in response to my touch as though I had trespassed on someone's private property. I was never really sure how much my care helped Arthur, although ten visits later he pronounced himself cured and I never saw him again. His was the classic profile of a Lost Satellite unable to reconnect.

Penetrating the Shell of a Lost Satellite

Occasionally it is possible to penetrate the shell of a Lost Satellite with often dramatic results. When I saw Marcia for the first time she defiantly informed me, "I've been through four therapists this year!" Here also was her unspoken challenge, "Watch out, or you'll be the fifth!" Ostensibly Marcia came to see me for tightness in her chest and upper back. Here, too, was an unspoken message in her body: a tight exterior—her chest and upper back—protecting a soft interior—her heart. From her educational background—she had several advanced degrees—I suspected that the other therapists may have failed because they engaged her strongest defense—a keen mind and sharp wit. Instead I chose to engage her body.

Without saying much I asked her to lie down and gently supported her with one hand underneath her upper back, the other resting lightly beneath her collar bones. My touch was extremely light, but within a few moments she began to protest. "Stop, you're hurting me," she said. Normally I would have removed my hand instantly, but I knew I was not hurting her physically. I sensed what she was really saying was, "Stop, this is causing me to face why I'm hurting." She escalated her protest. "Stop, you're really hurting me," she insisted. Biting my tongue slightly, I continued to gently hold the area while refusing to answer Marcia. I was sure that speaking to her would engage her intellect and move her away from the feelings welling up inside.

Each time she appeared to experience some emotion, her body would tense up as if she were fighting hard to hold back tears. She continued to protest my gentle touch, and this stand-off lasted ten or fifteen minutes until she gave in and said softly, "I'll tell you what I've never told anyone, not even my husband." The shell was broken and out came the story of a four-year-old girl sitting on the steps of her house. She watched her father, whom she adored, leave without saying good-bye, without even looking back as he walked away. She had not seen or heard from him in the twenty-five years since that time. Her tightness was fueled by her anger, pain, and rage. As she narrated the story she kept using the word "connection." Though she was nearly thirty now, she still longed for a connection with her father. She even sought that connection with other men and was having difficulty in a marriage to someone twenty-five years her senior. Marcia was a Lost Satellite attempting to reconnect.

Penetrating this shell allowed Marcia to get in touch with feelings she had held in for years. Throughout the two years of our therapy, Marcia worked hard at uncovering and addressing her pain and rage. Then her healing journey took a remarkable turn. She had just returned from her mother's home in eastern Pennsylvania, after a weekend of open discussion about her therapy. She got a surprising call. Out of the blue, after more than twenty-five years, her father called. Ultimately this led to a meeting with him. Face to face, she spoke of her anger and pain. For both people this was a rare and special gift of healing. Feelings can be locked in the body and touch can help unlock these feelings for a Lost Satellite, thereby contributing to healing and recovery.

The Submerged Self

If the Lost Satellite has difficulty bonding, the Submerged Self has difficulty separating. Early on the Submerged Self is the child unable to emerge from its initial bond with Mother. Mahler termed this early bond symbiotic, implying that for all practical purposes two different people functioned as one, and both mother and infant benefited from such a union. Symbiosis is an obvious fact of life before birth and natural immediately after birth, but eventually we must transcend this intertwined state.

Children who became Submerged Selves, Mahler observed, seemed unable to leave this orbit with Mother and treated her "as if she were part of the self, that is, as not separate from the self but rather fused with it." They developed a psychosis Mahler also termed symbiotic and lived to become severely dysfunctional adults. As children they never attained "a feeling of wholeness," she wrote, "of individual entity, let alone 'a sense of human identity.' " Their life was one of "fusion, melting, lack of differentiation between the self and the nonself—a complete blurring of boundaries." James F. Masterson summed up the dilemma of the Submerged Self in a sentence: "Although physically he is a separate, autonomous self, he doesn't feel, think, or act that way."

The Submerged Self results from a variety of causes that interfere with our psychological birth. Not all interference with our hatching results in the devastating psychosis Mahler referred to. While the nature of the interference determines the severity of our dysfunction, it is usually trauma in some form that delivers the message that separation is dangerous. For the Submerged Self, hatching leads to separation, which leads to fears of abandonment. To counter these fears the Submerged Self seeks to fuse, bond, and otherwise remain in the safety of the unhatched state. Even when it is time to leave the nest the Submerged Self seeks to remain. This state of bonding or fusion is a continuation of the first state of safety we experience after birth—bonding with Mother.

Often it is the mothering person who inappropriately continues the bond. For the infant to emerge from this thoroughly enmeshed dyad, the mother must willingly let go. If the mother also suffers from being a Submerged Self, her fears of abandonment may prevent her from allowing the child to hatch. Sometimes chance plays a role. If the mother dies or becomes seriously ill during the child's first years of life, the child may not hatch. Deliberate trauma can also have a hand. The child may be victimized physically or sexually when first emerging from the safety of the bond with Mother.

This message—bonding is safe, separation is dangerous—is incorporated into the child's developing personality, behavior, and physical body. Then when the need to separate from Mother arises—and at other times of separation or loss—the crisis of the Submerged Self ensues. A typical set of behaviors comes into play: clinging, denial of separateness, and alternation between avoidance and approach.

Clinging is one way a Submerged Self deals with crisis. Clinging preserves the illusion of oneness and soothes the fears of separation and loss. At a young age clinging is expressed through the body: A child clutches its mother as though the tighter it holds the more it becomes one with her. Clinging reinforces a lack of physical boundary between self and other that is characteristic of the Submerged Self. This is different from refueling, which is natural for a child exploring the emergence of its separate autonomous self. Refueling is the return from separation for reassurance that we can bond. Clinging is unwillingness to separate at all. By clinging, notes Masterson, the child "can act out his wish for reunion with the mother, making it seem in fantasy as if he and she are still a fused pair as they were before and immediately after birth." Clinging is not only expressed physically but also emotionally. As an adult it may be easier for a Submerged Self to cling to an abusive relationship, for example, than to leave. Clinging feels safe.

Denial of separateness is closely related to clinging. By acknowledging our separateness we recognize the existence of our unique individual self. It is precisely the emergence of this authentic, separate self that frightens the Submerged Self. Denying this authentic self is learned behavior. As a child, the Submerged Self, according to Masterson, "learns to avoid opportunities to express himself, or assert his wishes, or activate what is most unique in his personality, all of which could threaten his emotional equilibrium."

I am reminded of a story told by H. Steven Glenn. While sitting in a restaurant he observed two perfectly dressed children walk in with their perfectly dressed mother. The youngsters were obviously groomed to be adults-in-miniature. When the waitress asked the young boy what he wanted, he eagerly replied, "A hamburger, french fries, and a Coke." Whereupon his mother leaned over to the waitress and said, "But he'll actually have roast beef, a baked potato, and milk." Somewhat disheartened the child slumped back into his seat. Soon the waitress came with the order, setting down a hamburger, french fries, and Coke in front of an incredulous child. "Look Mommy," the youngster exclaimed, "She thinks I'm real!" Submerged Selves have not experienced their real self.

Submerged Selves are also unable to integrate bonding and separating. Their life is one of avoidance or approach—now you see me, now you don't—and they rigidly alternate between

the two. Unsure of their own boundaries, Submerged Selves feel
safety in holding on tightly or evading contact altogether. In
either case the Submerged Self avoids the challenges posed by
relationships with others. Submerged Selves were held onto at
times when letting go was needed for the emergence of an authentic separate self. They were reassured for remaining bonded
rather than reinforced for exploring their independence. Thus,
a deep memory in body and mind sends the message, "You will
be rewarded by avoiding life's challenges and keeping your true
feelings to yourself."

Somatic Therapy With the Submerged Self

Somatic therapy with a Submerged Self often brings this avoid-
ance/approach behavior to the surface. The body of the Submerged Self feels safety in being held or touched. Breaking
contact by letting go or not touching raises the specter of separation and confrontation with an authentic self that is threatening.

Jane was a woman in her late fifties, recently divorced and
working as a bookkeeper for the first time in many years.
Throughout the several months I saw Jane therapeutically she
seemed eager to work with me and amazed that touch could
reveal so much about her emotional issues. I was one of a string
of somatic therapists—chiropractors, rolfers, massage therapists—that she had seen in recent years. She complimented me
profusely and was eager to give me a big hug at the end of each
session. My own sense was that our work together was going
all too well, so I began to refuse her desire to hug me at the end
of each session. I explained to her that something didn't feel
quite right about hugging her. She made fun of my comments,
accusing me of being afraid to get close.

One morning, after I had not seen Jane for several weeks,
she seemed in a particularly agitated mood. I just sat quietly,
waiting for her to initiate conversation, or talk about her feelings. "Well," she barked, "what are we going to do now?" "I
don't know, Jane," I replied, "what would you like for us to
do?" "You're the doctor," she said, getting more agitated,

"you're supposed to know what to do. Why do you always sit there without saying anything? Why do you always ask me what I want to do?"

By sitting quietly, by not initiating the conversation, and asking her what she wanted to do, I was refusing to become enmeshed in Jane's drama of the Submerged Self. By default I was also beckoning her true self to emerge. The tension mounted and Jane became more insistent. "Touch me," she demanded, "that's what you're supposed to do. Touch me!"

"No, Jane," I responded firmly but softly, "it doesn't feel right for me to touch you now."

"Touch me," she ordered, "that's what you get paid to do!" Once again I politely but firmly declined her request for touch. This time, however, she jumped up from her seat and unleashed a barrage of anger in my direction.

"You're a horrible person," she screamed. "You have no compassion. You just sit there without saying anything and without feelings for anyone. That's why people I've referred to you don't come back to see you. You don't care about them and you don't care about me." Jane went on and on like this for at least ten minutes. I felt like a sailboat buffeted by strong winds and steep seas, but I held my course in silence. By now Jane was pacing back and forth, enraged and infuriated by my inaction.

"Jane, does this remind you of anything?" I asked, referring to her outburst. That startled her. After pausing for a moment and coming to the brink of tears she said, "Yes, it reminds me of what I've felt but never been able to say to my parents." This was the turning point in our work together. From here Jane was able to more directly confront those parts of herself that were submerged. Sometimes touch is most compassionate when it is withheld. For a Submerged Self withholding touch can counter the powerful forces in the drive to merge physically and psychologically. This can begin to create boundaries that were formerly absent and encourage the Submerged Self to hatch.

Emotional flooding is another way the Submerged Self deals with life. Flooding is a consequence of living without boundaries, the internal equivalent of merging. Flooding is the absence of boundaries around the emotions experienced by the

Submerged Self and others. When the Submerged Self is flooding, ordinary emotions are blown far out of proportion. What normally makes us sad causes a deep, dark sorrow; what normally makes us happy produces unbridled ecstasy; what normally makes us wonder causes mystical reverie. These emotions are uncontained and uncontrolled.

Martha had been in Twelve-Step programs for nearly twenty years before I first saw her. She was a vivacious fifty-year-old woman, distraught about the potential dissolution of her thirty year marriage. She felt she was no longer getting anywhere with "the program," as she referred to Twelve-Step programs. After taking a brief history I asked her to lie on her back. I went to hold her feet in order to evaluate the tension in her legs, hips, and lower back. No sooner had I begun this than Martha started to cry. She wailed and sobbed for ten or fifteen minutes. When she was through she thanked me and remarked how much better she felt. I was surprised by her catharsis and responded that she was obviously in touch with her feelings. Initially, I took this as a positive sign.

I saw Martha a week later. Again I approached her feet but before I could place my hands around them she began to cry and wail just as before. "Hmmm," I thought to myself, "there's more here than someone who's in touch with their emotions." I let her continue crying, and again Martha was pleased with her cathartic outpouring. This time, however, I was not so pleased, something didn't feel right.

The next week things came to a head. I had just walked into the room and spoken with Martha briefly. As I was rising from my chair to walk to the end of the treatment table she began to cry once more. Something flashed inside my head, I wheeled around, looked her in the eye and said rather forcefully, "Martha, stop crying!" She was startled. In all her years of therapy and Twelve-Step programs she'd always been encouraged to emote, no one had ever asked her to stop. But Martha had the symptoms of being a Submerged Self and right then emoting was the last thing she really needed.

Martha slowly reined in her tears. She found they had been obscuring other issues that lay at the root of her current distress. The tears diverted her away from the pain and anger from an abusive childhood and an alcoholic father. In each subsequent session I would remind her to stop crying, and over time she brought this tendency under greater voluntary control. Not all catharsis is emotional flooding and not all catharsis needs to be stopped. But Martha did need to stop flooding long enough to discover the real authentic emotions that often escape the Submerged Self.

Unlike the self-absorption of Lost Satellites, Submerged Selves seek to get their physical and emotional needs met through others. This is one reason they frequent the offices of healthcare providers. It's been my observation that Submerged Selves seem particularly attracted to somatic therapists—those of us who work with the body and use touch. I suspect this is partly because human touch can physically recreate the bonding that feels so safe for them. Unfortunately many somatic therapists are not trained to identify the personality and behaviors associated with Submerged Selves. I know all too well how this combination of an unaware practitioner and a Submerged Self can have unfortunate consequences.

I first began to practice as a chiropractor with virtually no training in the emotional dynamics of health care—very few somatic therapists do have such training. I saw a woman named Deidre who was in her early forties. Deidre was of Swedish descent, though she was born in Poland during World War II. Later her family moved to Germany where at sixteen she met and married an American GI. After his tour of duty he brought Deidre back to the United States and they settled in suburban New Jersey. They began a family and also began to encounter some serious problems. Deidre's husband was an alcoholic, and Deidre had many scars from living under a Nazi regime during the early years of her life. Then her husband became physically abusive, and he had a string of affairs with other women. Deidre sought help.

The first time I saw Deidre she told me about all the healthcare practitioners she had been to over the years to "fix" the various problems she had. She had been to a number of chiropractors, she informed me, but she was sure I was the one who could finally "make things right." I even called the previous chiropractor she'd seen to check on their relationship. He was very pleased—even relieved—that she was now seeing me. Still I had no clue what lay waiting.

At first our therapeutic relationship went well. It seemed I could do nothing wrong. Deidre told me how wonderful she felt, and how my treatment helped her as no other. However, as our sessions continued I began to notice a troubling pattern. Deidre might come in complaining of shoulder pain. While the pain might leave after working with her shoulder, it would mysteriously reappear in another part of her body. Sometimes clients will report the sensation of pain moving around the body, but Deidre's response was different. The pain always seemed to keep moving—from shoulder to lower back to neck to chest to head—and I seemed to be chasing the pain. This is a very frustrating position to be in. I never felt I could do enough and Deidre seemed to enjoy every moment of it. My sessions with her almost always went beyond our allotted time, which threw my entire daily schedule behind.

Gradually Deidre's attitude toward me changed as well. Why was the pain traveling all over her body, she wanted to know. Maybe I wasn't the great doctor she thought I was anyway. I was beginning to dread seeing her. After one treatment session she bumped her right leg against the doorknob while walking out of my treatment room. There was no visible bruising but something told me this was going to be trouble. From that point on I could do nothing right. The pain from that bump became the central theme of her life. She projected everything that was going poorly for her—her husband's alcoholism and extramarital affairs, her son dropping out of school, her mother being hospitalized for depression—onto this injury. She let me know I had made her life miserable.

Suddenly Deidre no longer kept appointments and I didn't hear from her for two years. One day I received a letter informing me that she was suing for malpractice. The documentation of malpractice bordered on being ludicrous. She had taken a photograph of her leg and used a pencil or pen to darken an area of the picture. Then she made photocopies of the photograph, which she contended showed the physical harm she had suffered. The evidence of harm done also included a letter detailing the many life tragedies suffered, she claimed, as a result of this injury. It was obvious that the evidence would never stand a test of law. To my surprise, my insurance company settled out of court for a mere two thousand dollars rather than assume the legal fees required to contest Deidre's charges.

Some years later I went back and read her final statement. It was only then I understood I had been engaged in the drama of a Submerged Self. Deidre had inflated me and deflated me, attempted to merge, and projected all her problems as far away from her troubled real self as possible. But her final statement said it all. "I am suing for the pain and anguish suffered," she wrote, "when I was injured by someone in whom I had placed all my faith." This is indeed the crisis of the Submerged Self: to place all their faith in others and little in themselves.

The Body and the Submerged Self

Lack of boundaries—a central theme for the Submerged Self—is also reflected in their bodies. Submerged Selves frequently have bodies lacking definition and tone. Where the body of the Lost Satellite is tight and bounded, the body of the Submerged Self is loose and unbounded. Submerged Selves feel little ownership of a separate, unique self and consequently they feel little ownership of their body, that first crucial expression of a unique self.

Externally, Submerged Selves may be overweight and out of shape. They often sense the need for psychological and physical boundaries without having a clue as to how to create them. One client told me, "I'm afraid of getting to close to other people, I know how quickly I want to merge with them. It's a lot easier for me to maintain this extra weight. At least it gives me distance." Internally, the Submerged Self can be unaware of large portions of the body. "It's all numb below my waist"; "I can't really tell where my upper body ends and my lower body begins"; "My left leg feels blank"; "My right side feels amorphous." These are typical comments reflecting the lack of body awareness—and therefore the lack of self-awareness—characteristic of the Submerged Self.

Two Studies in Dysfunction

The dysfunctional attributes of the Lost Satellite and the Submerged Self are almost directly opposed to each other. Yet both scenarios represent unhatched eggs—selves that are only partially born. The Lost Satellite is a self within a protective shell. Emotionally it is a grandiose shell of self-absorption and lack of emotional involvement with others. Physically it is an armored shell of tension, rigidity, and lack of bodily contact. Lost Satellites know little of bonding with others—physically or emotionally—though they continually seek the approval and admiration of others to support their inflated feelings of self-worth and self-importance. But their's is a hard shell protecting a soft core. This outer shell defends against inner feelings of emptiness, loneliness, vulnerability, and rage. Lost Satellites are often described as having a "narcissistic personality disorder."

The Submerged Self is also partially born. It has broken through the shell of the Lost Satellite but has not fully established itself as a whole, separate, unique human being. Boundaries are difficult for the Submerged Self to create and maintain—merging, however, feels safe. Lacking a sense of boundaries—physically and emotionally—the Submerged Self manages relationships with others through fusion, avoidance/approach, emotional flooding, inflation/deflation, and the other traits portrayed above. This state is often called a "borderline personality disorder."

Ideally we evolve beyond both the Lost Satellite and the Submerged Self, achieving psychological birth and its endowment of a separate, unique, whole sense of self. In this process we learn the dance of relationships—bonding with others and retreating to self when needed. At times we do not dance well; we find ourselves unable to bond, like the Lost Satellite; or unable to separate, like the Submerged Self. At times our dancing partners—parents, friends, lovers, mates, children, subordinates, colleagues—have difficulty bonding or separating as well. We can ignore these missteps and continue our dance, or choose to view them as opportunities for healing, recovery, and growth.

THE BODY'S ROLE IN DYSFUNCTIONAL BEHAVIOR

The Lost Satellite and the Submerged Self also highlight the body's role in the origins of dysfunctional behavior and in the healing process. Our bodies communicate simply through the presence or absence of touch. Touching is the body's way of bonding, withdrawing touch the body's way of separating. In fact the dance of bonding and separating could just as easily be called the dance of touching and not touching. Long before we learn the verbal skills of bonding and separating we learn these somatic skills. The somatic aspects of bonding and separating are so important they became the basis for Mahler and other researchers tracking the psychological birth of the human infant.

How do you investigate the mind of a child who cannot talk? This dilemma has plagued psychologists for years. It is not possible to ask an infant how it feels or what it thinks. One can't lean over the railings of a crib and say, "It's been three months since your birth, have you started the hatching process yet?" A six-month-old baby has no verbal answer to the question, "Is Mommy giving you enough room to grow and explore?" Instead, investigators found answers to these and many other questions through observing the infant's body.

Observing a child's body, Mahler says, "permits one to infer what is going on inside the child; that is to say, the motor phenomena [what happens in the body] are correlated with intrapsychic events [what happens in the mind]. *This is particularly true in the first years of life* [Mahler's emphasis]." The body is the womb of our psychological birth. Mahler felt behavior that could be verbally investigated later in life could be traced to early somatic roots:

> The young child's rich and expressive affectomotor (gestural) behavior of his entire body, as well as the back-and-forth movement of approach and appeal behaviors and distancing between infant

and mother—their frequency, amplitude, timing and intensity—served as important guidelines, furnishing many clues to phenomena we encounter through verbal communication at later ages.

Touch is the first sensory system to develop in the fetus. Movement is present from the beginning of life. It should come as no surprise that our body, through movement and touch, is so important to the later development of our emotional and psychological being.

EXPLORING THE BODY CRUCIBLE

Touch, movement, and body awareness are the three main ways our body contributes to our emotional experience. Using these three factors we can investigate our body's role in our emotional life. We can discover some of the issues that challenge us and how we might work with those issues through the body. I'd like to propose a set of experiments, or experiences, to explore our body's role as a crucible for our emotional life. The following exercises recreate some aspects of the body's role in our psychological development. The exercises all require that you work with a trusted friend. Before undertaking these exercises please read them through. If any of the exercises feel awkward or uncomfortable, do not attempt them. If you have any questions about whether you should attempt these exercises, discuss them with a therapist or qualified health care provider first. **Do not attempt these exercises with someone you do not know well, or someone with whom you have never shared a touch.**

PREPARATION

Find a quiet, comfortable place to work. There should be few distractions, even pleasant distractions like music or outdoor sounds. You and a friend can be sitting in chairs or on the floor facing each other. Throughout these exercises you will be designated the **Traveler** and your friend will be known as the **Guide.** Maximum value will come from doing the exercises in the order they are presented here. The Traveler should record any reactions or impressions after each exercise—a note on a piece of paper will do just fine.

The Guide should pay special attention to remaining an active and not passive partner during these exercises. Even though the focus of the exercise is primarily on the Traveler, the Guide should be aware of his or her experience somatically (in the body) and psychologically (mentally and emotionally). Most of the time the Guide remains silent, saying only as much as the instructions ask. Even in this silence the Guide can keep the following question in mind: What is my experience like right now? At the end of each exercise there is an opportunity for both parties to discuss their experience. The Guide can report to the Traveler what his or her experience was like. Guides may also find paper and pencil useful.

Exercise 1: Finding a Safe Place to Touch

This exercise must be done before any of the other exercises are attempted.

1. Allow the Traveler to relax.
The Guide asks the Traveler to relax using the relaxation script in the appendix of this book or one of the Guide's own choosing.

2. Traveler scans body to find a safe place.
The Guide asks the Traveler to find a safe place to be touched using the following intervention or one similar to it:

> Would you slowly scan your body from head to feet. When you find an area you feel is safe for me to touch, let me know.

The Traveler can have his or her eyes open or closed during this step. Regardless of how well the Traveler knows the Guide this safe place should have a very low emotional, physical, or sexual charge. Hands, knees, shoulders, elbows, forearms, and feet are some examples of areas that may be safe. The Guide should not influence the Traveler's decision of what area feels safe.

3. Traveler reports the safe area to the Guide.
The Traveler reports this safe place to the Guide using the following simple statement or its equivalent:

> My———feels like a safe place for you to touch.

Touch should not take place yet. The Traveler has simply found an area that will be used in the following exercises.

EXERCISE 2: SIMPLE TOUCH
The objective of this exercise is to have the Traveler become more aware of his or her somatic and emotional reactions to being touched. This exercise will familiarize the Traveler and Guide with the basic process used in the subsequent exercises.

1. Allow the Traveler to relax.
The Guide asks the Traveler to relax using the relaxation script in the appendix of this book of one of the Guide's own choosing.

2. Ask Traveler to focus on the safe area.
With eyes open or closed, the Traveler is asked to focus on his or her safe area using the following intervention or its equivalent:

> Please bring your awareness to [Traveler's safe area]. At some point I'll touch this area. Once you feel my touch, make note of how your body reacts and please say the first word that comes to your mind.

This exercise works most effectively if the Traveler does not attempt to edit the physical sensations or emotions that arise in response to being touched. Simply being aware of how the

Traveler's body reacts to touch, and the first word that comes into the Traveler's mind is sufficient. In verbalizing the first word that comes to mind, the Traveler is asked to be aware of the emotions that arise in response to being touched. This awareness is "free association." Any word that arises is all right and the Traveler should make no attempt to edit what word is spoken.

3. Guide touches Traveler's safe area.
The Guide gently touches then removes his or her hand from the Traveler's safe area.

4. Traveler reports his or her reactions.
The Traveler describes the physical sensation of being touched and verbalizes the first word that comes to mind in response to the Guide's touch. The Traveler may wish to consider some of the following questions in regard to being touched by the Guide:

> What's it like to anticipate being touched? What reaction did my body have to being touched? What's the first thing that came into my mind upon being touched? What did I desire the Guide to do (leave hand, remove hand, etc.)?

5. Guide records the Traveler's responses.
The Guide should also have paper and pencil to record the Traveler's response in the following manner:

Physical Sensation
———————————————
First Word

6. Repeat steps one through five.
The Guide and Traveler should repeat steps one through five at least three times and the Guide should write down each response.

7. Traveler concludes exercise.
The Guide asks the Traveler to slowly open his or her eyes. The Traveler is also given an opportunity to write down any

thoughts, feelings, impressions, or ideas that come from doing the exercise.

8. Traveler and Guide discuss the exercise.

The recorded responses of the Traveler should be discussed and both parties should describe their reaction to this exercise. This basic exercise on touching is meant to set the stage for the following two variations. Each variation illustrates a particular somatic aspect of bonding and separating.

EXERCISE 3: BONDING

This exercise is similar to Exercise 2 with the exception of step three. Instead of removing his or her hand from the Traveler's safe area, the Guide now continues to touch the Traveler. The Traveler should not respond immediately to being touched by the Guide. Instead he or she should be aware of the difference between momentary and continuous touch. **Once the Traveler begins describing his or her reactions to the Guide, the Guide's hands should be removed from the Traveler's body.**

My experience with this exercise reveals two different types of responses. As touch continues there is often a feeling of bonding or merging. Some Travelers will report their body seems to soften, relax, and more easily accept the Guide's touch. There is often a report of merging boundaries between Traveler and Guide. It becomes difficult to distinguish where the skin of the Guide stops and the skin of the Traveler begins. Both Traveler and Guide will often report they did not want to stop touching.

The other response is just the opposite. As touch continues the Traveler's body tightens more and seems to defend against the intrusion of the Guide. Travelers will report muscular rigidity and the feeling that their body wanted to pull away from the Guide. There is often a sharp boundary between the Traveler's and Guide's skin. The Traveler will report wanting the Guide to stop touching, while the Guide will describe being very uncomfortable while touching the Traveler. Of course other possible responses fall between these two extremes. For example, a

Traveler may oscillate back and forth between a merged and an armored response to prolonged touch.

The objective of this exercise is to explore bonding. Evidence of physical relaxation and acceptance of touch are somatic and emotional components related to bonding. Conversely, physical tightness and aversion to touch are somatic and emotional experiences opposed to bonding. In part, Travelers reporting such aversions share an experience common to the Lost Satellite. There may be many healthy reasons why someone recoils from touch. I am not suggesting that such a Traveler is a Lost Satellite, but that when the objective is bonding through touch and the experience is being armored to touch, this is similar to the experiences of a Lost Satellite. In fact, this is the point of the exercise: to experience in body and mind what it is like to attempt to bond through touch.

EXERCISE 4: SEPARATION

This exercise is substantially the same as Exercise 3 with one exception: **At some point while being touched the Traveler decides to pull his or her safe area away from the Guide's hand.** Depending upon where the Traveler's safe area is, this exercise may require movement of a hand or a knee, or the Traveler may need to move his or her entire body away from the Guide. Whatever is necessary, the Traveler should move away from the Guide's touch without informing the Guide when this is about to happen. Meanwhile the Guide should offer no resistance to the Traveler's effort to pull away.

Throughout the exercise the Traveler should be aware of how soon after being touched he or she felt compelled to pull away, what the physical sensation of moving away was like, and what the emotional sensation of moving away was like. The Guide should be aware of his or her response to these same issues.

There are a range of interesting responses to this exercise. Some Travelers report a slight tightening of the body and pulling away with ease after a reasonable period of time. A word that frequently emerges from this Traveler is empowerment.

Other Travelers report only desiring to be touched for a short period of time, tightening the body forcefully, and pulling away quickly. Here the Traveler may have feelings of anger. Still other Travelers tell of difficulty in deciding to pull away at all. The Guide's touch felt comforting, reassuring, or inviting and the Traveler did not want to break contact. There is some fear at the prospect of separating. Often these Traveler's will lose touch with how their body feels but will report concern about the Guide's feelings of abandonment.

Here the objective is separation. Moderate physical tightness and movement away from touch are naturally associated with separation. Heightened awareness of physical boundaries is also related to separation. On the other hand, loss of body awareness, confusion around pulling away, and overt concern for the Guide's feelings are contrary to separation. These experiences are comparable to the Submerged Self. This in no way implies that a Traveler who reports confusion about pulling his or her body away from the Guide's touch is a Submerged Self. However, the feelings in body and mind are similar.

Guides can have a range of experience similar to the Travelers'. Some Guides will speak of feeling glad and relieved the Traveler made the decision to break contact. Other Guides report feelings of emptiness, abandonment, or frustration when the Traveler pulled away. Often Guides will speak of a rejection and a lack of support, as if a part of the body caved in when the touch of the Traveler was withdrawn. He or she might experience feelings of inadequacy. Said one Guide, "It felt as if I just couldn't do the right thing no matter how hard I tried."

This exercise also demonstrates the reciprocal nature of touch—that one cannot touch without being touched. The Guide's perceptions are important because they inform us about what happens when bonding is attempted by one party but resisted or rejected by the other.

THE INFLUENCE OF SIMPLE TOUCH

I used an exercise like this with a Traveler named Sally, a competent, middle-aged law professor with only two living relatives. She had never married and struggled with issues of loneliness, neglect, and abandonment. For this exercise, we switched places—she took the role of the Guide and I took the role of the Traveler who pulled away. After the exercise I asked what it felt like in her body for me to pull away. "It felt as if the rug was being pulled out from under me," she said. "I was reminded of my father, who I felt disliked and discounted my feelings and ideas," she continued. "Whenever I had something to say he managed to disparage it or change the subject. Eventually I learned to shut up and keep my feelings to myself. That's when I first began to feel isolated and alone inside myself."

Using similar techniques, Travelers can explore a range of emotional experiences through their bodies. Couples can also benefit from these exercises, which explore the somatic issues of partnership and intimacy. By alternating roles between Traveler and Guide, each partner has the opportunity to experience the somatic effects of bonding and separation. Taken alone these exercises are neither diagnostic nor therapeutic for a given physical or emotional condition. However, they do show the profound influence that simple touch has on our emotional experience. They hark back to a time before we could speak about our feelings, a time when our body, through movement, gesture, and touch, was the basis of our relationships.

THE SAGE WITHIN THE TEMPLE

Our bodies first learn the dance of bonding and separating through touching and withdrawing from touch. What we first learn somatically becomes the basis of our emotional and psychological development. Our bodies contain a record of our life experience at this dance of bonding and separating. Through our bodies we can examine how well we dance. We can make changes somatically that show themselves emotionally. We can be in touch with emotional experience by being in touch with our bodies. Our bodies are great teachers. Reflecting on the traditional proverb at the beginning of this chapter, one Guide observed that the body is not only a temple for the soul, it is also the sage within the temple.

4.

TOUCHING THE CHILD WITHIN

Our Child Within flows naturally
from the time we are born
to the time that we die and
during all of our times and transitions in between.
We don't have to do anything to be our True Self.
It just is.
—CHARLES L. WHITFIELD

The "inner child" or the "child within" are phrases now synonymous with healing and recovery from dysfunctional relationships. This alive, creative, authentic part of us also has been called the "divine child," "wonder child," "true self," "real self," "higher self," "deepest self," and "core self." Dysfunction results when this part of us is stifled, blocked, or otherwise denied full expression. Recovering this child within and allowing it fuller expression in our life is a key element of physical and emotional healing.

PSYCHOLOGICAL BIRTH AND THE CHILD WITHIN

The psychological birth of the human infant occurs at that critical time between birth and three years of age. This psychological birth gives rise to our real self—the child within. Interfering with psychological birth leads to a false self masking this real self—a "wounded child within" I described as a Lost Satellite or Submerged Self. Bodily experience profoundly influences our psychological birth—our body, in effect, acting as a crucible for our child within. There are somatic origins of our dysfunctional behavior as adults, and ways the body might be enlisted in our healing and recovery. In this present chapter we'll explore further the body's role in healing and recovery by investigating the somatic reality of the child within.

BEYOND VISUALIZATION AND AFFIRMATION

To consult the many books, tapes, videos, and workshops for healing the child within, one would think our inner child was primarily verbal and visual. Most therapeutic techniques rely on a combination of seeing, talking, and listening to explore the thoughts, feelings, and experiences of the child within. Consider a hypothetical individual recovering from alcoholism. As part of her healing process she is **asked** to go back to her childhood, which she does by **visualizing** herself at age three. She is further asked to engage in a **dialogue** with this **image** of her inner child. This woman will **listen** as her inner child **tells** her about particular feelings or **describes** events that occurred in her family. She may be asked to **talk** about the feelings that emerge as she interacts with her inner child. She may also discover the inner child's **tapes** (negative **messages** the child **heard** over and over again), and it may be suggested that she provide **affirmations** to counter these negative messages. Most therapy is similar. Regardless of the specific techniques, this is audiovisual (AV) therapy.

Much good comes from such therapy. However, I am always struck by the absence of bodily experience. Our inner child was somatic before it was verbal or visual. And this somatic reality continues even when our verbal and visual experience becomes more pronounced. Although as adults we mostly talk about our feelings, as young children we experienced and enacted our feelings through our bodies.

Carmen was a forty-three-year-old mother of two who was raised in an alcoholic family. She was also married to a man who was a recovering alcoholic. Carmen continually struggled with her readiness to be her husband's caretaker and codependent behavior that resulted. At the beginning of one therapy session she happily announced that she had some good news.

"I stood up for myself," she beamed. "He promised to drive the kids to a birthday party on Friday. So I planned to take a walk along the riverfront for exercise after I came home from work." Friday came and Carmen's husband failed to return from work early enough to keep his promise. She ended up driving their children to the party and forgoing her opportunity to take a walk. Later her husband explained that he was over-burdened at work and simply forgot.

"It wasn't the worst thing that could happen," she noted, "but I did feel hurt and angry." Once at home with her husband she waited until her initial anger subsided. "I asked him to sit down and told him I had something to say," she recounted. "I said I felt hurt and angry not only because he broke his promise but also because he hadn't called me. Normally, I would have just blown it off and told him I understood how hard he worked. I was a little nervous but I said this all without hesitating or crying."

It was obvious how proud Carmen was of standing up for herself. In fact, her body literally stood up as she talked. Her head was held high, her shoulders were placed back, and her arms were by her sides. However, shortly after narrating this story, Carmen spoke of another event that happened several days later. "I overheard a coworker talking about her son being arrested for shoplifiting," she recalled, "and I immediately started to cry. I can't explain why, but I burst out in tears at her story."

Carmen's body assumed a completely different posture for this second tale. Her head was slumped down, her shoulders were rotated forward, and her arms were slumped over her legs. "Please, don't say another word," I asked Carmen. "Close your eyes for a moment and be aware of how you're holding your body right now."

"What's that like?" I asked after she'd had her eyes closed for several minutes. Carmen started to cry again. "This is how I held my body as a young child of three or four," she replied. "I'd listen to my drunken father yell and scream at my mother," she continued, "while standing in a corner just like this, ashamed and afraid to look at them." The body often provides direct access to the child within.

THE SOMATIC RIGHTS OF THE CHILD WITHIN

The bodily experience of our child within is based on several important rights. They are

- The right to experience one's body separate from the body of others
- The right to bond through touch, or separate through avoiding touch
- The right to ownership of one's entire body
- The right to experience one's body as a normal source of pleasure and pain

When these rights are met they provide our inner child with a normal, healthy environment in which to grow and flourish. When these rights are not met, or are trampled upon, our inner child's environment is unhealthy and dysfunctional.

The Right to Experience One's Body Separate From the Body of Others

Our sense of self is based on being able to experience our body separate from the body of others. During the period immediately after birth we sense our body as a part of our mother's body. We sense our self as a part of her as well. The hatching process leading to the birth of our child within—our true self—begins as we physically separate our body from the body of our mother.

Touch, movement, and body awareness help our child within accomplish this independent bodily experience. We develop our first boundary through our skin and sense of touch. Awareness helps the inner child realize what is within the skin is **self**, what touches the skin is **other**. Through movement our child within first experiences this world of self by pulling back from the world of Mother and others.

The freedom to experience our body separate from the body of others is not always respected. Sexual and physical abuse trample upon this fundamental right. From the perpetrator of such abuse our inner child receives the message "Your body is not separate from mine." Indeed, the body of a survivor of abuse has been used and abused at will.

Tampering with this basic body right may also be more subtle than overt physical or sexual abuse. Since our child within first learns about establishing and maintaining boundaries through its body, the body is also involved when confusion about boundaries exists. Codependency, for example, frequently reveals confusion over boundaries: Codependents often confuse their needs with the needs of others. This confusion leads to the caretaking and rescuing behaviors of typical codependency. A codependent's body reflects this confusion as well.

Such caretaking and codependent behavior is illustrated in the case of Ann, a woman in her late thirties, a wife and mother of three children. She initially sought my help for chronic pain between her shoulders. During our first treatment session I asked her to focus on that painful area. "It feels as if my shoulders are being weighted down," she said bluntly. While she spoke I walked behind her and with her permission began pressing down on her shoulders. This intensified the discomfort she was experiencing.

"Ann, when's the first time you remember experiencing a sensation like this?" I queried. After a moment's pause she recounted her earliest memory of shoulder pain. "I was a young child of four or five," she recalled. "Each time I'd hear my parents argue I'd tense my shoulders. I wanted to stop them and I believed it was my fault they failed to get along together."

"Do you remember other times you experienced this tension?" I inquired. Ann also recalled incidents during her adolescent years when her older brother quarreled with their mother. "I tried to make peace between them," she said, "but I never could. Even today, years later, it still makes me tense to be around them when they argue." "Go on like this," I suggested, "let yourself discover the various times in your life when this shoulder tension was present."

She spoke about current times. When her daughter angrily accused her of favoring the other children, Ann was deeply hurt and angry herself. "But I was afraid to say anything to Cindy," she observed, "afraid I'd upset her even more. Her anger scared me. And the tension in this shoulder mounted." There was also her husband. "Marty doesn't talk much about his feelings," she lamented, "and he's made it clear he doesn't like hearing about mine either." Ann's husband was a truck driver who spent a lot of time on the road. "When he's home," Ann related, "I tiptoe around my feelings in order not to upset him."

Ann finally came around to herself. By now the reasons for her shoulder pain were pretty obvious. "I don't know who Ann is and what she wants from life," she cried softly. "This shoulder pain reminds me how well I take care of others," she sobbed, "and how poorly I take care of myself." Meanwhile my hands were still on Ann's shoulders: symbols of her confusion with others; reminders of her inability to identify and act upon her own unique needs. "When you're ready," I suggested, "reach up and slowly remove each hand from your shoulder." I continued to press down so removing my hands required some effort on Ann's part.

She struggled to lift my right hand off her shoulder and this made her angry. At first she directed her feelings toward her parents and her brother, saying out loud what she previously had felt compelled to hold within. Next Ann removed my left hand and the anger continued. Now it was directed at her children and her husband. We repeated this process several times. Eventually Ann's feelings were directed within rather than at others—her anger turned into fear. She removed my hands for the last time. "I guess I'm frightened of discovering who Ann really is," she concluded. "But I'm willing to try." Breaking the cycle of codependency means asserting the fundamental right of our child within to experience its body separate from others and, therefore, experience a separate self as well.

The Right to Bond Through Touch, or Separate Through Avoiding Touch

The healthy child within grows to discover it can set aside boundaries and bond with others, or establish boundaries and remain to itself. Relationships with others are a continual movement between these two choices. Our inner child first explores these options somatically as it forms and dissolves bonds through physical contact. When this right is infringed upon we lose the ability to choose between bonding and separating. Trauma often infringes upon this right.

Sexual and physical abuse violate this right to choose. Although the body is an object of abuse it can also be an ally of recovery by helping our inner child reassert this right of choice. Jennifer was a thirty-six-year-old woman who worked as a ting inspector for commodities entering this country by She was divorced for seven years when I first saw her. In the therapy she entered during her divorce she was also she was a survivor of childhood sexual abuse.

Jennifer had the classic profile of a Submerged Self. In particular she had difficulty bonding and separating in relationships. Right after her divorce she went through several years of promiscuous relationships. "I didn't discriminate who with," she noted, "if they were available so was I." However during the last few years she had distanced herself from people—forming neither intimate relationships nor close friendships. She also had gained forty pounds. "The extra weight," she added, "made it easier for me to keep people away."

We began working together with a simple exercise. First, I asked her to find an area of her body where she felt safe about being touched. She identified that area as the back of her right hand. I then asked her to give me permission to touch her right hand when she was ready. With permission granted I lightly touched the back of her hand and instructed her to ask me to stop touching when she was ready. Our exchange went like this:

J: Clyde, I give you permission to touch my right hand in a
         appropriate manner.
Dr. F: [Touches back of right hand without saying anything.]
J: [After several minutes of silence.] Clyde, would you stop
         touching me *now*. [Word is emphasized by client.]
Dr. F: [Immediately ceases touching without saying anything/
         Exchange is repeated several times.

However simple, this exercise uses the body to reinforce th
inner child's right to choose bonding or separating. Through
out the months we worked together Jennifer's right to choos
was reinforced. We made an agreement that whenever I needee
to touch her therapeutically, I would first ask her permission.
would also wait for her to ask that our physical contact b
broken. Sometimes I'd forget and reach out to touch her with
out first asking. She'd look up as though she'd caught me in the
act and say half-smiling, "Gotcha!" Although I was a little embarrassed, I was glad to see her asserting her right to choose.
    Over time this simple exercise began to pay off. Jennifer met
a man whom she liked and they began dating. During one session she described their first sexual encounter. "I told him I
enjoyed him and I too wanted our relationship to become more
intimate," she said. "But I asked if he would first obtain my
permission before touching me," she added, "just as we've been
doing here." Jennifer informed me how awkward it was to ask,
but she was elated when her request was accepted. "He asked
for permission to touch me and I could hardly believe it," she
exclaimed, "nobody had ever asked me this before and I never
realized I had the right to insist upon it." Through our body,
our child within can recover and reassert this essential right of
choice.

The Right to Ownership of One's Entire Body

Our child within is entitled to its entire body. This entitlement
follows from the right to maintain our body as separate and
distinct from the body of others. At first it may seem that ownership of one's body is a fact of life without question. But the
body often tells a different story. Survivors of physical and sex-

ual abuse, for example, will relate how portions of their body feel unavailable to them. When asked to describe sensation in an arm, a leg, or an abdomen, they are unable to do so. "It's all dark there," said one person attempting to describe what she felt in her abdomen. "I can't get to it," said another of the entire lower half of her body. "It's split off from the rest of my body," said a man when asked to describe the sensation in his legs.

I'm reminded of a patient whose gangrenous leg is amputated to save his life. To survive abuse our psyche adopts a similar strategy: The trauma of abuse is compartmentalized in one area of the body and that area is then emotionally removed from the rest of us. But neither amputation nor compartmentalization guarantees freedom from pain. Phantom leg pain can plague an amputee, unresolved feelings, no matter how well compartmentalized, can give rise to physical or emotional pain.

John was a forty-two-year-old father of two. He was married and the owner of a small architectural firm. When I first saw him he described a history of sexual and physical abuse. John had been in and out of therapy over the past ten years regarding this abuse. He reassured me that he was well aware of the issues surrounding his abuse, and said he had come to see me for a painful left shoulder. "If I could just get rid of that pain," he stated, "my life would be fine."

Something in his reassurance that "everything in life was fine except for this shoulder pain" rang untrue. I couldn't put my finger on it, so I decided to play along with him for the first two visits. During these sessions we did only gentle manipulative therapy to his shoulder and surrounding parts of his body. Each time he left feeling better only to return feeling the same pain.

Our efforts had not seemed to help. From our discussions I learned of John's passion for acting. He frequently appeared in the productions of a local repertory company. At our third session I decided to appeal to his thespian talents. I first asked him to stop talking, to stand, and to focus all his attention on his painful left shoulder. "When you're ready," I suggested, "act out what you're experiencing in that shoulder right now, without saying a word."

John stood in silence for several minutes. Then, like an actor in a black-and-white silent movie, his body began to speak. He started by facing me, then slowly turning away. As he swiveled around his body began to crumple: He dropped his head, let his knees buckle, bent his arms, and drew them into his chest. His body movements were intense and he proved himself an excellent actor—the feeling he conveyed was unmistakable. John remained in that collapsed standing position for several minutes before sitting down. He was emotionally spent and managed only a single word. "Shame," he uttered, "shame."

Eventually John's voice returned. "I've been walking around with the shame of my abuse locked in this shoulder," he observed, "because it was too painful to cope with directly." Thus, John began to reown his entire body, including the shoulder that stored such shameful feelings. This is what reowning our body means: recovering those parts that have been emotionally severed and reclaiming the feelings that have been locked away.

The Right to Experience One's Body as a Normal Source of Pleasure and Pain

The healthy inner child should grow to experience its body as a normal source of pleasure and pain both physically and emotionally. This right to the bodily experience of our emotions stems from our right to own our entire body. We were designed to experience and express emotions through our body. We become dysfunctional when we are disconnected from this bodily source of emotional life.

Bodily experience of emotions must have conveyed a tremendous evolutionary advantage to our ancestors. Most animals simply react to their internal or external perceptions: when hungry they eat; when threatened they retreat or attack. However, the bodily experience of emotions allowed us another option: *in-action* for a period of time. In-action is not the same as doing nothing. It really means "inner action," or constant attention to the bodily sensations giving rise to our emotional experience. In-action is actually the definition of emotion. Emotion is a conjunction of two Latin words, *ex* (meaning out of) and *motion*. So emotion literally means out of motion.

THE EVOLUTIONARY BENEFITS OF EMOTIONS

Eons ago the scenario may have unfolded like this: Suppose our ancestors came upon a large, threatening animal. Their normal response would have caused them to either stay or fight, or turn and flee. Fear would have surely been the emotion connected with such an encounter. Instead of always responding to the perception of a threat through fight or flight, suppose our ancestors sometimes chose in-action. They simply monitored their fear without doing anything. The animal, surprised by this response, moved in quickly for the kill. But it is unaware of our ancestor's compatriots hiding in the brush on either side. Leaping high in the air to pounce on its victim, the animal exposes its flanks to a series of deftly thrown spears that quickly kill it before it reaches our fearless predecessor. In-action has delivered its reward.

Feelings lead to either motion or emotion. Feelings are our perceptions of events taking place in the world-out-there or the world-in-here. We respond to these perceived feelings through motion and emotion. Motion is an external response, emotion by definition is a process out of motion—an internal response. Motion allows us to express our feelings through our body.

Emotion allows us to explore our feelings through our body. Through emotion we can store our feelings long enough to have the opportunity to respond rather than react. In other words, we can take the process out of motion long enough to choose how to place it back into motion. At least, I believe this is how it's supposed to work.

NORMAL AND DYSFUNCTIONAL EMOTIONAL CYCLES

The normal emotional cycle I've just described can be summarized in three steps: experience, store, express. This normal cycle is shown in Figure 4.1. Problems occur when something interferes with this cycle. The interference usually involves the body. When the cycle goes awry it frequently means we go through the first two steps (experience and store) without ever getting to the third (express). For example, if we are abused as children we go through the steps of experiencing and storing the trauma often without an opportunity to express our fear, rage, and anger. Likewise, we may find our need to bond, which enables us to experience and express love, is frustrated. We experience the need and store the experience without expressing it. At some point emotion needs to become motion or the charge of storing emotion builds so high we can no longer safely discharge it. Figure 4.2 is a diagram of this dysfunctional emotional cycle.

I recently received a manufacturer's notice about the battery charging unit for my portable marine radio. I have the radio in the event of an on-the-water emergency when I'll need to contact the appropriate authorities. But the manufacturer's notice warned of overcharging—leaving the charger plugged into a wall receptacle for longer than eighteen hours. This, the proviso cautioned, could lead to excessive heat buildup and the destruction or malfunction of the battery unit. Our emotional cycle can malfunction in a similar way.

Dissociation, a Dysfunctional Emotional Cycle

Continuing to experience and store feelings without expressing them leads to excessive buildup and dysfunction. The

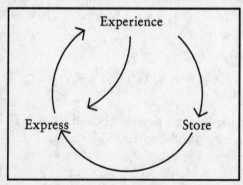

Figure 4.1 The normal emotional cycle

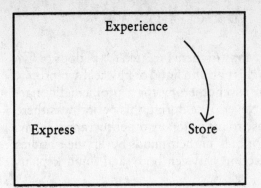

Figure 4.2
A dysfunctional
emotional cycle

buildup may be such that at some point we actually discon-
nect from our body experience. **Dissociation,** for example,
would be one way of disconnection. This is a common way
survivors cope with abuse. When asked about her body from
the waist down, Sharon, a sexual abuse survivor in her late
twenties, gave a typical account. "I can't feel it," she said,
"it's not part of me." Upon further questioning Sharon described how this lack of feeling came about. "After a while I
realized I could no longer protect this area from my father,"
she recounted, "I had to let go of it in order to survive. I
handed over this part of my body during the abuse and re-
treated to my mind." Abuse shredded Sharon's normally in-
terwoven experience of body and mind.

Most survivors do not share Sharon's exceptional awareness of this disjunction between body and mind. In the years I
practiced as a chiropractor without attention to the emotional
and psychological dynamics of my clients, I saw many people
unaware of this disjunction. A composite profile of this client
easily comes to mind. She is between twenty-five and forty-five
with an unknown history of sexual abuse. Her physical complaints are vague but chronic. A typical complaint from my
clients was generalized lower back pain. She has difficulty forming or maintaining relationships with men, and by contrast our
therapeutic relationship seems exceptional to her. Attention to
physical symptoms—through a variety of manual therapeutic
techniques—brings varying periods of relief. Sometimes this client will go for weeks or months without pain, but the initial
discomfort always seems to return.

I cannot count the number of clients I saw that fit most

aspects of this profile. Many of them I treated for periods of five years or more through this ebb and flood of physical symptoms. Some were actually in psychotherapy for a problematic marriage or relationship. Never once during this period was there mention of sexual abuse to me or to any other therapist. It was a secret well hidden not only in their minds but in their bodies as well. This disconnection between body and mind kept us both in the dark.

One day my innocence was shattered. A simple physical examination unintentionally evoked a body memory of incest in a client. Thus, I became more open to the possibility that other clients had similar experiences stored in their bodies. One by one bodies began to talk. They told stories that amazed me and astounded my clients. One by one it became obvious that their physical pain was a plea to listen and take action on long-held emotional pain. Only then did chronic physical symptoms start to change. As these patients confronted their abuse their bodies let go of the related physical pain.

EMOTIONAL CONTAINMENT

The normal cycle of emotions has three steps. Some individuals have difficulty in containing their feelings at all. Their dysfunctional cycle seems to move directly from experience to expression; from step one to step three, bypassing the second step entirely. This dysfunctional pattern is shown in Figure 4.3. Emotional storage is a natural process that involves the body. Inability to contain emotions is also dysfunctional and represents another kind of boundary problem. Instead of confusion

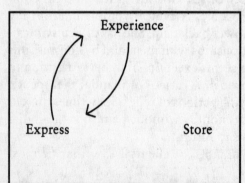

Figure 4.3

A dysfunctional emotional cycle

about forming boundaries between self and others, there is confusion about forming boundaries within one's self.

I often ask for volunteers when demonstrating techniques during my workshops. Most participants raise their hands and I randomly select one person from the audience. At one workshop a woman rushed forward without raising her hand, jumped on the treatment table, lay on her back, looked up and said, "Work with me!" Her name was Carol and I didn't seem to have much choice so I proceeded with this eager participant. I asked her what area of her body felt as though it needed attention. "My neck," Carol informed me. I reached out to gently hold her neck, intent on demonstrating a very specific technique. But Carol seemed to have a completely different agenda. No sooner had I touched her when she began to undulate. First it was her head and neck, then her back, arms, and legs until finally Carol's entire body was engaged in this bizarre display. She swirled and writhed and arched herself backward. At times Carol moved so much I was afraid she would fall off the table.

Such an expression of movement is not unheard of when working with the body. It has been called an unwinding or a somatoemotional release. But there's a quality, a certain authenticity that a true release has. When it feels right I'm dancing with a client who's the leading partner. We're in sync as I follow and support the movements of the client's body. This experience was different. My presence seemed irrelevant. It was as though I had let go of the key on a wind-up doll. At one point Carol moved suddenly and I lost touch with her body. It didn't matter, she continued without me.

Every therapeutic instinct I had told me this was a bogus display. I leaned over and said in a caring but firm way, "Carol stop moving and allow your awareness to return to your neck." "No, I don't want to stop," she said, "this is my way, it feels good." So I intervened somatically. Instead of following her movements, I offered barriers to them. If she rotated her head left I kept my hands in place neither forcing her to move back nor following her movement in that direction. Anger seeped into Carol's voice, "You're not unwinding me," she snapped, "this is what I need." By now my internal voice was whispering,

"Seduction Clyde, you're being seduced." I felt as though she was baiting me into "her way." So I brought the process to conclusion. "In the next minute," I said, "find a place to stop and ask me to remove my hands." She did this only begrudgingly, making sure I knew how displeased she was.

The process lasted only ten minutes but I felt quite tired afterward. Although the demonstration had not gone as I anticipated, it contained some valuable lessons. With Carol's permission I solicited the reaction of the other participants in my customary way: they could offer only the feelings that emerged for them during the demonstration. "Frustration," "anger," "conflict," "power struggle," "confusion," participants called out. I also asked Carol to report her experience. She informed us that she'd been to another workshop where the leader encouraged her into a bizarre unwinding. She also found a somatic therapist in her hometown who "unwound" her regularly. "How often do you unwind?" I asked Carol. "Every time he touches me," she said. "Have you made some progress with your physical and emotional issues this way?" I continued. "I can't control it," she observed, "I feel good while it's taking place but I keep returning and unwinding time after time."

By now Carol and the other participants got what I was hinting at: Something's amiss with a process repeated over and over again like a record stuck in a groove. I thanked Carol and asked her to take her seat. Without further reference to Carol I spoke about boundaries and emotional containment. In fact, she demonstrated the body equivalent of the emotional flooding that often besets people who form boundaries poorly. Everything about my interaction with Carol suggested the unbounded confusion of a Submerged Self. What Carol's body needed least was further expression of emotional content. What she needed most was normal containment and storage of emotions.

THE ALEXITHYMIC BODY

There are some individuals in whom the split between body and mind is so great that even the initial experience of emotions seems impossible. Often referred to as *alexithymic* (literally meaning without emotional feeling), they deny being able to experience feelings. When asked how they feel about a particular event or experience they routinely respond, "I don't know." This disconnection of feelings and awareness even extends to the body, as I learned from the one alexithymic individual I've seen in my years of practice.

Allen was a forty-two-year-old insurance agent who had seen several psychotherapists before coming to see me. He was very cerebral and a workaholic in a failing marriage who told me, "I can't understand why my life is falling apart." When I asked Allen to relax, he informed me he didn't know how. The muscles in his neck were taut so I suggested he describe the physical sensation in this area of his body. "I can't feel anything except your touch there," reported Allen. I removed my hand, thinking it may have been a distraction, and once again asked him to tell me about his neck. It appeared he was trying hard and I sensed frustration as he again advised me of his inability to discern sensation in his neck. I thought he might at least be aware of his frustration. "What's it like to be unable to describe how this area feels?" I queried. "Oh," Allen said in a flat tone, "it's pretty much the way I am all the time."

This impasse continued for the next ten visits and I began to seriously question whether my skills and knowledge were adequate to help Allen. I referred him to another therapist for consultation and treatment. Several weeks later I spoke with the therapist and then with Allen. Nothing had changed. Allen and I tried working together for several more sessions but it was obvious we were going nowhere. With a great deal of puzzlement and sadness I released him from care.

THE BODY'S ROLE IN THE EMOTIONAL CYCLE

At a west coast workshop I demonstrated the body's role in the normal emotional cycle. A young woman named Theresa volunteered as a subject. She came down from among the hundred or so people in attendance and lay on the treatment table at my right. I asked Theresa to relax and let her awareness turn to the most predominant emotional issue she was dealing with in her life. Without informing me of the issue, she was to let me know her awareness of it with a simple head nod. After she nodded her head, I asked Theresa to find an area of her body that seemed related to this issue. She pointed to her neck, which I then held with her permission. The only instructions I gave Theresa were to periodically report the sensation she experienced in her neck.

As I sat at Theresa's head holding her neck with both hands I could feel the tension in her muscles. Several minutes into the process Theresa reported feeling pain in her neck. "Just stay with the pain," I counseled, "and follow it wherever it leads." Several minutes later when Theresa reported feeling angry I again suggested that she simply follow that anger. Like the layers of an onion, Theresa peeled off several layers of physical and emotional sensation. Pain led to anger; anger led to fear; fear led to sadness; and sadness led to a strange sensation of floating. "I feel as if I'm in limbo," she said, "not sure of which way to go next."

Throughout this process I specifically avoided delving further into the experiences reported by Theresa. Most people in the audience were massage therapists. My point was to demonstrate that without engaging a client in verbal dialogue, an emotional process could take place through the body. I had Theresa give verbal feedback only so the audience could experience the movement of her process. Otherwise the demonstration would have been quite boring to everyone except Theresa and me. I was simply holding her head and neck. Everything else was taking place out of sight within her body and mind.

As Theresa described her different physical and emotional sensations I could feel her neck muscles gradually relax. By the time she portrayed herself "in limbo," her neck was limp. I debated concluding the demonstration then but something urged me on. One more time I offered simple guidance, "Stay with the feeling of being in limbo and follow it wherever it leads." For several minutes nothing seemed to happen. I imagined myself in the audience looking on. "He's not doing anything," I'd be thinking, "he's just sitting there holding her neck. How strange!"

Suddenly something shifted. After a brief sigh Theresa's head began to sway. I followed it to the right, then left, and held on as she traced a gentle figure eight. This was a true unwinding. We danced like this—her head in my hands—for at least ten minutes, her movement slowly winding down. At the end she took some deep breaths then opened her eyes. I asked her to help us understand what had taken place.

"My issue was self-expression," she reported. "Often I don't feel safe expressing my feelings. I'm sure it began as a child. Feelings weren't freely expressed in my family. We weren't allowed to cry, and certainly not to get angry. 'Keep your feelings to yourself,' is a statement I heard a lot. I've gone through most of life," Theresa reflected, "believing that to be loved and accepted I needed to hide what I felt."

Then Theresa commented about the demonstration. "At first I was tense and unsure of where it would lead. The pain of holding onto my feelings was lodged in my neck. But I was also aware I had the choice of letting go. That was new and scary. When I realized what a struggle it has been to express my feelings I did become angry and when I looked back over all the years I'd hid them I just felt very sad. Being in limbo was interesting," she noted, "I still wasn't sure it was safe to express myself and I really didn't know what I would do. But you continued to hold my head and neck and that gave me the confidence to continue. The movement was freeing and wonderful," Theresa beamed in reference to the unwinding, "I felt like a young child running, singing, and playing. I was not afraid to feel and to express those feelings freely."

Through her body, Theresa came to terms with a normal range of emotional experience, pleasurable and painful. She was aware of how and where she stored her feelings, and she was also aware of her ability to express those feelings. Most of Theresa's process occurred nonverbally through body awareness, movement, and the presence of human touch. In this way she reclaimed the gift of self-expression stolen from her child within.

Embodying Functional and
Dysfunctional Relationships

Learning about relationships is a somatic process that begins with our mother then gradually moves out to encompass the strangers we encounter. I've described this body-based learning as a back-and-forth dance between bonding and separating. What we first learn through our bodies influence how we make and break relationships throughout our lives. Our body is the classroom for our inner child.

Healthy (functional) and unhealthy (dysfunctional) relationships have roots within our body. To illustrate this, psychiatrist William S. Condon microanalyzed filmed interactions between two individuals. Each frame of a 16mm film was studied linguistically (parts of words spoken) and kinesthetically (parts of the body moved). When speech and movement were compared, Condon observed a repertoire of micromotions— small, subtle movements of the body—accompanying an individual's spoken words.

A more astonishing finding occurred when he compared speech and movement between a speaker and listener. "Further intensive microanalyses of sound film of human interaction have revealed a very startling phenomenon," Condon noted. "Listeners were observed in precise shared synchrony with the speaker's speech." There was no discernible time lag between the speaker's utterance and the listener's movement—a phenomenon he termed "interactional synchrony." Furthermore, the synchronization continued when the speaker became the listener.

Condon described this as "a new concept of response" based on "an almost immediate entertainment of bodily organization." In other words, we first respond to verbal communication by an immediate change in our body. Our body then continuously changes in synchrony with the speaker's words. When it is our chance to speak, our voice similarly entrains the listener. This is not unlike two tuning forks of the same frequency. Striking either one and bringing it close to the other will cause the second tuning fork to vibrate. In effect Condon demonstrated that people in a relationship resonate somatically with each other. "Communication is thus like a dance," he observed, "with everyone engaged in intricate and shared movements across many subtle dimensions, yet all strangely oblivious that they are doing so."

Condon then went on to show that dysfunctional relationships resulted from interruptions and alterations of these shared body movements. He compared the shared movements of normal individuals to those found in dysfunctional children—children with autistic symptoms, developmental difficulties, and learning disabilities. Every dysfunctional child studied had delayed entrainment to a speaker's words. Like the motions of actors out of sync with a film sound track, the bodies of these children were out of sync with the spoken word.

Dysfunctional relationships are thus linked to body changes that precede our emotional or behavioral response. To heal and recover from dysfunctional relationships, the child within must confront its feelings and behavior. But this inner child must also turn to its body.

THREE GENERATIONS AND THEIR BODIES

I had the opportunity of simultaneously working with three generations of women around the dysfunctional bonds they shared: Sally was the thirty-two-year-old daughter, Judith was the fifty-year-old mother, and Ann was the seventy-two-year-old grandmother.

I had been working with Sally for more than a year. She had two children, a four-year-old and a six-year old, from two previous marriages. Both of Sally's children lived with their fathers. Sally was recently divorced for the second time, unemployed, and had moved back into the family home where she grew up. Her mother, Judith, and her stepfather lived at home along with her grandmother, Ann, whose husband had died several years previously. Sally's stepfather was confined to his bed most of the time with an advanced case of emphysema. No other family members lived at home. Primarily, this was a home that housed three generations of closely bonded women.

Unfortunately, their bonds were not always healthy. All three women had been in and out of Alcoholics Anonymous and Adult Children of Alcoholics programs over the years. Though none were practicing alcoholics, codependent behavior was an obvious facet of their relationship.

The chain of command among these women was well established. Sally and Judith called Ann "Momma", and despite her age Momma pretty much ran the show. Both daughter and granddaughter attributed Ann's domineering manner to the three years she worked as a foreman welding airplanes during the Second World War. "If she'd have been on Patton's staff," they often joked, "the war would have been over a lot sooner." Many things about these women suggested their degree of enmeshment. Adjusting for their nearly equally spaced age differences, their bodies were remarkably similar. Their voice pattern, inflection, and cadence were identical. They used similar colloquialisms and had similar mannerisms.

Their shared mannerisms piqued my interest. I saw the mother, Judith, for a brief period of time. However, it was long enough to pick up the similarities in body patterning between mother and daughter. Under stress or in contact with difficult emotions both mother and daughter had a typical body response: they raised their eyebrows, opened their eyes wide, turned their upper lip to one side, and made a short sweeping motion with one hand in front of their body. It was a body message that seemed to say, "Oh, this can't be that important, can it?"

Furthermore, throughout my therapeutic work with Sally and Judith, I always felt that Ann was a silent participant. On several occasions when answering questions, they responded with descriptions of Momma's thoughts, ideas, or feelings on the matter. A daily focal point for all these women was the evening "walk with Momma." All three women loved nature and Momma insisted they walk around a nearby lake each evening. However, the beauty of this mutual love for the outdoors was marred by the dysfunction displayed in regard to this walk. These walking sessions were often times when Sally and Judith would tell all while Momma would listen and then dispense advice, approval, and condemnation. Judith resented her mother's pressure to take these walks but found herself unable to stand up to her. Sally, meanwhile, claimed not to mind the walks but felt terribly guilty when she missed them.

At first, mother and granddaughter were adamantly opposed to my suggestion that Momma was pivotal to their healing and recovery. I continued to see Sally after Judith ended therapy and repeated my suggestion that her bond with Momma prevented her moving on in life. Amazingly one day Sally said, "I'm ready to get rid of this unhealthy bond I've got with Momma." Still surprised, I responded, "We can only do that if all three of you participate together." "You mean all three of us together in a session with you?" Sally queried. "Yes," I emphasized, "all **three** of you." "I'll have to think about that," she concluded, "and I'll have to talk it over with my mother and Momma." Several weeks passed before Sally mentioned the joint session again. "We want to do it next month," she informed me at the end of one appointment, "Momma and mother have agreed to participate."

On the appointed day these courageous women met at my office. I excused myself while they sorted out their seating arrangement. They sat in a semicircle in front of me. Not surprisingly, Momma sat in the middle with Judith and Sally at either side. Together they were quite astonishing. Their physical features, voice patterns, and gestures really did span three generations. The power arrangement between them was predictable—Judith and Sally deferred to Momma. Before we got started I asked each woman if she had any thoughts, concerns, or feelings about the journey we were embarking upon. Momma answered first, expressing her gratitude to me for helping her "girls." She also informed me she wasn't exactly sure what would be accomplished during this session but she was, naturally, glad to help. Momma stared directly at me while speaking.

Sally spoke next and was more straightforward about what she hoped would happen. "I feel a need to let go of the negative feelings that bond us," she said. "That's what I hope we're able to do." Judith, on the other hand, was clearly uncomfortable with the proceedings. She voiced skepticism saying she felt no strings between herself and either her mother or daughter. "I only have good feelings for them both," she insisted. Interestingly, neither Sally nor Judith looked at me directly. After each statement they first glanced toward Momma and then toward me. These opening statements accurately reflected the dysfunctional family roles each woman played—the commander (Ann), the rebel (Sally), and the caretaker (Judith).

I asked them to close their eyes and relax. They brought their awareness to the person on their right and observed what body sensations and feelings surfaced. Then they focused on the person to their left and observed what they felt physically and emotionally. "Where in your body are you connected to these people?" I inquired. "And how does that connection feel to you? Are there parts of this connection you would like to do away with?" I continued. "And are there other parts you would like to keep?" The atmosphere in the room began to shift as each woman seemed to confront the nature of the task that lay ahead.

After several minutes of this silence I asked them to open their eyes so I could explain how we could proceed. True to form, Momma opened her mouth as well. She began to explain what she had experienced during the silence. I stepped in and informed her that from this point on each person would be given an opportunity to speak and while that person was speaking no one else would be allowed to comment. I further described the process we were about to engage in. We'd work in pairs of two. Each person would have the opportunity to identify what she felt was healthy and unhealthy about her bond with the other person. Furthermore, each person would have the opportunity to discover what area of her body felt bound by these dysfunctional qualities. Then she could physically remove the dysfunctional bond from that area of her body. The order of pairing was: Sally and Ann; Sally and Judith; Judith and Ann.

We began an epic journey of several hours. It was Sally's turn first. She scanned her body and noted several locations where she felt bonded to Ann. "My throat, my shoulders, my chest, and my stomach," she said. "Face Ann and tell her how you feel about those bonds," I advised. "If any of them feel like they don't belong, reach to that area of your body and slowly remove the bond from yourself."

"Grandma, I love you," Sally began, "but I feel I'm not heard. My feelings and thoughts don't seem to matter much. When I express what I feel, I'm not taken seriously. I often feel judged by you." Then reaching up to her throat as if to grasp a hand that was choking her Sally slowly pulled away one per-ceived bond and said, "I'm removing this bond of your judg-ments about me." Next Sally moved to her shoulders. "I feel held back by your insistence that I participate in activities that are important to you," she said. "I'm trying to rebuild my own life separate and apart from you and mom." She reached over to each shoulder and slowly pulled off this bond. "I need my freedom and I no longer want this bond of feeling stifled by your desires."

Sally then moved to her chest and stomach where feelings of being bound by shame and fear emerged. She also pulled these bonds away and verbally relinquished the hold they had on her. Ann, meanwhile, was obviously uncomfortable. Her eyes teared on occasion and her body moved with desire to respond to Sally. But to her great credit, Ann just listened. Sally con-cluded by saying, "Grandma, now that I've removed the bonds I don't want, I want to create a bond between us that feels good." Sally pointed to the middle of her chest and said, "This bond starts in my heart and extends out to you. It's made of my love for you and through it I hope to receive your love and support." The simplicity, candor, and beauty of Sally's words and actions were riveting.

Ann was next. "I guess I never realized how you felt," she began. "But I don't want us bonded in a harmful way." Ann closed her eyes for a moment, then said, "I feel bonds in my head, my throat, and my stomach that I want to remove. From my head," and Ann reached up to remove the bond there, "I want to remove the bond that says you are incapable of making it in the world on your own. And from my throat I want to let go the bond that attempts to control you. The bond in my stomach is more difficult for me," Ann observed. "It reflects my fear of being alone in the world as I age. Perhaps that is why I've wanted you and your mother so close now. But I know it needs to be released. So here it goes." After physically removing these bonds, Ann said to Sally, "I too want to keep this bond at my heart. I accept the love you extended to me and I offer mine to you in return."

Meanwhile, Judith was silently observing the transaction between Sally and Ann. I purposely had her sit out the first two rounds of this process because of her stated ambivalence. I was pretty sure she could not watch what transpired between her daughter and mother without reflecting on her own dysfunctional bonds with them. Sally and Judith had their turn next. Judith went first. At first she could only identify nurturing bonds that existed between her and her daughter—bonds of love, support, encouragement. But I asked her to tune into the physical sensation in the areas related to these nurturing feelings and something changed. Judith allowed herself to open up to the pain in her chest. "I miss my grandchildren," she said softly, "it hurts not to be able to see them." After this she was able to speak more openly about her feelings and her bonds with Sally. She removed the bonds she didn't want and created a bond of love to extend to Sally. Sally, now the veteran at this process, identified and removed bonds between herself and her mother. She then accepted her mother's bonds of love and extended hers back to Judith.

Ann and Judith were the final pair. They each went through a familiar process of identifying and removing unwanted bonds, then creating a desired bond between them. To conclude this long ordeal Sally, Judith, and Ann sat with closed eyes and focused on their bodies a final time. They observed those areas where bonds had been removed and felt the new bonds they had created between each other. "This is our graduation," Sally said as they left the room, "we can all go on from here."

The story of these three women is a very touching example of the body's role in freeing our child within from unhealthy, dysfunctional relationships. This is yet another important way our body becomes part of our healing and recovery.

5.

SAFE TOUCH: THE SOMATIC REALITY OF SEXUAL ABUSE AND RECOVERY

I never realized how much of this trauma I carried in my body. Releasing it was like giving birth to a new me.

—*A SEXUAL ABUSE SURVIVOR*

For survivors of sexual abuse, long after physical injuries have healed, emotional and psychological scars remain in both mind and body. Healing the mind is not enough, the body also has a prominent role in the process of recovery. Often the body holds the first clues to a history of sexual abuse, though such clues may lay hidden beneath more ordinary circumstances. Many of my clients initially sought treatment for bodily complaints—an ache, a pain, a tight muscle, or a sore lower back. Sexual abuse was far from their minds.

Even when the body's clues surface they are often veiled: One client gags as if to vomit; another stiffens his body while being touched; persistent lower back pain is unchanged after many treatments; someone begins coughing violently; someone else's pain apparently moves from place to place; one client feels pain when she is being touched gently; another asks for deeper and deeper touch because he feels nothing. Are these ordinary therapeutic responses or do they point to something else?

Sometimes when I have initially accepted such signs at face value I have been wrong. Continued therapeutic care offered little benefit. Months or even years of frustrating treatment, referrals to specialists, and the suggestion that the complaint was psychogenic (a polite way of saying "it's all in your head") left the client not much better than when he or she first sought care. Even referring a client for psychotherapy—a logical decision in a case like this—often failed to identify a history of abuse. Some survivors of sexual abuse ask us to listen to their bodies not their minds. They are able to face their abuse somatically before coming to terms with it cognitively. Unfortunately we do not always hear and understand what the body has to say—and the body is then left out of the healing and recovery process.

I have also encountered another group of survivors whose bodies have been left out of the healing process. These are individuals who know their history. Frequently they have sought professional care for their traumatic past and this care has been sensitive and helpful. They have openly discussed their sexual abuse and taken many important steps to heal their wounds. Then one day a physical symptom develops that causes them to seek additional care. It might be a toothache, lower back pain, or intestinal cramps for which a dentist, chiropractor, or internist is seen. The client is touched in a routine therapeutic way—an open mouth inspection, a lower back or intestinal examination—and somehow the abuse is relived in that moment. While we call these episodes flashbacks, I suspect they might also be a way the body beckons for inclusion in the healing and recovery process.

We can take the survivor's body seriously. We can listen beyond symptoms and see beyond flashbacks. Many times the body has a story to tell that is quite different from the mind. In fact this dissociation between body and mind is a hallmark of the trauma suffered by survivors of sexual abuse. For survivors, body/mind dissociation ranges from inability to describe physical sensation, to full blown multiple personality disorder (MPD).

Unfortunately most therapy addresses dissociation in mental terms only. *The Diagnostic and Statistical Manual of Mental Disorders* (DSM-III-R)—the Bible of psychological diagnosis— defines dissociation as "a disturbance or alteration in the normally integrative functions of identity, memory or consciousness." This definition contains no hint of the body's crucial role in normal personality integration or in abnormal dissociation. Excluding the body from diagnosis is a sure way to exclude it from treatment.

THE BODY'S ROLE IN RECOVERY FROM SEXUAL ABUSE

Why is it so important that the body be brought into the process of healing and recovery from sexual abuse? A story from a surprising source might help us understand why. It begins nearly forty years ago in the laboratories of neuroscientists attempting to understand the connection between bodily states and behavior. Surgical removal of the amygdala caused rats who were otherwise satiated to eat voluminously (see Chapter 2 for additional information on the amygdala). At one point researchers terminated the experiment because many rats died from overeating a sawdust and axle grease mixture. Apparently the surgery had severed the animal's ability to discern a bodily condition (hunger) and take appropriate action in regard to that condition.

Years later researchers had a chance to examine human patients who had undergone surgical removal of their amygdala to treat cancer. Like the rats, these patients also ate tremendous quantities of food. Weight gain of up to one hundred pounds a year was not uncommon. Now, however, these human subjects could be asked what it was like to feel hungry all the time.

Neuroscientist Karl Pribram describes his encounter with one such patient. In a consultation room before lunch she was asked how she felt. Was she hungry? "No," she replied. Would she like a piece of steak? "No." Would she like any food? "Not really." She expressed only a mild interest in some candy. However, when the doors of the consultation room were opened, she bolted toward a long table where other patients were seated and already eating. Pushing the others aside, she stuffed her mouth with food with both hands. Pribram immediately recalled her to the consultation room. Wasn't she really hungry? "No." Didn't she really want some food? "No."

She was unable to register what she felt—her body was dissociated from her mind—and therefore she was unable to act appropriately on her feelings. This is where the rats, the amygdala, the body, and sexual abuse intersect. The surgical dissociation of this patient mirrors the traumatic dissociation seen in survivors of sexual abuse. What are we to believe? If we rely solely on the mind—the verbal and cognitive reports of clients in therapy—we miss what the body has to say. Months, or perhaps years, of verbal therapy may proceed to a point where the survivor verbally reports resolution of key emotional issues. Then the survivor's body is touched, moved, or engaged in a way that recreates the original abuse. The rawness and intensity of the trauma seem unabated and we question what was really gained through therapy. We end up calling it a flashback. This is equivalent to only believing the verbal reports of the woman described above. She said she had no feeling of hunger, yet she overate.

On the other hand, if we observe only the body we can also be misled. Survivors often have physical complaints that might appear unrelated to the trauma they have suffered. If we address only the physical symptoms we may never discover the underlying trauma with its pervasive emotional and psychological scars. This would be equivalent to believing only the overeating behavior of the patient described above. If we knew nothing about her surgery we'd conclude she was lying about her feelings of hunger and we'd never look any further for the source of her dissociation. The survivor who is unaware of a history of abuse may report only a nagging lower back pain—a verbal report of sexual abuse may not surface. If we attend only to the physical pain, months and years may go by before we discover the real trauma underlying this pain.

INTEGRATING BODY AND MIND IN THE TREATMENT OF SEXUAL ABUSE

Rather than choose between body or mind, we can believe both. Body and mind are equally involved in our emotional cycle. In an earlier chapter we described this emotional cycle in three steps; experiencing feelings; storing feelings; and expressing feelings either through action (motion) or attention without action (emotion). Like an underground stream this emotional cycle continuously flows within the body. Normally we are able to tap into this flow with our minds. But trauma or surgery can sever our connection to this somatoemotional flow.

The survivor's body receives the trauma, the physical insult of sexual abuse, and the body responds. Muscle tighten to resist intrusion, a protective posture is assumed, and sensation to certain areas is temporarily shut off. But when trauma overpowers the survivor's capacity to respond—as it almost always does in sexual abuse—the only recourse is to cut the circuits from the overload. Once cut, control is lost. Momentary tightness becomes chronic pain, attempted protection becomes constant rigidity, and temporary loss of sensation becomes enduring numbness. If the overload is too great, new construction may be undertaken. A different emotional, psychological and physical entity—a multiple personality—is created to handle the overwhelming traumatic energy.

BODY-BASED EMOTIONAL SCARS

The persistent emotional and psychological scars of abuse have a strong somatic component. Guilt and shame—an abiding legacy of sexual abuse—are centered around the body. Survivors may feel guilty for having participated in sexual acts even though their body's participation was against their will. And they may feel guilt, shame, or betrayal because their body was aroused or climactic in spite of their efforts to the contrary. Lowered self-image is body-based as well. Our sense of self— our image of who we are—is first and foremost an image formed through our body. Sexual abuse delivers a message that despite our best attempts we are unable to protect this foundation of our self-image. This in turn leads the survivor to feelings of lowered self-esteem, lowered self-worth, and a sense of helplessness and powerlessness. Repetition compulsion, self-mutilation, and perpetration of abuse by survivors are some of the body-based behavioral consequences of sexual abuse.

With the body so directly involved in the long-term consequences of sexual abuse, I've sought ways to more directly involve the body in the treatment of abuse. My work with survivors is divided into three phases: a beginning, an intermediate, and an ending phase of therapy. At the start of therapy I am mostly concerned with getting to know the somatic reality of the survivor and developing a therapeutic rapport based on safety and trust. In the middle stage of treatment the survivor's body gets to tell its story. We then compare and contrast the body's story with that told by the mind. This presents an opportunity for somatoemotional resolution through jointly addressing the somatic and emotional scars of the abuse. Ultimately a point of conclusion arises: Therapeutic gains are consolidated and the survivor emerges with greater empowerment to continue living, healing, and recovering.

The Somatic Reality of the Survivor

I use touch, movement, and body awareness to assess the somatic reality of the survivor of sexual abuse. It is a process that begins with the handshake or hello of our first meeting. *Body habitus*—normal posture and movement—say a great deal about underlying emotional and psychological issues. I have no particular system by which I assign significance to a given body posture or movement. I prefer to be open to what strikes me most about how someone holds herself and how she moves. Usually an overall feeling is communicated through posture, gesture, and movement. It's similar to the feeling you get from observing a painting, listening to a symphony, or watching a sunset. Trying to extract the details of that feeling may destroy its essence. After all this is just the first meeting and there will be time for specificity later.

I pay attention not only to the survivor's posture, gesture, and movement but also my own. How does my body feel upon first encountering this person? Am I relaxed, tense, or anxious. Within my own body I find important signs about the therapeutic adventure we are about to embark upon. I know that many of my decisions as a guide on this journey will be based on gut-feelings. Now is the time to first read those feelings and lay a basis for comparison in the future.

Of course the normal verbal exchange occurs with the survivor—all the facts, figures, questions, and answers that constitute an initial therapeutic session. Even here I am listening for more than just what is said. I sometimes imagine myself in the role of a neuroscientist questioning a client whose amygdala has been surgically removed. I want to hear the verbal response but I also want to sense how the body responds. I am concerned about the trauma of abuse disrupting the survivor's connection between body and mind.

Physical examination provides yet another means of assessing the somatic reality of the survivor. Rather than a casual inspection of posture, for example, I may precisely check for symmetrical height at the hips, shoulders, and head. At these locations many people show an inequality of height when both sides of the body are compared. Similar analysis of posture can be obtained from the side. A plumb line dropped from the ear lobe ought to pass through the shoulder, elbow, hip, knee, and ankle joints on that side. Postural deviations often indicate chronic patterns of muscle tension, spasm, and pain. Posture is also part of our emotional anatomy: How we hold ourselves somatically is related to how we hold ourselves emotionally and psychologically.

BODY MAPS—A TOOL FOR HEALING AND RECOVERY

So far assessment of the survivor's somatic reality has been based solely on my observation. An even more important source of this assessment comes directly from the survivor. Typically I begin my work with sexual abuse survivors by creating a **body map** that is unique for them (a detailed description of creating body maps is found in Chapter 6). The body map provides a tremendous source of information relating areas of the survivor's body with prominent emotional and psychological issues.

Figure 5.1 is the partial body map of a woman named Lynne, a forty-two-year-old social worker who is an incest sur-

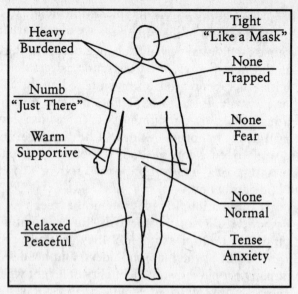

Figure 5.1 Body map of Lynne, incest survivor

vivor. I obtained Lynne's body map by simply asking her to relax and bring her awareness to various areas of her body. Beginning with her head and face she provided two pieces of information for each area: the physical sensation she had (i.e., tight, tingling, relaxed, hot, cold, painful, swollen) and a related nonphysical quality (i.e., a feeling, thought, image, voice, color). I charted her responses by writing the physical sensation over the top of the nonphysical quality.

Lynne was disheartened upon examining her completed body map. "It's depressing to look at," she said, "I'm a wreck." "No," I countered, "it's actually very hopeful. It gives direction to the work we'll be doing." I went on to explain what I saw in her body map. First I noted Lynne's central core—upper chest, abdomen, and pelvis—had no apparent sensation. This did not mean that Lynne had a neurological condition affecting these parts of her body. Had these areas been struck with a needle, or accidently touched a hot surface, I'm sure she would have felt it. However, it is not uncommon for survivors of sexual abuse to psychologically and emotionally turn off areas of their body.

Once this has occurred they will typically be unable to describe their awareness of these areas. This, as we noted earlier, is one form of body/mind dissociation.

COPING WITH ABUSE BY TURNING OFF THE BODY

Survivors "turn off" areas of their body for many reasons. Continued awareness of the physical sensations in an area may be too overwhelming. Physical violence may have been part of the sexually abusive behavior and some areas of the survivor's body may have been in chronic physical pain. Turning off sensation to such an area of the body is a way of coping with physical pain. Survivors may have also experienced normally pleasant body sensations during sexually abusive behavior. The discrepancy between unwelcomed abuse and normal body sensation from sexual stimulation can cause survivors to believe their bodies have betrayed them. One solution for betrayal is to turn off sensation. Survivors frequently report feeling helpless and powerless because they were unable to protect their body from abuse. Turning off an area of the body they cannot protect is another way of coping with the abuse. Very closely related are those survivors who feel their bodies colluded with the perpetrator. They often express feelings of guilt directed at their bodies for participating in the abuse even though this participation was coerced through force and threats. A phrase I've heard on several occasions is "I don't own that area of my body." Turning off a disowned area of the body is a way to cope and survive.

Lynne spoke more about the absence of sensation in her central core. "My heart feels trapped like a caged bird," she noted. "It feels safer to keep my thoughts and feelings inside of this cage," she said pointing to her chest. Lynne discussed her abdomen and her fear of getting in touch with her feelings surrounding the incest. "It's overwhelming," she sighed, "and I'm afraid I might not be able to handle all of my feelings." Finally she spoke about her pelvis, which bore the brunt of the actual abuse and harbored many of the emotional scars as well. "I've never felt it was part of me. I couldn't afford for it to be part of me when he touched me," Lynne observed in reference to her father. "Even as I grew older and he stopped I didn't like this part of my body because it reminded me of the abuse," she mourned.

Next we talked about other areas of Lynne's body map. Her arms, for example, symbolized the powerlessness she felt as a victim. Lynne's right leg represented that part of her that felt good about pursuing her healing and recovery from incest. Her left leg, however, felt tense and anxious about those very same issues. Lynne's shoulders seemed to represent the accumulated stress of many aspects of her life. Lynn's face and head were more perplexing. "I never really show people who I am," she mused. "They always get the happy, smiling Lynne not the frightened, sad Lynne." Lynne chose to comment about her hands last. "Sometimes I lie in bed, close my eyes and I swear I can feel light in my hands," she beamed. "They're warm and aglow. I feel my spirit within my hands. I want my whole body to be like my hands."

I ended this session by telling Lynne my feelings about body maps. When I look at survivors' body maps I see epic journeys: they tell where the survivors have been and about the pain they've endured. They tell where the survivors are in life right now. A body map also tells me where they're going with their life journeys and the obstacles they will encounter along the way. Finally, a body map points to the inner resources they possess to overcome the obstacles and to see the journey of healing and recovery through.

"I have a homework assignment for you," I concluded. "Take your body map with you and see if you can locate all the elements of your journey of healing and recovery."

TAKING A BODY HISTORY

Body maps are an effective tool for helping survivors link their body with prominent issues in their healing and recovery. The body history is another tool I use in a similar way. While a body map deals with many areas of the body, a body history focuses on one area only. In taking a body history we start at the present and work backward (see Chapter 6 for additional information about the body history). For each stage in his or her life the survivor relates a physical sensation and a nonphysical quality for that area of the body. If the survivor can't remember what physical sensation or quality was there, imagining works equally well. The process regresses as far back as the survivor's experience in the womb. Many people are amazed at how much they can recall and recollect from their early life.

Where the body map has one sensation and quality for many areas, the body history has many sensations and qualities for one area. Let's look at the body history for a survivor named Jeffrey. Jeffrey is a fifty-year-old carpenter who was sexually abused from ages eight to eleven by an uncle with whom he spent his summers. His major physical complaint was lower back pain, so we took a body history of this area. After asking Jeffrey to relax, I had him begin at the present and slowly work his way back in time. His body history chart is shown in Figure 5.2

Just as concentric tree rings record the layers of environmental events that have affected a tree, a body history records

Jeffrey M.—Lower Back		
TIME	PHYSICAL SENSATION	EMOTIONAL QUALITY
Present	Chronic pain	Despair
One month ago	Chronic pain	Frustration
Six months ago	Chronic pain	Anger
One year ago	Chronic pain	Hope
Two years ago	Chronic pain	Tolerable
Five years ago	Intermittent pain	Paid no attention to it
Early 30's	Blank	No recall
Early 20's	Strong	Can do anything with it
Around puberty	Blank	Unprotected
Late childhood	Blank	Scared
Early childhood	Flexible	Playful
As an infant	Supple	Protected
At birth	Soft	Vulnerable
In the womb	Warm	Supported

Figure 5.2 Body history chart of Jeffrey

144 . . . DR. CLYDE W. FORD

the layers of physical and emotional events that have affected an individual. Jeffrey's case shows patterns that are common to many of the body histories I have obtained and examined. We could begin by observing three major periods within his body history: an early period from the womb through early child-hood; a middle period from late childhood to his early thirties; and a current period from five years ago until the present.

The early period displays a typical sequence of events and emotions—from a warm, nurturing, all encompassing womb, through the trauma and uncertainty of birth, to progressive degrees of self-assurance and self-identity. Jeffrey's comments on this period were:

> Being in the womb felt warm and safe. At birth I imagined how the air would feel on my lower back, which had grown accustomed to a warm, liquid environment. I'd feel scared, weak, and vulnerable. As an infant I either remember or imagined my mother holding me and supporting my lower back with her hand. I felt protected then. As I grew older and began to walk there was a sense of elation and playfulness. My body was helping me explore a new world.

An obvious gap in an otherwise normal sequence of events and emotions happened for Jeffrey in late childhood. Skip ahead for a moment and you'll notice the entries under "early twenties," seem as if they should appear under "late child-hood." Of course this is the period when Jeffrey was subjected to repeated sexual abuse by his uncle. The familiar survival pattern of turning off body areas is found in Jeffrey's body history during this time. There also appears to be a reversal of emotional growth as feelings of fear and vulnerability resurface. When Jeffrey spoke about this period, he described his overwhelming sense of guilt and shame about participating in sexual acts with his uncle.

Five years prior to my first visit with Jeffrey, another epoch began. It was characterized by pain progressing from intermittent to chronic and emotions progressing from tolerance to despair. By the time we finished the body history it was obvious to Jeffrey that his lower back pain had to do with more than just his physical condition. Jeffrey's physical and emotional pain was chronic and unresolved. "I never realized how much I was affected by what happened with my uncle," he said. "I thought my despair was about my lower back pain, it's also about that awful period in my life."

THE MOVEMENT OF HEALING AND RECOVERY

Body movement is another way of connecting the physical and emotional issues surrounding abuse. Jane was a twenty-eight-year-old commerical artist whom I saw on referral from a psychotherapist. Her body map revealed stiffness in both legs though she was unable to describe any emotions or qualities she experienced in regard to that stiffness. Upon further questioning she described feeling that stiffness especially when she walked along the city streets. I asked Jane if she would feel comfortable walking around my office as though she were walking in public. She agreed and began to walk in circles around the office. Her only task was to focus her attention on her legs as she walked. After five minutes of walking I asked her to stop and reflect upon that experience. "I get it," she blurted out, "I'm really scared and I don't feel protected. My legs are trying to hold me back from what feels like a threatening and unsafe world."

Movement is often direct and straightforward. It can be an especially valuable tool when assessing a survivor's early life experience, or any experience that the survivor has difficulty talking about. Before we could verbally express emotions we somatically expressed them. Psychologists call this somatic expression of emotions *affectomotor responses*. Though most pronounced in early life, we exhibit affectomotor responses throughout our life. A smile is a good example of an affectomotor response. As children and infants our entire body, not just the muscles of our face, are involved in affectomotor responses.

Asking a person to move and bring his or her attention to a particular body area or a particular life event sets up a body-wide affectomotor response. I often use a simple suggestion that begins with "Would you move as if . . ." It's completed with the idea of moving as if the survivor were a particular feeling, thought, area of the body, person, event, or other relevant issue. After moving for a period of time the survivor is asked to stop and reflect on the physical sensations and other qualities produced by the movement. Moving in front of a therapist is not acceptable to all survivors—it may suggest exhibitionism. In that case I simply ask the survivor to sit comfortably and imagine moving as if. . . .

SAFE TOUCH FOR SURVIVORS

Of all the assessment tools, the most valuable is the Safe Touch protocol I developed after several years of working with survivors of sexual abuse. In part this is because the protocol is simple yet it provides a great deal of insight into the survivor's journey of healing and recovery. Moreover, the same protocol can be used to assess, build therapeutic rapport, and work with the survivor's issues of healing and recovery. In an age when Safe Sex is promoted to prevent the spread of AIDS, I believe that Safe Touch should be promoted to prevent the spread of sexual abuse.

Safe Touch came about because of my need to touch some survivors. In fact, as a somatic therapist many clients came to see me with physical conditions that required hands-on therapy. My awareness that touch could reenact sexual abuse was rudely awakened nearly ten years ago by a client with a sharp mind and often biting wit. Karen was a young psychotherapist whom I saw only for chiropractic manipulative therapy. She had injured her lower back and neck in an automobile accident. In the beginning of her care I saw Karen frequently and we had the chance to get to know one another. As is customary in many healthcare facilities, patients at our clinic went into a small treatment room, removed their street garments, got into a mint green clinic gown and lay down on a comfortable table. I always had soft music and soft lights in the rooms to foster relaxation.

One day Karen stopped me as I walked into her treatment room. "You know Dr. Ford," she said wryly, "outside of my husband you're the only man for whom I come into a dimly lit room with soft music, take off my clothes, slip into something scanty, lie on my back and allow myself to be touched." We chuckled briefly but the poignancy of her remarks was not lost in this humor. Karen was not a survivor, but she could have been. I knew that I had treated, and would continue to treat, women and men who were survivors.

Most somatic therapists, regardless of their specialty, receive virtually no training about how their touch might be perceived by survivors of sexual abuse. It seemed that something had to be done to respect the issues that Karen so indelicately brought to my attention. Safe Touch was born out of this need to respect the use of touch when working with survivors of abuse.

Five guidelines form the basis of the Safe Touch protocol. We've discussed these guidelines in various ways throughout the book but it's helpful to bring them together here.

1. The physical boundaries of an abuse survivor need to be respected at all times.
Without permission or consent, touch is a violation of an individual's physical boundaries. In this way even innocent touch can reenact past instances of abuse when one's physical boundaries were violated. Permission or consent to be touched can be either explicit or implicit. There are individuals in our lives who implicitly have permission to touch us—our children and our mates, for example, although there may be time when even these loved ones need to explicitly ask us for permission to touch. Other individuals normally need to ask for permission and it is our choice to grant that permission or not. When a therapist is using touch with a survivor of sexual abuse I believe explicit permission to touch needs to be given. I'll say more about the nature and frequency of that permission when we review the steps of the Safe Touch protocol.

2. Permission should be given before touching a survivor of abuse.
This guideline follows directly from the first and simply emphasizes the importance of respecting and validating the sanctity of the survivor's physical boundaries.

3. Any area of the body can access emotional issues.

Emotional recall is not just related to areas of the body commonly associated with sexual or physical abuse. Any area of the human body can be sensitized by past trauma. In this and previous chapters we've examined the many reasons why this might happen. It is particularly important to remember that an area of the survivor's body that seems "safe" to a therapist may not be at all safe for the survivor.

Another personal experience illustrated this for me. I was attempting to slowly introduce touch into the treatment of one survivor. I decided to lightly touch her shoulder so she could begin to experience my touch in a nonthreatening way. My well-intentioned plans quickly unraveled. No sooner had I touched her right shoulder than she started to cry and move her body as if to push me away. I was surprised by her behavior and asked her about it. "My father would restrain me by pinning my shoulder down," she informed me. "When you touched me there it reminded me of that fact." Therapists should never make assumptions about the safety of any area of a survivor's body. Instead the survivor's help should be enlisted to discover what areas do feel safe.

4. Avoid directly touching sensitive areas.

With limited exceptions there is rarely a need to touch a body area directly involved in sexual abuse—breast, buttocks, or groin. However, I have witnessed somatic therapists who, in my opinion, violated this guideline. I am reminded of one workshop I attended on somatoemotional technique where a woman participant was dealing with sexual abuse issues. She was lying on a treatment table and it was obvious her physical sensation and body movement were focused in her pelvis. In the name of helping her, the workshop facilitator pushed the flat surface of his palm between this woman's legs and directly into her groin. The woman began to cry even more deeply. Such a radical use of touch was unnecessary and inappropriate. I was uncomfortable witnessing this interaction, which so clearly reenacted the original abuse, but the workshop facilitator assured us he knew what he was doing.

On those rare occasions when it is necessary to touch a survivor (or anyone for that matter) at or near a sexually charged area of the body, I have a hierarchy of techniques: first, the survivor can touch the area and I can guide that touch verbally. If that won't suffice, then the survivor can touch the area and I can touch the top of their hand. If I still feel a need to directly touch that area of the body, then I do so with the survivor's hand on top of mine. Our understanding is that my hand can be lifted off at any time for any reason with no explanation needed.

5. Therapists need to be aware of their feelings about abuse that surface while touching a survivor.
We have already seen how feelings are transmitted through touch. When I touch a survivor I therefore need to be aware of what feelings arise for me regarding sexual abuse. For example, during many sessions with survivors I am aware of my own anger and outrage. "How is it," I say to myself, "that one human being could do such things to another?" That anger is a perfectly normal reaction to the horror of sexual abuse. However, if it continues unchecked I run risk of transmitting my anger to the survivor. Try touching someone in a gentle way when you're harboring anger and outrage—it's difficult if not impossible to do. I need to be aware of and separate my feelings about sexual abuse from my feelings about working with the survivor.

With these guidelines in mind I always introduce the Safe Touch protocol during my first session with a survivor. The steps of that protocol follow.

Safe Touch Protocol

1. Describe process to client.
2. Relaxation (eyes open or closed).
3. Allow client to find a body area where he or she feels safe being touched. If none exists switch to Safe Space.
4. Client gives permission to touch: "Clyde, I give you permis-

sion to touch my _____ in a _____
way."
5. Therapist lightly touches area.
6. Client observes touch.
7. Client requests cessation of touch: "Would you stop touching me now!"
8. Therapist immediately stops touching client.
9. Repeat steps four to eight several times.
10. Assess client's response.

The Safe Touch protocol is deceptively simple—there's more here than initially seems apparent. First, let me suggest that you try the protocol with someone else. It matters not whether you are a survivor of sexual abuse. Don't rush through it and whether you're in the role of the Traveler or Guide pay attention to your feelings and thoughts. The next few paragraphs contain some observations about the process.

Steps one and two are a way of helping a survivor understand what is about to take place and relax as the process begins. Before even beginning this process I often ask survivors if they feel all right about how close I am to them. Obviously, I have to be close enough to reach out and touch. Some survivors, however, will feel uncomfortable if I am within touching distance of them. If this occurs I ask them to suggest a better position for me, which is still within touching distance. If such a position cannot be found, I do not proceed with the Safe Touch protocol; instead I switch to the Safe Space protocol, which I'll describe later.

I often use a simple statement of explanation such as, "I'd like to demonstrate a way of touching that will help create safety and trust between us. Do you feel comfortable with that?" I might also add to this by reminding the survivor, "If at any point during this process you feel uncomfortable for any reason, just let me know and we'll stop immediately." When it comes to touching, it is important to let survivors know they are in control.

In step three survivors are specifically asked to find a "safe" area of their body to touch. Some survivors do not have an idea of what that means, so I might help them by saying:

> Find an area of your body you feel safe and comfortable about me touching. It could be the back of your hand, your shoulders, your arms, your legs, ankles, or feet. It could also be another area of your body I haven't mentioned. When you find that area let me know. And if for any reason you don't seem to be able to find an area of your body that feels safe for me to touch, that's also OK.

If the survivor can't find a safe area of his or her body I immediately stop the protocol and switch to a protocol I call Safe Space. Assuming a safe area can be found, I ask the survivor to specifically point to it so I have no confusion. In step four I ask the survivor to explicitly give me permission to touch, and also to inform me what kind of touch feels most appropriate. Here I am looking for qualities such as "in a healing manner," "in a respectful way," or "in an appropriate way." Some survivors are eager to be touched by someone else—even a stranger—although it can be a way of repeating the scenario of their abuse. For many survivors caring and abuse are connected—especially when a parent or loved one was the abuser.

At one workshop I asked for someone from the audience to participate in a demonstration of this Safe Touch protocol. Although I gave this woman the explicit instructions I have described so far, she gave me permission in the following way. "I know I'll like your touch," she said. "You can touch me whenever you're ready." It is precisely this response that the Safe Touch protocol attempts to correct. At first she found it difficult to understand why I would not accept her permission in that way. We rehearsed several different statements until she finally arrived at one that placed her in control of her boundaries around being touched.

The Guide lightly touches the Traveler in step five. Step six asks the Traveler to allow touch in this safe area for a period of time while the Traveler observes his or her reaction to it. This period of time is determined by the Traveler and not the Guide. Step seven, then, lets the Traveler know whenever he or she is ready the Guide can be asked to stop touching *now*. I suggest they emphasize the word **now**. It is very important that the Guide immediately honors this request and stops touching the Traveler, step eight. Step nine asks the Traveler to go back through steps four through eight without prompting from the Guide. Finally, after several cycles of this protocol, a discussion between the Guide and Traveler should take place. When I first began to use the protocol I felt very awkward. The logic of each step made sense but it felt stilted to actually rehearse them with a Traveler. My initial discomfort was quickly dispelled by what survivors had to say.

The focus of the process is in step four where permission to touch is given and step seven where cessation of touch is requested. About giving permission, survivors commented, "I felt respected," "I felt honored," "Someone finally listened to me," or "I didn't realize I had the right to do that." About requesting the cessation of touch the universal comment was, "I felt empowered." I began to get excited as I realized that positive therapeutic benefits were happening from such a simple protocol. But I also had more to learn about Safe Touch. I started asking survivors different questions about the process: Was it easier to give permission or request cessation of touch? Some individuals found it much easier to give permission for touch and more difficult to request that touch stop. For others the reverse was true. I guessed this had something to do with how easy it was for a survivor to bond (give permission to touch) or to separate (request that touch be withdrawn). My hunch seemed supported by use of this protocol with Travelers who were not survivors.

Individuals with difficulty forming boundaries found it easier to give permission to touch than to request an end to being touched. On the other hand, those with difficulty bonding found it harder to give permission to touch and easier to request an end to being touched. So the Safe Touch protocol could identify problems of bonding and separating. Often sexual abuse is the origin of such boundary problems, even if the person is unaware of a history of abuse. The protocol also became a way of screening for individuals who might be survivors.

The more I worked with the process the more I realized it

was unnecessary to ask Travelers which portion (permission or cessation) was easier for them. When shaking someone's hand there is an implicit sense of time duration: You know when someone has held your hand too long or too short. You even make some assumptions about the person based on the time duration of their handshake. I discovered the same thing is true of the Safe Touch protocol. After observing the protocol with hundreds of people you develop a sense of what is typical. After being given permission to touch, if I am not asked to cease touching within a certain period of time I begin to feel strange. "This is going on too long," I find myself saying silently. Or I may be asked to withdraw my touch so quickly that I also feel strange.

When I've asked survivors what was going on during this time they've reported, "I was trying to get up the courage to ask you to stop"; "It felt good and I didn't want you to stop"; "I was angry you asked me to do that"; "I didn't know how to ask you to stop"; "I could feel things stirring inside of me from being touched and I needed them to stop quickly"; or "I got irritated the moment you touched me." The protocol itself was able to bring up many of the survivor's primary issues of healing and recovery.

In some instances I don't go any further than this protocol for the first several weeks of treatment. Just enacting the steps of this process brings many important issues to the surface. But the protocol also has built-in therapeutic applications. For example, if a survivor has difficulty forming boundaries I might suggest the following: "Take me through this process again. Now, however, shorten the time between giving me permission to touch and requesting that I cease touching you." We might do this for several cycles. Each time the survivor shortens the duration between giving permission and requesting cessation. Similarly, if a survivor has difficulty bonding, at some point I might suggest, "Take me through this protocol again. Now, however, lengthen the time between giving me permission to touch and requesting that I cease touching you."

Safe Touch for Assessing Dissociation

The usefulness of Safe Touch doesn't stop with boundary issues. We spoke about body/mind dissociation earlier and this protocol can help identify how wide a gap exists between the body and mind of survivors. I became aware of this during a workshop in Miami. Of the three hundred people in attendance a woman in the front row volunteered to demonstrate the Safe Touch protocol. I took her through the steps of the process and she identified the back of her left hand as a safe place for me to touch. She then gave me permission to touch her, but as I reached out she offered her hand to me, then withdrew her hand slightly, then finally let it drop on top of her leg where I touched it gently.

Her ambivalence was obvious. When I questioned whether she was indeed comfortable with me touching her. "Yes," she said, "I feel comfortable with your touch." But her body told a different story. I could feel her tight and rigid wrist and forearm. Verbally her message was "yes," somatically her message was "no." A very observant participant raised her hand and said she also felt this woman did not really feel safe about my touch. We asked my volunteer about this again, and again she denied feeling anything but safe. Throughout her denials I imagined myself as the neuroscientist with the amygdalectomized patient whose body felt something other than what her mind described.

Safe Touch for Building Therapeutic Rapport

The Safe Touch protocol is also an excellent means of building rapport between a Guide and a Traveler. This simple process is, in effect, a model-in-miniature of the survivor's journey of healing and recovery. We have already mentioned how Safe Touch deals with the important issues of bonding and separating. It addresses issues of trust, safety, intimacy, and empowerment as well. Sometimes I have been unable to touch a survivor during our first session because an acceptable level of safety was not present. One woman was uncomfortable because I was male and she was abused by her father; another initially felt unsafe because she was alone in the room with me and no one else was in the building; still another survivor experienced no part of her body as being safe to touch. It was not until we began the Safe Touch protocol that these important concerns were voiced. This allowed us to first create a safe environment for touch: I could listen and respond to the survivor's concerns about my gender; we could wait until the next visit when a female friend was brought along; or we could practice ways of creating a Safe Space before we attempted Safe Touch.

Safe Touch for Creating Safety and Trust

Safety can be created more rapidly than trust. Since trust depends on consistency over time, Safe Touch is a good way to begin creating trust. I do not use the entire protocol each time before touching a survivor. Instead I ask for active permission to touch and I seek active permission to cease touching. I insist on active rather than passive permission. Active permission, for example, requires the survivor to say, "I give you permission to touch me in a healthy way." Passive permission only requires a "yes" or "no" to my request, "May I touch you in a healthy way?" Active permission is often more difficult but it is also more empowering for a survivor. At the end of a session I seek permission to remove my hands from a survivor. This is yet another opportunity for empowerment around the survivor's physical boundaries; another time when the survivor's verbal request is respected and acted upon immediately.

Safe Touch—A Beginning Lesson in Intimacy

As trust is built I may modify how and when I ask for permission to touch. In the beginning of treatment I usually ask for permission to touch each and every time I move my hands from one body location to another. Eventually it feels appropriate to decrease the frequency with which I ask for permission. I may only do so when moving from one region of the body to another, say from the upper body to the lower body. Ultimately, some survivors will give me global permission to touch at the start of a session by saying, "Dr. Ford you have permission to touch me in a healthy appropriate way."

Safe Touch is a beginning lesson in intimacy. It focuses on safety and trust, conditions that must exist for healthy intimacy to occur. It provides a clear set of guidelines for bonding and separating, the basic steps of the dance of intimacy. Safe Touch is also a beginning lesson in empowerment. Responsibility in this process resides with the survivor: The survivor initiates bonding and separation. Feeling empowered around bonding and separation is fundamental to healthy, functional human relationships. Sexual abuse wrests this ability from survivors, Safe Touch places it back in their hands.

Safe Touch and the Therapist/Guide

The Safe Touch protocol affects the Guide as well as the survivor. Many professionals treating survivors are not survivors themselves. While empathy with a survivor of sexual abuse may come easily, the somatic reality of the survivor is often more difficult to grasp. In my workshops for therapists I have used the Safe Touch protocol with a slight modification to convey the somatic reality of the survivor. Each therapist takes a turn giving and receiving touch. When the person receiving touch requests that it stop, the person giving touch ignores the request. The impact is profound. While this exercise should not be done with a survivor, it is a dramatic teaching tool for therapists of all backgrounds. Participants are quite shaken by their inability to control their physical boundaries. They describe feelings of powerlessness, victimization, subjugation, oppression, anger, and fear—the range of emotion experienced by survivors. They also describe somatic feelings of vulnerability, lack of ownership, and muscular tension, similar to the survivor's body experience.

There are other lessons for the Guide in the protocol as normally used. Many somatic therapists are not accustomed to clients initiating and concluding the use of touch. So this protocol often places them in an awkward position. Many have confessed after working with Safe Touch they actually feel relief as the survivor takes greater responsibility in the healing process. Safe

Touch is nondirective, which means that unlike some therapeutic methods the Guide does not control the show. Instead a partnership is sought between the Guide and the survivor.

Finally, Safe Touch is a convincing demonstration of the power of somatic techniques in healing and recovery from sexual abuse. I know of no more simple process that touches so many different aspects of the survivor's healing and recovery. Very little is said during the process but much is experienced. Issues of bonding and separating, of safety and trust, of intimacy and empowerment form the somatic reality of the survivor of sexual abuse. These issues are dealt with simply and directly through the use of Safe Touch.

SAFE SPACE FOR SURVIVORS

There are times when even the Safe Touch protocol is not "safe" for a survivor of sexual abuse. Initially, a survivor may feel unsafe about the therapeutic relationship with the Guide. The mere thought of being touched by a stranger is unacceptable. Or a survivor may be unable to discover any area of the body that feels safe to touch. At these times I have substituted a protocol called Safe Space. It is similar to Safe Touch but eliminates physical contact. Still, many benefits of the Safe Touch protocol are retained.

In Safe Touch the skin becomes a boundary. The survivor then regulates bonding and separating across that boundary. In Safe Space a less threatening boundary is defined away from the survivor's skin. However, the survivor still regulates bonding and separating across that boundary. The protocol is conveniently divided into two parts. First the survivor discovers Safe Space, then the survivor regulates bonding and separating in that Safe Space.

Safe Space Protocol

1. Describe process to client.
2. Relaxation (eyes open or closed), client and therapist sitting or standing.

3. Ask client to verbally move you back until he or she feels comfortable.
4. Client notes safe space boundary.
5. Client gives permission to enter: "Clyde, you have permission to enter my space in a respectful manner."
6. Client observes therapist's presence.
7. Client requests therapist to leave: "Would you move out of my space now!"
8. Therapist immediately moves back across the boundary into safe space.
9. Repeat steps five to eight several times.
10. Assess client's response.

For obvious reasons the protocol is very similar to Safe Touch. Figure 5.3 is a top-down view of how a survivor finds Safe Space, in steps three and four. The Guide is continually asked to move back until the survivor feels a sense of safety. At that point the survivor notes the boundary. I often ask the survivor to draw an imaginary line on the floor, or note a partic-

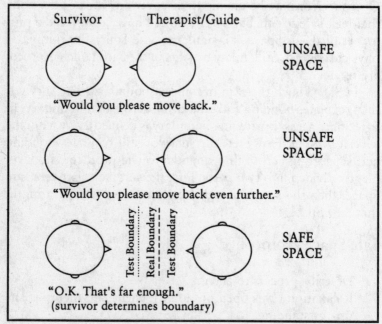

Figure 5.3 Safe Space Protocol, Part One

ular spot on the wall. If there is any question about the actual boundary, the survivor can ask the Guide to move forward beyond the apparent boundary. While this is taking place the survivor should be aware of any uncomfortable feelings. This will help establish what is really a Safe Space boundary. Once the Safe Space boundary is determined the therapist should move back on the "safe" side of that boundary.

In steps five through eight the survivor regulates access to and withdrawal from this Safe Space in a manner similar to the regulation of touch in the Safe Touch protocol. These steps are depicted in Figure 5.4.

Finding Safe Space With a Survivor

I have used the Safe Space protocol at several points during my work with survivors. Most often I use it in the beginning of therapy when it is apparent that Safe Touch is too threatening. But I have occasionally reverted to this protocol during the course of therapy when it seemed relevant to a particular issue or situation. In one instance a forty-two-year-old woman

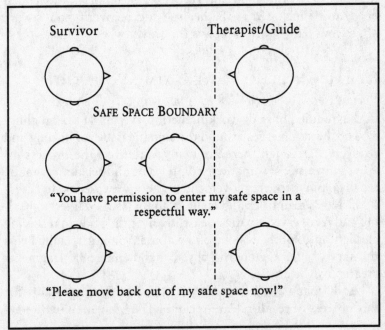

Figure 5.4 Safe Space Protocol, Part Two

named Sylvia had recurring middle back pain, which was aggravated in the presence of her mother. Though her mother was not the perpetrator (her father was), Sylvia described feeling enmeshed with her mother.

Asking Sylvia to find Safe Space away from her mother was actually humorous. I played the role of her mother and she backed me up. First, she backed me up about half-way across the room. Then she backed me up against the door. That was still not enough, so she backed me out of the door and continued backing me up until I was way across the adjoining room. I could hardly hear her giving me instructions! We practiced the protocol and Sylvia found she could move me closer without feeling threatened. Eventually Sylvia was able to establish a Safe Space boundary closer in, yet one that she felt empowered to maintain.

The same elements found in the Safe Touch protocol are also found in Safe Space protocol—bonding, separating, safety, trust, intimacy, and empowerment, but now these issues are a step further removed from the skin boundary of the survivor. This additional margin of safety may be required to explore these aspects of healing and recovery. Ultimately Safe Touch needs to be included in the healing and recovery from sexual abuse, but Safe Space can pave the way.

RECALL, RELEASE, RECLAIM: SOMATIC PROCESS IN THE TREATMENT OF ABUSE

In the middle phase of working with survivors of sexual abuse a basic theme emerges around the somatic issues of healing and recovery. Although there are many variations the process involves three steps: somatic recall, release, and reclaim. Somatic recall employs touch, movement, and body awareness to access a survivor's memories and feelings about issues related to healing and recovery. Somatic release involves the body in resolving and letting go of the residue of the abuse. Somatic reclaim helps the survivor reintegrate the physical and emotional fragments created by the abuse.

Body maps and body histories provide starting points for this process of recall-release-reclaim. The body map of a forty-two-year-old librarian and mother of five named Joan showed an upper abdomen and solar plexus devoid of sensation and emotion. Previously I attempted the Safe Touch protocol with Joan but she felt too threatened so we switched to Safe Space. After successfully completing the Safe Space protocol we again tried Safe Touch. This time Joan felt safe enough to allow me to touch her, but as I did she began to feel herself leaving her body. For the rest of the session she maintained an awareness of leaving her body.

Over the next several sessions I had no occasion to touch Joan and the dissociation experiences were not present. Then at one session touch seemed an appropriate course of action. I sought her permission, which she gave me, and proceeded to touch her. But shortly after doing this she once again reported feeling as though she was leaving her body. I stopped touching her immediately and we talked about the "leaving" experience. She informed me that she was accustomed to feeling this way whenever she felt threatened or under stress. So I gave Joan a homework assignment: At our following visit she was to report the changes that took place in her body just prior to a "leaving" episode. What follows is a partial transcript of that next session with Joan.

TRANSCRIPT OF A CLIENT SESSION

Joan: You asked me to tell you what's taking place in my body when I leave.

Dr. F: Yes.

Joan: First I tighten up here [points to abdomen]. Then I start thinking about something unrelated to my feelings. I'll usually have a smile on my face. On the outside people think I'm fine.

Dr. F: You mean how you appear on the outside and how you feel on inside are exactly the opposite?

Joan: Yes.

Dr. F: What's it like to feel split in that way?

Joan: I guess it's the way I use to avoid facing my feelings.

Dr. F: Joan, what would happen if you allowed yourself to face your feelings?

Joan: I might not be strong enough. I feel too much anyway. I empathize with others. At work I can feel what others are feeling. It's too much. I don't know how to protect myself I guess.

Dr. F: I understand that you feel too open to other's feelings. We were talking about feeling **your** feelings though. You said you don't feel able to face them.

Joan: [Cutting in.] Yeah.

Dr. F: Would you touch the area [Dr. F. points to his upper abdomen] that you first notice tightening when you're about to "leave."

Joan: [Joan touches her upper abdomen.]

Dr. F: Find the amount of pressure that is similar to the feeling you get when you're about to leave. Let me know when you have it.

Joan: [After experimenting with differing amounts of pressure for several moments.] OK.

Dr. F: What's your body feel like there?

Joan: Tight.

Dr. F: Joan, would you stay with that tightness and follow it wherever it leads? Periodically, tell me what you're experiencing.

Joan: [After a few minutes of silence.] It feels dark, like a black hole.

Dr. F: Stay with that darkness, Joan, and follow it wherever it leads.

Dr. F: [After several more minutes of silence.] What's it like now?

Joan: It feels very confused in here.

Dr. F: Just stay with that confusion.

Joan: [After a period of silence.] I can feel things starting to happen in my head. There's a swirling feeling here [points to head].

Dr. F: I know you're aware of these feelings in your head. I wonder if you would bring your awareness back to the place you're touching on your abdomen?

Joan: [A few moments pass.] I can feel myself starting to leave now.

Dr. F: Joan, bring you awareness back to the physical sensation beneath your hand. What's it like there?

Joan: It's numb there now.

Dr. F: Take however long you need to find the tightness that was originally in that area. When you've gotten back in touch with that tightness, let me know.

Joan: [After a long pause.] OK.

Dr. F: What's it like there now?

Joan: It's painful.

Dr. F: Could you stay in touch with that pain?

Joan: [Pausing] I have to move away.

Dr. F: That's fine. Move away as far as you need to while still staying in touch with that pain.

Joan: [Long pause of several minutes. Appears to be experimenting with how much pressure is being applied to the abdomen.] I can feel this energy shooting back and forth between the front of my body and my spine. [Begins to motion in direction of energy.]

Dr. F: I understand you're aware of the movement of that energy. Can you bring your awareness back to the place you're touching on your abdomen? Allow yourself to be back in touch with that pain.

Joan: [Another long pause.] I had to move away again.

Dr. F: That's fine. What's it like there now?

Joan: [Face reddens, appears to be on the verge of crying.] I have an image of being wounded, like someone shot an arrow that pierced through my body right here. It's how I felt when my mother, or someone else, would hurt my feelings. I'd get it right here and I'd tighten up my body so I wouldn't feel anything.

Dr. F: Stay with whatever you're feeling in that area.

Joan: [A long pause.] Anger. No one should have treated that little girl [referring to herself] like that. All she wanted to do was grow and explore the world. She was always made to feel wrong when she spoke about her feelings or asked questions.

Dr. F: Stay with that anger, Joan, and follow it wherever it leads.

Joan: [Face still red, but not crying, body beginning to rock.] Sadness. [Eyes begin to well up.] It's so sad she had to go through that.

Dr. F: Once again stay with that sadness, make some room inside for it.

Joan: [Obviously exhausted.] OK.

Dr. F: [After a long pause.] Joan, slowly bring your awareness back to your breathing. Take a moment to reconnect with what this experience has been like for you. Then when you're ready you can stop touching your abdomen.

Joan: [Several moments pass. Joan stops touching her abdomen. Looks directly at Dr. F.]

Dr. F: It appeared to me that you had enough strength to be in touch with a range of emotions.

Joan: Yes, but still I had to move over here [Points to a location about one foot in front of her body].

Dr. F: You did and yet you didn't leave altogether, you stayed present with your feelings. What was that like?

Joan: It's the first time I can remember being in touch with those feelings.

Dr. F: I have a homework assignment for you. The next time you feel yourself leaving touch your abdomen and only move away as far as you need to stay present.

This transcript demonstrates the use of touch and body awareness to access feelings and deal with dissociation. Joan first described the internal processes leading to dissociation: tightening of the diaphragm, distracting thoughts, and inappropriate facial expression. Sensation in her upper abdomen had been shut off for some time. She was afraid to feel the sensations and emotions in that area.

I decided to take a straightforward and simple course. We would use touch to focus her awareness on the physical sensation around her diaphragm. Whenever her awareness strayed I would gently ask her to bring it back to her abdomen and stay present with whatever changes in sensation and emotion were taking place. I also decided to approach

Joan's dissociation head on. Using touch we worked right at her edge between staying and leaving. The results were gratifying.

From my previous work with Joan I knew I would be unable to touch her. Physical contact would be difficult for her to handle, and full-blown dissociation would probably occur. However, I felt she could touch herself, which I asked her to do. Experimenting with pressure to mimic the tightness before the dissociation is a somatic technique I call *mirroring* (see Chapter 6 for more information). I felt mirroring was a safe way for Joan to explore the somatic and emotional events leading to dissociation.

In the early portion of the transcript Joan informs me that directly confronting her emotions seems too threatening. "I might not be strong enough," she said. By keeping her awareness at the level of physical sensation, those same emotions might surface somatically in a less-threatening way.

After Joan found the pressure that mirrored how she felt right before dissociating, a chain of important events was set in motion. Joan's awareness of this area began with tightness. But tightness led to darkness, darkness led to confusion, confusion led to numbness, numbness led back to tightness, tightness then led to pain, pain to anger, and anger led to sadness. At first Joan was primarily aware of her physical sensation. The darkness and confusion were messengers that something more was present. Right at the point of transition when physical sensation would have naturally led to emotional experience, Joan started to dissociate. In effect the pressure was becoming more than she could tolerate.

Like the top of a pressure cooker, touch was critical. It was her control valve—a physical and symbolic way of releasing enough pressure to stay present with the emotions that were about to surface. Instead of dissociation, Joan reexperienced the pressure and tightness. But this time tightness led to pain and pain led to her underlying unexpressed emotions.

It's fortunate that this chain of events was reported so clearly. In this process we see the use of touch and body awareness to help a survivor access a range of emotional experience previously unavailable to her. There is no specific way somatic therapy is used to recall emotional experience. But given the relationship between the body and emotions we've described so far; given the sensitivity and creativity of the Guide; and given the willing participation of the survivor, many ways can be found. Joan's story is a hopeful illustration of somatic therapy used to uncover and recall unexpressed emotions.

Somatoemotional Release

Somatic release is the second part of a therapeutic triad used in helping survivors of sexual abuse. Somatic release sometimes involves an actual physical or emotional letting go of unwanted feelings. At other times it becomes a way of resolving feelings and reducing their detrimental impact on the physical and emotional well-being of the survivor. When working with somatic release, I frequently use a process called *image/counterimage* (see Chapter 6 for a full description of this method).

Every feeling is represented by some arrangement of the body. At a macroscopic level, feelings involve observable states of muscular tension, heart rate, breathing, and blood flow (blushing). At a microscopic level, feelings involve more subtle arrangements taking place within our biochemistry and nervous system. These macroscopic and microscopic arrangements form the somatic images related to feelings. A frown is an example of a somatic image: an arrangement of our muscles of facial expression related to feelings of sadness or despair. A smile, on the other hand, is the counterimage of a frown: an arrangement of our muscles of facial expression related to feelings of joy or contentment. We can use the notion of somatic images and counterimages to release and resolve troubling emotions.

Valerie was a thirty-two-year-old graduate student in psychology. She had been in psychotherapy for several years as an incest survivor. Valerie came to see me because of abdominal pain she felt might be related to her ongoing process of healing and recovery. During one session I lightly touched her abdomen and asked her to bring her awareness there.

COMPASSIONATE TOUCH . . . 167

"What's it like there?" I queried. "It's painful," she replied, "and I have the image of a pocket of thick, black fluid trapped in here." "Just stay with your feelings in this area," I suggested, "you needn't say anything for a while." Several minutes later Valerie offered her feelings about the pain and the black fluid. "Symbolically, they represent what the incest left inside me," she observed, "the physical and emotional residue of being raped by my father." I let the weight of what she'd just said hang in the air for awhile, then asked what she wanted to do with this fluid.

"I've struggled so long with my feelings of guilt and shame," she sighed, "and in therapy I've spoken about feeling dirty and disgraced." Anger and tears swept into Valerie's voice as she stated her intention. "I want it out," she asserted, "I want this stuff out."

Getting It Out of the Body

Expulsion images—something painful inside that needs to come out—are not uncommon among the survivors I've worked with. However, many survivors are unaware of the relationship between their physical pain and this desire to expel something from their body. Making this connection, then helping the survivor expel whatever has been retained, can be a powerful and important step in the healing and recovery process. Usually the expulsion takes place through an orifice, and frequently this is not the orifice directly related to the sexual abuse. I have worked with survivors who chose "cough it out," "push it out" (as in giving birth), or "excrete it" from their bodies. On other occasions survivors have opted to create a symbolic orifice for this expulsion. I gave Valerie the choice of how the expulsion should proceed.

"It feels as if it should be drained from here," she noted, pointing to an area on the left side of her abdomen just below her rib cage. "When you're ready to create an opening and drain the fluid out, let me know," I responded. It took several minutes for Valerie to summon the courage and strength to take this step. "I'm ready," she said finally.

I pressed and twisted my right index finger into Valerie's side.

Her job was to tell me how deep we needed to bore to reach this pocket of fluid. As this was taking place Valerie began to cry though she tearfully continued to direct the creation of this opening. "That's it," she whispered, "you've tapped the fluid now." For the next fifteen minutes we drained the fluid. She pushed from her abdomen while I kneaded her body tissue toward this symbolic opening. Valerie moved through a range of emotions in this process. At times she screamed while angrily pushing this fluid out, and at other times she sobbed softly, apparently content to let it ooze from her body. While taking a break to rest she even quipped, "This is like an oil change, isn't it?"

An oil change was not a bad metaphor! Once the fluid had been drained an empty cavity was left. Valerie had the choice of how to refill this space. "I want to fill it with love," she told me, "with the love I need to have for myself. A love that lets me know I'm not dirty, I'm not guilty, and I'm not to blame."

"Take however long you need to fill yourself with this love," I replied, "then let me know when you're ready to close the opening."

"I'm filled," she said after awhile, "you can close it now." And so I slowly removed my finger from her side.

Through touch and body awareness Valerie realized the existence of a somatic image (the pocket of fluid) connecting the physical and emotional residue of her abuse. She then discovered an appropriate counterimage (draining the fluid out through her side). Valerie's healing process unfolded as this image was transformed into its counterimage and ultimately replaced by a new image (filling her insides with love) of special importance to her. There is an exquisite privilege in participating in a process like this. It is yet another opportunity to experience the simple elegance and deceptive power of bringing the body into a survivor's journey of healing and recovery.

Reclaiming the Body

Somatic reclaim is the final part of this therapeutic triad we're examining. Reclaiming an area of the body and its related emotions often happens through a process similar to Valerie's. However, I feel reclamation deserves special attention because it is such a prominent feature of the somatic reality of abuse. Earlier we noted that survivors frequently feel they do not own parts of their body. For them it is too painful to claim title to body areas that could not be protected against abuse—even though it was not their fault.

Nowhere is the lack of body ownership more evident than in multiple personality disorder (MPD). Often it is possible to bring forward a new personality simply by touching a different area of a multiple's body. Here, tragically, individuals have not only given up areas of their body but also created entire personalities to handle the trauma of abuse. The following example shows how reintegrating portions of the survivor's personality goes hand-in-hand with reclaiming portions of their body.

Jodi, a forty-five-year-old woman, had her childhood stripped from her through the sadistic physical and sexual abuse of parents involved in cult worship. To cope with the severe trauma, she developed MPD with more than thirty different personalities surfacing at various points in her life. For most of her life these personalities remained separate. They ranged from a housewife, married with two children (at one point Jodi was married with two children) to a little girl of six wandering the streets (when this personality was active, Jodi actually would be found walking the streets alone).

By the time I saw her she had been in psychotherapy for several years with a specialist in MPD. She had integrated more than half of her multiple identities and was managing to work as a nurse's aide. Her physical complaint was a painful right shoulder, but she suspected her pain was related to her abuse. I touched her right shoulder, which was indeed tight and tender. While gently holding her shoulder I asked her to relax. Immediately her voice changed and a new, angry voice emerged.

"That's Sarah," Jodi blurted out, "she's filled with anger about our abuse and has resisted integration into the rest of us." One primary strategy in treating MPD is to find the integrated self helper (sometimes called the ISH) personality. The ISH (and there may actually be more than one) is then encouraged to function as a collection point for the other disparate identities. Over time the more peripheral personalities can often be integrated into the center provided by the ISH. As with the other identities, the ISH often has its own body location. I hoped we could discover Jodi's somatic center of integration.

"Where in your body are these integrated personalities?" I asked, referring to the eighteen personalities she had successfully integrated under psychotherapy. Jodi pointed to her solar plexus. "May I touch that area of your body?"

After consulting with this center Jodi gave me permission to touch her. I rested my hand gently over her solar plexus. "Ask this integrating center if it is ready to receive Sarah," I said. After several minutes of silence Jodi tearfully replied, "Yes, and Sarah wants to come home now."

With my right hand on Jodi's shoulder and my left hand on her solar plexus, bringing Sarah home was a mythic journey. I gently kneaded Jodi's muscles down her back, around her midsection, and toward her solar plexus. At various points I could feel her body tense under my hand. When this occurred, I held still and asked what Sarah was experiencing. Sarah would invariably experience feelings about Jodi's abuse—primarily anger, resentment, and rage. We always stopped long enough for Sarah to let go of these feelings. I knew this letting go had taken place when Jodi's body would finally relax under my hand.

When we were about six inches away from her solar plexus, I stopped again. This time Jodi's integrating center became fearful of accepting Sarah back. Jodi had complete freedom to stop the journey if she felt her center was unable to accept Sarah. But after five or six anxious minutes, she announced that her center had "opened the door to Sarah." Then with a final push my right hand joined my left hand at her center. Sarah had finally come home.

Welcoming Back the Body

As with the other portions of this therapeutic triad, there are many ways to help a survivor reclaim the somatic and psychological fragments left over from the abuse. Reclamation ranges from the intensity of Jodi's journey to a celebration of reunion. One survivor, for example, hosted a body party where she welcomed the return of her legs and pelvis back into the rest of her body. During the party my role was applying pressure from the bottom of her feet. This pushed her legs and pelvis into her torso and gave her the physical sensation of being reunited. Too much is at stake to ignore the importance of returning ownership of survivors' bodies to them. Owning our body is how we own ourself. There must come a point in the healing and recovery process when survivors reclaim their bodies—not just their minds—from the abuse.

EMBODYING EMPOWERMENT: A FINAL STAGE OF HEALING

The journey of healing and recovery from abuse is not unlike a mythological journey where the hero or heroine must travel into a dark forbidding land to reclaim a lost treasure. Of course the treasure is none other than those parts of the survivor lost to the abuse. The body has a role at the conclusion of therapy when it is clear the hero or heroine has captured the lost treasure, and it is time to return from the journey.

Toward the end of the therapeutic journey, empowerment is a measure of capturing this lost treasure. Survivors feel empowered to express and handle emotions that appeared difficult before—empowered around their personal boundaries, empowered around owning their bodies, empowered around the choices they have in their lives, empowered around creating and maintaining healthy relationships, and empowered around their ability to seek help and make progress in healing and recovery.

In concluding treatment with a survivor—and in concluding this chapter—I'd like to recount the final session I had with a female survivor named Charlene. We met Charlene at the opening of this book. She was an adult survivor of sexual abuse I had worked with for many months. During our work we uncovered deeply held feelings within her body and worked to reclaim areas of her body and psyche taken away by the abuse.

In our final session, I asked Charlene to work with another body that was involved in the abuse. I asked her to inhabit the body of the perpetrator, her uncle. I want to emphasize that this is not something to be done with every survivor or abuse, not something to be done lightly, and certainly not something to be done in the beginning stages of healing and recovery. But Charlene had come a long way on her healing journey. Still, my request startled her. With some reluctance she agreed to try. As she closed her eyes and began to imagine herself in the body of her uncle, a remarkable transformation came over Charlene. She was first aware of his fear and pain. "He was a very fearful and scared person," she noted. "I can feel that in my body now."

Charlene, who had worked long at forgiving herself, surprisingly now found herself with an attitude of forgiveness toward her uncle. "I hate what he did," she said, "I hate how he hurt me. It was not right. But he was a human being with so much pain and anger. I can forgive him." In the next few minutes an even larger force took over. "I feel this tremendous surge of energy flowing throughout my body," she gasped. "I feel this power. It's the power he thought he gained by abusing me. It's mine now," she shouted excitedly, "It's mine now, and not his!" And with this outburst Charlene opened her eyes in amazement. She had embodied the transition from victimization to survival to empowerment—she had the power now.

Charlene was an exceptional Traveler on the journey of healing and recovery from sexual abuse. Not all survivors reach the point she did, but certainly many can and many do attain a similar sense of empowerment. My final journey with Charlene shows the hope and promise that exists for all survivors when the body becomes an integral part of their healing and recovery. The body, which is the survivor's symbol of abuse, can become a symbol of hope. And like Charlene, survivors can embody this transition from victimization to survival to empowerment. They can reclaim their power.

6.

THE ART OF COMPASSIONATE TOUCH

Learn your techniques well,
but be prepared to drop them
when you touch the human soul.
—C. G. JUNG

When I demonstrate working with the body it often seems that nothing happens. For twenty minutes I can gently touch a volunteer in front of two hundred and fifty people. My hand barely moves throughout the process. This is a strange place, a fishbowl before so many expectant onlookers. I imagine myself in the minds of the audience. "He's not doing anything," one bemoans. "I don't see a thing," another remarks. "He must be a magician with a trick up his sleeve," decries another silently. Sometimes I have similar thoughts, "Oh, this is a terrible demonstration nothing *really* is happening." Then the process draws to a conclusion and the volunteer speaks. A kaleidoscopic movement of feelings, thoughts, sensation, color, and visions is reported. Change has taken place, something has shifted right beneath my hands; right before everyone's open eyes. I am sure I hear the audience join in a collective sigh of relief. The demonstration has not come to a disastrous conclusion—something *has* taken place.

Soon my audience finds its central question, "We don't know what took place, but whatever it was, how did you do it?" Routinely my answer is, "I didn't do anything." Groans of frustration and protest are raised. "We came to learn what you do," some say. "If you watch what I do you'll miss what takes place," I counter. "Then what is there to learn?" asks another. "There is much to learn but little to do," I reply. I am sure I must sound like a Zen monk answering the koan, "What is the sound of one hand clapping?" The koan shows that answers are not always at the same level as questions. This is my purpose too. Answering the question "What did you do?" is not always the best way to learn about the body's role in healing and recovery.

THE TECHNIQUE MAZE

Somatic therapy is often dogmatic in insisting on technique. There is an underlying belief that the right technique produces the right outcome—physically or emotionally. Like searching for the Holy Grail, practitioners expend much effort searching for the perfect technique. Practitioners usually spend time and money attending technique seminars. They listen to someone who claims to have developed a more perfect technique. They watch, imitate, and practice what they see. When they do not obtain the results promised by the technique guru, their quest continues. They may attend more advanced seminars on the same technique, or look elsewhere for the next more perfect technique. There are many somatic techniques—from Acupressure to Zero-Balancing—all promising a better way to effect physical and emotional healing. Clients fare little better in this technique maze. Some believe there is a perfect technique for them and travel from practitioner to practitioner in their quest. Others, having experienced a technique they like, are convinced nothing else will work. Their first question to a prospective practitioner is, "Do you do the———technique?"

Somatic techniques amuse and frustrate me. Many years ago a woman sitting next to me on an airplane flight inquired about my work. "What do you do?" she asked. I promptly listed the techniques I'd become proficient at as if they were merit badges of my fitness to be a somatic therapist. "But what do *you* do?" she insisted. I got her point and I was embarrassed. It was difficult to define what I did outside of the techniques I practiced—and that bothered me. She taught me a valuable lesson. From that day on I stopped describing myself in terms of the techniques I knew. I started searching for what I did as a somatic therapist.

The following simple experiment always reminds me of the difficulty of relying on technique. With the fingertips of either hand, gently touch your clavicle, (collar bone) and follow it in toward your sternum (breast bone). Right where the two meet let your fingertips drop down over your clavicle into the soft space between the sternum, clavicle, and first rib. You're now touching an area diversely connected to your physical and emotional health. Some say this is a point that when stimulated balances the energy flow throughout your body. Others say this is an area related to the drainage of lymphatic fluid from your upper body. Still others label this emotionally as the area of grief and loss. In yet another system, this area is related to the thymus gland and its effect on the overall health of the body.

Depending on whom, and what, you believe you may need to rub this area, deeply goad it, hold it lightly, or not touch it at all. Each different way of understanding and working with this area of the body will have a different name. The number of named somatic techniques is staggering: acupressure, bioenergetics, craniosacral therapy, chiropractic, structural integration, functional integration, psychostructural integration, Reiki, Mari-El, applied kinesiology, behavioral kinesiology, educational kinesiology, transpersonal kinesiology, thymokinesiology, Hellerwork, Trager, and Zero-Balancing, just to name a few. Not surprisingly one technique or system often looks unfavorably at others. This can lead to heated debates among practitioners, resulting in splits and splinter groups even within a given technique.

In response to this confused state of affairs, I ask myself what the body knows. Can the body possibly know that at any particular moment I'm using acupressure as opposed to functional integration or rolfing? Of course not. Can the body know I'm interested in a particular emotion when I touch an area? I don't believe so. What, then, does the body know? When stated in this way it's possible to describe somatic therapy without reference to a specific technique. There is a somatic language of touch, movement, and awareness our body knows well. Perhaps it would be better if we attempted to understand what the body knows and not impose upon the body a technique of our choosing. In the remainder of this chapter, I'd like to outline this somatic language and show how it can be used to include the body in the process of healing and recovery.

THE LANGUAGE OF TOUCH

Languages are composed of primitive objects, like words or sounds, and rules of usage, like grammar or phonetics. Using these primitive objects according to rules allows us to convey meaning. The language of touch is no different. Here the primitive objects are simple: physical contact through the skin, or no physical contact. Added to this are only three rules that govern this language of touch: depth, direction, and duration—the three *D*'s of touch. While the primitive objects of this somatic language—touching or not touching—are straightforward, the rules need a little more explanation.

Depth of Touch

Depth refers to how deep one is touching. Depth of touch ranges from "touching" off the body, to gentle touch at the skin surface, to deep pressure. Each level transmits different messages to the body. For example, deep touch activates our *proprioceptive system*. This is our positional locator system. Stretch your arm out to your side. Point your index finger and close your eyes. Now in a wide arc sweep your index finger around to touch the tip of your nose. You need an intact proprioceptive system for that task—locating the position of your nose on your body. Proprioception is also related to body movement, in particular the ability to locate the position of various body parts in the midst of moving the entire body.

It is possible to touch lightly without activating the proprioceptive system. Light touch is related to another body system called the *spinothalamic system*. This system, which we encountered in an earlier chapter, transmits pain, temperature, and light touch from the skin surface to the brain and nervous system. Neuropeptides, we noted, are intimately involved in the first stage of this spinothalamic system. Even touching off the body conveys information. This was illustrated in an earlier chapter where I described research showing changes in the electromagnetic field interaction between two individuals, and reviewed the work of Békésy, the Nobel laureate who studied our ability to project touch away from the skin's surface.

Direction of Touch

Direction is the second rule of the language of touch. Direction also conveys meaning. The scientific term for directional meaning is *orientation selectivity*. It comes from vision research. The cells in our brain resonate to different aspects of our environment. Cells in the auditory system, for example, resonate to different frequencies of sound. Cells in the visual system resonate to different orientations of lines (among many other things). Draw a heavy dark line on a piece of paper. Close one eye and slowly rotate the paper in front of the other eye. If you could simultaneously record from cells in your brain (the experiment was actually done on monkeys) you would find a different response as you rotate the line. When the line is vertical some cells will respond vigorously while other cells will be dormant. When the line is horizontal other cells will respond while those that responded to the vertical line are silent. At all orientations between vertical and horizontal the same response pattern exists: Some cells will react maximally while others will remain quiet. The cells that react maximally to a given position of the line are said to be selective for that orientation, hence the term orientation selectivity.

Years later the same response was found through the skin. Open your left palm so it's facing you. Now with your right hand touch a spot in the middle of your palm. Trace a line from the middle of your palm straight up to twelve o'clock. Next trace a line from the middle to one o'clock, then two o'clock, then three o'clock—all the way around an imaginary clock face.

At each orientation some cells in your somatosensory system (the system that processes touch) will react maximally and others will not. Your entire body has orientation selectivity to touch. This means the direction of touch conveys specific messages and calls forth specific actions from the body. Perhaps "being rubbed the wrong way" is a metaphor based in truth.

Duration of Touch

Duration is the last rule of this language of touch. Duration, like its two predecessors, conveys specific meaning. The eyes again give us a clue to the meaning of duration. Fix your gaze on a single point in front of you without moving your eyes. Done long enough and with enough diligence that point will disappear. Our vision has habituated. Now just move your head or eyes ever so slightly and vision returns. Your visual system has oriented. The same phenomenon appears through the skin. Hold a pen in your hand without moving it for several minutes. Eventually touch habituates and you can no longer feel the pen. Then move your hand ever so slightly and you will feel the pen again as your body orients to the stimulus. Habituation says things are all right the way they are—don't change! Orientation says something new just took place—better check it out and make adjustments.

CONVEYING MEANING THROUGH TOUCH

Together these three *D*'s describe most therapeutic methods of using touch. You don't have to learn specific technique. You can simply learn these three rules that describe the language of touch: depth, direction, and duration. Still, speaking a language involves more than simply knowing the grammatical rules. Words placed together must convey meaning. Touch used according to these three rules must also convey meaning. Touch informs our body in four ways: it **mirrors, intensifies, counters,** or **monitors.**

I might observe a Traveler with a tight middle back. Perhaps I am aware of this tightness because I can see small muscle spasms occurring between the shoulder blades. But the Traveler may be unaware of, or simply accustomed to, this tightness. To heighten awareness I might ask the Traveler to help me gauge the pressure needed between the shoulder blades to mimic the sensation in this area. Thus, touch **mirrors** an event taking place within the body.

At other times heightening awareness is not enough. It may be useful to explore a physical sensation further. If a Traveler feels slight tension in one shoulder, I might exert just a little more pressure than needed to mirror that tension. Thus, I would be **intensifying** a physical sensation. Finally there are times when I would want to touch in a way that is opposite of a particular physical sensation. If someone has a tight muscle, I may choose to touch in a way that relaxes it. My touch now **counters** given physical sensation. By varying the depth, direction, and duration of touch we can either mirror, intensify, or counter nearly any process taking place within the body. At times the practitioner also might use touch for one other purpose: to **monitor** events happening within the body. For example, I might palpate the muscles up and down a Traveler's spine to find which are relaxed and which are under tension. Monitoring is a way of using touch to assess what is taking place within the body.

A SOMATIC LANGUAGE OF EMOTIONS

Depth, direction, and duration of touch are related not only to events taking place within the body but also to underlying emotional experience. In landmark studies spanning several decades, pianist and neuroscientist Manfred Clynes studied the connection between feelings and touch. He constructed an apparatus that measured pressure along two axes: forward-backward and upward-downward. Think about the movements of a typical car seat and you'll understand the nature of Clynes's device. The forward-backward direction of the seat allows you to slide closer to or further away from the steering wheel, while the upward-downward direction of the seat allows you to move higher or lower relative to the car's ceiling. Instead of a car seat, Clynes constructed a button connected to an electrical recording device that measured pressure in these directions.

Clynes asked hundreds of subjects to press this button while experiencing certain feelings—love, hate, grief, joy, reverence, anger, sex, and an absence of feeling. As his device recorded the depth, direction, and duration of pressure in response to these feelings, a remarkable finding emerged. Similar pressure patterns existed for all the subjects. Clynes called these shapes *essentic forms,* whose purpose was to communicate feeling. Figure 6.1 shows the major essentic forms discovered by Clynes. The top lines represent pressure exerted in an upward-downward direction, the bottom lines represent forward-backward pressure. "Essentic form is biologically given," Clynes observed, "and appears to be genetically preserved." Clynes illustrates the elemental emotional qualities communicated by the body's language of touch.

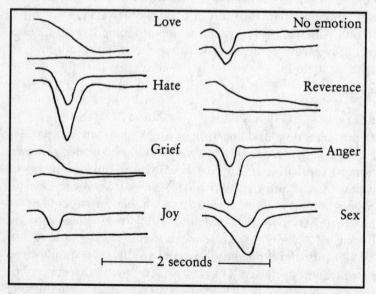

Figure 6.1 Essentic forms of about two seconds duration
(After Clynes, 1989)

INTENTION AND HEALING

There is one intangible aspect of this somatic language: the intention between Guide and Traveler. Although difficult to identify, intention is still an important part of a therapeutic exchange. The word intention comes from the Latin *intentus* and has the interesting somatic connotation of literally meaning to stretch out or to stretch toward. One element of intention resides in the will of the Traveler and Guide—the conscious and unconscious hopes, expectations, and drives each brings to the therapeutic partnership.

In the first chapter I mentioned a research project conducted by the National Institutes of Mental Health that measured psychotherapeutic effectiveness. Clients were randomly sent to either trained and untrained therapists, with little differentiation in the outcome of their sessions during the first six months. The untrained therapists were taught a technique of empathic listening. In effect, these untrained therapists simply had the intention of "holding the client in highest positive regard." Initially, this intention alone was enough to sustain a positive therapeutic outcome.

A complementary study further examined a client's response to therapeutic intention. Joseph Weiss and his colleagues tested two assumptions about how people in therapy change. One assumption (a traditional psychoanalytical one) held that the therapist's intentions toward a client caused frustration. According to this view, a client represses issues he or she needs to examine. Many powerful forces of body and mind block the client's awareness of these crucial issues. But the therapist takes no position. He or she assumes a noncritical stance toward the client's issues. This neutrality fuels the unconscious material repressed by the client. Like hunger in a person denied food, the intensity of these unconscious issues mount until they must find conscious expression. Significant material is then brought forward to be explored and examined.

The alternative hypothesis proposed that the client unconsciously tests and senses the therapist's intentions. Like a person gingerly placing a foot in a tub of hot water, the client continuously probes the therapist's intentions. When those intentions appear to create a safe, noncritical environment, the client brings forth repressed issues. These two assumptions about intention and therapeutic change are exactly opposite. One says the therapist tests the client's readiness to change. The other says the client tests the therapist's readiness for change. Using an extensive series of tests, Weiss found support for the latter: Clients probe and monitor a therapist's readiness for them to change.

While these studies say much about the importance of intention in therapeutic change, they say little about how intention actually causes change to happen. Intention may produce subtle changes in the body. A shift in body position, a twitch, a movement of an arm or leg may all communicate intention. In an earlier chapter I described how important it was for somatic therapists to monitor their feelings. In my training groups I often suggest a simple exercise: touch someone lightly without varying depth, direction, or duration. Instead vary the intention. Through intention alone I have participants convey different messages: deeper or more superficial touch, emotions like love, anger, hate, fear, or guilt. The recipients of this touch try to sense what quality is intended. Without changing the nature of the physical contact nearly all recipients can sense changes in intention.

A few scientific studies even suggest the power of intention to affect animate and inanimate objects. One study by William Tiller, at Stanford University, described a gas-filled glass tube sensitive to intention. The tube was placed across the room from volunteers who were not connected to it in any way. When a volunteer was asked to concentrate on the tube, the gas began to discharge and the tube began to glow.

Carroll Nash, a biologist at St. Joseph's University in Philadelphia, studied the effect of intention on the genetic mutation of bacteria. Two strains of *E. coli,* bacteria normally found in the human digestive tract, were used for Nash's experiments. In test tubes one strain, A, is colorless while the other strain, B, is red. Ordinarily both strains mutate back and forth between each other. Fifty-two volunteers were asked to focus their intention on promoting or inhibiting the mutation of the bacteria. There were nine test tubes in the experiment. In three tubes volunteers attempted to inhibit the mutation of strain A to strain B. In three other tubes promotion of mutation was intended. The remaining three tubes were left alone as experimental controls. The results were significant and surprising. There were more strain B bacteria in the promoted group than the control group. Intention not only affects inanimate objects, like gas in a tube, but living organisms as well.

William Braud and his colleagues at the Mind Science Foundation performed a related set of experiments with humans. They connected electrodes measuring the electrical activity of the skin (called EDA) to the palms and fingers of the experimental subjects. Another group of volunteers were seated sixty yards away in a different room. This second group was asked to influence the EDAs of the first group. They succeeded even when the subjects were unaware of their attempts. Although it goes against the grain of conventional wisdom, the intention of one person affects the body and mind of others.

The EPR Paradox

While these studies are provocative and suggestive, they still fail to explain how intention produces such effects. A more tangible answer may lie in the misgivings of a great twentieth century scientist. Albert Einstein was a central figure in a debate regarding the best description of reality. On one hand were the relativists, among them Einstein, who proposed a commonsense approach: Reality can be described based on observations made and measured. Quantum theory opposed this view. Reality cannot be observed and measured with certainty said the quantum theorists. Only tendencies or probabilities about reality can be described. "God does not play dice," countered Einstein. The details of this debate are not as important as Einstein's attempt to disprove quantum theory.

In the 1930s Einstein, with two colleagues, Podolsky and Rosen, proposed that if quantum theory were true the following preposterous assertion also would be true. Take any two particles first joined in a system. Now separate them to the furthest ends of the universe, then change one and instantaneously the other changes as well. It's not a change in one causing a change in the other. According to quantum theory both would change simultaneously. This, according to a commonsense interpretation of reality, seemed implausible. The Einstein–Podolsky–Rosen (EPR) paradox, as it became known, was a thorn in the side of quantum theorists. Eventually experimental equipment was devised that could test the veracity of the paradox. To the amazement of many, the paradox was proven true! In a research laboratory a pair of particles was separated by distances too great for any known physical forces to operate. The spin of one particle was altered and instantaneously the spin of the other changed.

What does the EPR paradox tell us about intention? The paradox points to an order of reality in which wholeness, not separation, is fundamental. Intention may well operate in this order of reality. The particles described by the EPR paradox need not be photons or electrons isolated in the experimental apparatus of a research laboratory. When one human reaches out to touch another, the conditions for the EPR paradox are staged over and over again—many millions of times.

Consider the following sequence of events. You reach out to touch another's hand. Inches away from the skin and seconds before contact the EPR paradox is already in effect. Atoms and subatomic particles that once clung to you have spun off and are now clinging to your partner. In a similar way your partner's particles are now part of you. This process happens millions of times a second with particles switching sides so many times it's impossible to say to whom they really belong. When you finally touch, your particles have been joined in a system for eons of time when measured by subatomic standards. Even if you never touch and just stay close, the system of particles still exists. Now, according to the EPR paradox, you can separate from your partner but if something changes within you a complementary change occurs simultaneously within your partner. A feeling or thought about someone else would be capable of producing such a simultaneous change within your partner. Whether intention will ever be fully understood in terms of quantum physics remains to be seen. Regardless, intention is an important variable that joins with depth, direction, and duration to form the basic grammar of a somatic language.

SOMATIC INTERVENTIONS

Throughout this book I've presented many situations where somatic therapy was used to foster physical and emotional healing. I'd now like to examine in greater detail this use of touch, movement, and body awareness, using the somatic language. There's an exercise associated with each method we'll explore—somatic process is often better understood through experience than description. The exercises are designed for two people, but they can be adapted for individual use.

Body History

The body history is a way of helping a Traveler relate the emotional and physical issues of healing and recovery. The technique is simple and I frequently use it as a warm-up exercise for participants in my workshops. It is helpful to have the Guide verbally direct the Traveler through the body history, but it is not necessary that the Guide touch the Traveler's body. When doing this exercise the Traveler should decide beforehand if the Guide will actually be touching. If the Guide is not touching the Traveler, modify the appropriate steps of these instructions.

TAKING A BODY HISTORY

1. Explain the process to the Traveler.

Tell the Traveler you will be touching selected body areas, and asking for his or her awareness to be brought there. Once there, you will ask the Traveler several questions about that area of the body. Reassure the Traveler that there are no right or wrong answers—whatever emerges is all right. Encourage the Traveler to be open and spontaneous.

186 . . . DR. CLYDE W. FORD

2. Select an area of the body to work with.

In consultation with the Traveler, choose an area to work with. This could be an area that is in pain, one that was previously injured, or one that is of special importance to the Traveler— for instance, the legs of a dancer, the hands of a painter, or the arms of a carpenter. This could also be an area of the body the Traveler is simply curious about.

3. Guide the Traveler through relaxation and inner focusing.

Consult the appendix for a sample relaxation and inner focusing script, or use one of your own.

4. Lightly touch the area of the Traveler's body you are working with.

It may have been determined that the Guide will not touch the Traveler. In that case the Traveler may be able to touch the area of the body. This should be done in a way that is comfortable and feels appropriate in front of another person. Touching the area is not required, and the Traveler can simply keep his or her awareness in this area.

5. Ask the Traveler to bring his or her awareness to this area.

It is often easier for the Traveler to have his or her eyes closed during this process, but it is not necessary. The Guide can use the following intervention or one similar to it to focus the Traveler's awareness in this area:

> Bring your awareness to the area of your body I'm now touching. Without trying to change, control, or analyze it, allow yourself to experience this area of your body.

6. Help the Traveler retrace the somatic history of this area.

Ask the Traveler to listen to your questions, and answer them silently. Remind the Traveler to take as much time as needed to let the answers emerge. Use the following questions, or similar ones, in the order given:

(a) When is the most recent time you remember being aware of this area? What was that awareness like? (pleasurable, painful, loving, fearful, joyful, angry, etc.)

(b) One week ago, what was your experience of this area of your body like?

(c) Let yourself go back a month ago. What was your experience of this area like then?

(d) Six months ago, allow yourself to recall your experience of this area of your body.

(e) Continue this process of taking the Traveler back in time—one year ago, five years ago, ten years ago, in the Traveler's forties (depending on current age), in the Traveler's thirties (depending on current age), in the Traveler's twenties, around the time of puberty, during late childhood, during early childhood, at birth, and finally in the womb. At each point give the Traveler permission to **remember** or **imagine** what this area of the body was like.

Allow yourself to go back to———, remember or imagine what your experience of this area of your body was like then.

7. Have the Traveler come forward in time.

Once the Traveler has taken this journey back to the womb, suggest that he or she bring the process forward. Tell the Traveler:

Now reverse this process bringing it forward from your birth to the present time. At each age let yourself remember or imagine what your awareness of this area of your body was like. Take your time and let this journey move at a comfortable pace.

8. Ask the Traveler about the meaning and importance of this area.

After a sufficient time has elapsed for the Traveler to bring this process forward in time, the Guide should ask about the meaning and importance of this area of the body:

188... Dr. Clyde W. Ford

(a) If this area of your body had a message for you right now, what would that message be? Take a moment to listen to your body deliver that message to you.

(b) If you had a message for this area of your body, what would that message be? Imagine you can hear yourself delivering that message to your body.

(c) How important is this area of your body to you? What's it like to realize the importance of this area?

(d) What new awareness do you now have of this area of your body? How might you incorporate this new awareness into your life?

The Guide should make sure the Traveler is given plenty of time between each question for answers and impressions to emerge. Don't rush this step.

9. Guide the Traveler out of the exercise.

The Guide can use the following intervention or one similar to it:

> Bring your awareness back to your breathing. When you're ready take several deep breaths, stretch if you need to, then open your eyes.

10. Discuss the Traveler's experience.

First, give the Traveler an opportunity to jot down whatever feels important to remember from the exercise. An exercise like this is similar to a dream. When we first awaken we remember the dream in exquisite detail, but a few moments later we can barely recall the content. Writing about an experience immediately afterward can help the Traveler retain what was meaningful and important. Then the Traveler and Guide can discuss the exercise.

Reviewing a Body History

Travelers show an interesting range of responses to this exercise. Many notice an immediate change in the area of the body just from taking the body history—the body area feels better afterward. In exploring their body history many Travelers experience gaps or blank periods when no recall was available. Sometimes this is a reflection of a Traveler's body shutting off because of pain or trauma. Some Travelers find it surprisingly easy to remember, or imagine, this area of the body being formed in utero, being born, and its development in the early years of life. This is because our bodies have such paramount importance to us at those times. Other Travelers find it easier to go forward in time, while still others find going backward with the body history easier. There may be a different sensation in the area going forward in time from the sensation when going backward. Frequently the gaps present during regression are filled in when the process is brought forward.

Many Travelers can also hear the messages this area of their body has for them—these messages can be powerful and laden with meaning. In the chapter on sexual abuse I analyzed a body history taken from a survivor. It showed layers of meaning corresponding to the events taking place at different times in his life. The body history makes deeper body memories available to our conscious mind. In this way it can serve as a guide on our journey of healing and recovery.

Body Maps

Developing relationships between what's going on in the body (somatic process) and what's going on in the mind (mental/emotional process) is at the heart of using somatic therapy for healing and recovery. Creating these links between body and mind is like constructing a map that describes the features of a given landscape. As mapmakers we can begin at either end. We can delineate the features of our somatic language in mental/emotional terms, or we can describe our mental/emotional landscape by referring to our body. Regardless of where we start, we are left with a way of traversing the terrain between body and mind. This can be extremely useful when we deal with mental/emotional issues somatically, or when we address somatic issues through the mind.

Body maps can be prepared in two ways. One way is to look

up physical symptoms on a prepared chart and read off the related mental or emotional issues. For example, if I have a pain in my lower back I might consult a popular book on the subject. Looking up back pain I'd find it is related to lack of support in my life. I might then repeat some affirmations and do some counseling or visualization about creating more support for myself. If I discovered pain in my right shoulder I would again look up the meaning of that pain and take a similar course of action. While this approach to body mapping helps people understand the significant connections between body and mind, it is often too sketchy. Not everyone with back pain feels a lack of support. Not everyone with shoulder pain feels burdened. And not everyone with neck pain feels inflexible. Perhaps the biggest difficulty with this approach to body mapping is that individuals will try to fit themselves into the categories they find. Even if I don't experience a lack of support in my life, for example, once I've read about back pain I might believe support is the main issue I should address.

I've adopted a different approach to body mapping, one that allows each individual to evolve unique, personal meanings and correlations between physical and emotional experience. This technique for creating body maps is very straightforward.

CREATING A BODY MAP
Creating a body map begins by having the Traveler in a relaxed and comfortable position: lying on a comfortable surface or seated in a comfortable chair. Then the Guide can follow these steps:

1. Draw a simple stick figure like the one shown in Figure 5.1.
On a separate sheet of paper draw a simple stick figure and label it with the Traveler's name. If you like you can use a photocopy of the body assessment form found in the appendix.

2. Explain the process to the Traveler.

Tell the Traveler you will be touching selected body areas, and asking for his or her awareness to be brought there. There are many ways people describe their awareness of an area:

(a) Visual images (I can see————)
(b) Kinesthetic images (This area feels as though————)
(c) Auditory images (It's as though I could hear this part of my body saying————)
(d) Simple impressions (I'm aware of————related to this area)

Reassure the Traveler that there are no right or wrong responses. The process works best when the Traveler is as honest as possible with whatever emerges.

3. Guide the Traveler through relaxation and inner focusing.

Consult the appendix for a sample relaxation and inner focusing script, or use one of your own.

4. Lightly touch the next area of the body you wish to map.

The body assessment form shows ten areas of the body. The first several times you do this exercise take one area at a time and proceed through the entire exercise. Later you may selectively choose one of these areas to work with, or apply the exercise to any other area of the body. Usually different issues are related to the different sides of the body. Therefore, map right and left legs and arms separately.

5. Ask the Traveler to bring her or his awareness to this area.

You can use the following intervention, or one similar to it:

Bring your awareness to the area of your body I'm now touching. Without trying to control or analyze this area, just allow yourself to experience it.

6. Ask the Traveler for the physical sensation in this area.

Use the following interventions, or ones similar to them:

(a) What sensation do you experience in this area of your body?
(b) How does your body move in this area?
(c) Does this area of your body feel the way you would like it to?
(d) Are you comfortable with this area of your body?

7. Ask the Traveler to be aware of the emotional or physical content related to this area.

Use the following interventions, or ones similar to them:

(a) What's the experience of this area like for you?
(b) How do you experience this area now?
(c) What emerges for you as you experience this area of your body?
(d) What quality does this area express for you?
(e) What story does this area of your body have to tell?
(f) What message does this area of your body have for you?

8. Wait patiently for whatever emerges from the Traveler.

Do not rush the Traveler to identify the issues underlying a given body area. Trust the Traveler's inner wisdom by accepting whatever emerges. Although you have asked for physical sensation first, emotional issues may surface first. If the Traveler is having difficulty mapping this area try another intervention. If that does not work, skip this area temporarily, go on to another area, and return to this area later. In some areas neither physical sensation nor emotional experience may be available for the Traveler, and that's all right.

9. Validate the Traveler's experience.

Actively listen to the Traveler's responses. Note the physical sensation and process-oriented material (feelings, images, issues, qualities, etc.). Confirm your sense of the Traveler's experience by repeating to the Traveler:

(a) So, there's some sadness associated with the tightness in this area?
(b) The warmth in this area is like a river moving through rapids.
(c) It sounds like this burning has something to do with your relationship.

10. Label the Traveler's body map with the physical sensation and the emotional/psychological material discovered in the previous steps.

Draw a line from this area of the body out to the side. On the top of this line write in a few key words that summarize the physical sensation in this area (pain, tightness, relaxed, warmth). Below the line write a few words or a phrase that summarizes the emotional/psychological issues underlying this body area.

11. If you are finished with all body areas, then go to step twelve, otherwise, repeat the process beginning with step four.

12. Guide the Traveler out of relaxation.

You can use the following intervention, or one similar to it:

Bring your awareness back to your breathing. When you're ready take several deep breaths, stretch if you need to, then open your eyes.

Analyzing a Body Map

Once the body map is complete, the Traveler and Guide should discuss what they've created. There are many ways to read a body map. I first note whether it was easier for the Traveler to get in touch with physical sensations or nonphysical qualities like feelings, thoughts, or images. This often suggests which avenues of communication and expression are most available for the Traveler, and those which are least available. The general sense of the body map is also important. Is each area filled in, or do gaps exist where no sensation or emotion is found? Do consistent physical and emotional themes emerge from the body map?

Polarities are found in almost every body map: One area of the body expresses feelings and sensations directly opposite of another area. A Traveler's right arm may be tense with related angry feelings while her left arm may be relaxed and filled with a sense of peace. The left leg may be heavy and sad while the right leg may be light and happy. Right-side versus left-side polarities are the most common but similar opposites may exist front-to-back or top-to-bottom. Polarities are frequently related to unresolved portions of a Traveler's personality that appear in conflict.

The two most frequent questions I'm asked about a body map are (1) Do they change over time? and (2) Will a different Guide elicit the same body map from a Traveler? People are dynamic, they constantly attempt to extract meaning and purpose from the situations they encounter. Body maps reflect this dynamism. Physical sensation and emotional experience shift and these transformations will be reflected in a body map. From one day to the next the body map will not necessarily be the same. Areas of a body map that change most easily are usually of lesser importance than those areas that change least. In fact, creating a series of body maps over time can pinpoint the physical sensation and the related emotional issues that are most significant for a Traveler.

Therapy is based on interaction between two or more parties, particularly therapy based on touch. Just as body maps can change from day to day, they also can change depending on who helps the Traveler create them. Here, too, I view this as a benefit not a hindrance to their use. Many emotional issues stem from our attempts to establish and maintain relationships with others. Each Guide will have a different presence, a different touch, a different intention that is sensed both consciously and unconsciously by the Traveler. If our body truly reflects our dynamic inner experience, a body map should change based on our interaction with whoever helps us create it.

Varying the Detail of Body Maps

At times I am very specific and detailed about creating a body map. For example, in Chapter 5 I discussed creating body maps with survivors of sexual abuse. Here a body map is a very useful tool for assessing both the physical and psychological elements of this trauma. At other times I'm much more informal about the body map. I forgo drawing a figure and systematically mapping each area of the body. I may ask a Traveler to tell me about physical sensation in one area of her body, and relate that to a given emotional experience. In this way I am simply using this map between body and mind to guide the journey of healing and recovery.

Grandma's Hands

I have my grandmother to thank for using body maps. When my sister and I were young children one special treat was lying in a bed with our grandmother who'd tell us stories in a very special way. She'd have us turn over on our stomach and illustrate the stories on our backs. She'd assign various characters different locations on our body and have them interact with each other by walking her fingers across the surface of our skin. We laughed and giggled with delight. Once Grandma was gone, the stories remained, and to this day I carry Grandma's hands and her stories within my body. In a similar way we carry our life stories in our bodies. Our hope and fear, joy and sorrow, anger and contentment, love and hate, these and more are carried not only in our hearts and minds but also in our bodies. Body maps are one way of allowing our body to tell these stories of where we've been in life, where we are, and where we hope to be headed.

SIMPLE AWARENESS

At the beginning of the book I mentioned that the oldest recorded techniques of somatic therapy stem from 2,500-year-old Buddhist teachings. The story, part truth part mythology, has it that Prince Gautama—who was to become the Buddha—kept searching for the path to enlightenment. He went to teacher after teacher looking for the perfect technique that would purify his mind, making him fit to be the enlightened Buddha. With each teacher a similar scenario unfolded. Gautama would learn in a few days a difficult spiritual technique that took others years to learn. After perfecting the technique he would discover to his dismay that impurity remained in his mind—he was still unfit to be the Buddha, the enlightened one. Gautama would then ask that teacher whom he should seek next. The young prince would be referred to an even more advanced spiritual master where a similar sequence of events transpired.

Ultimately Gautama grew tired of this endless round of searching and studying only to find himself still with impurity. Alone in deep meditation one day he had a sudden flash of insight whereupon he realized his error. "I have been trying to purify the mind with the mind," he observed, "this cannot be done." To Gautama this was like trying to clean cloth by washing it in the same dirt that caused it to become soiled. Another substance must be used to cleanse the cloth. Instead of the mind Gautama discovered that the other substance was the body.

Gautama developed a technique that focused on the bodily sensation beneath thoughts and feelings. As I described this technique earlier, you stay aware of bodily sensation until that awareness shifts to the biochemical reactions that produce the bodily sensation. You stay aware of those biochemical reactions until you become aware of the molecular constituents that give rise to the biochemical reactions. You stay with the molecular constituents until you become aware of the most fundamental particles that cannot be further subdivided—the so-called *kalapas*. These kalapas, though appearing as solid particles, are actually vibratory waves. Out of this vibratory energy, sensation and feeling arise. Into this vibratory energy, sensation and feeling dissolve. Upon practicing this technique of focusing on bodily sensation, Gautama's mind became clear and he became Siddhartha (the one who has obtained his goals); the enlightened Buddha.

Within this myth is an important lesson: One cannot just contemplate emotional issues—the so-called impurities of mind—they must be addressed directly. But trying to address the mind with the mind is a difficult task. Addressing the mind with the body aids in finding resolution and clarity. Touch can be incorporated into this technique of body awareness as the following exercise demonstrates.

AWARENESS THROUGH TOUCH

1. Explain the process to the Traveler.

Inform the Traveler you will be touching a body area and asking him or her simply to be aware of the physical sensations in that area. If thoughts, feelings, or images enter the Traveler's awareness that's all right. The Traveler should simply be prepared to bring his or her awareness back to the physical sensation present in this area.

2. Guide the Traveler through relaxation and inner focusing.

Consult the appendix for a sample relaxation and inner focusing script, or create one of your own.

3. Select an area of the Traveler's body to work with.

There are many ways to do this. If you've already done a body map you can simply ask the Traveler to choose an area from the map. There may be a location that troubles the Traveler, or one that interests him or her. The Guide also might suggest an area from the body map related to the issues the Traveler is dealing with. One of my favorite ways of selecting an area of the Traveler's body is through a quick mini-map. There are two ways to do this. One can start with an emotional or psychological issue then proceed to an area of the body. Or one can start with an

198 . . . DR. CLYDE W. FORD

area of the body and discover the related emotional or psychological issue. When I begin with the Traveler's emotional issues I often suggest:

> Let yourself be aware of the most predominant feeling, thought or issue that is present in your life now. When you are aware of that nod your head to let me know. [I pause and wait for acknowledgment from the Traveler.] Now scan your body with your mind and when you discover an area that seems most related to this feeling, thought, or issue let me know where that area is.

Notice I haven't specifically asked about the Traveler's issue. I've simply asked the Traveler to be aware of that issue and relate it to an area of the body. Once this is done I can go on. The second way of creating a mini-map is very similar, only you begin with the body:

> Scan your body with your mind and let yourself be aware of whatever area seems to call for your attention most. This could be an area with an ongoing physical condition, an area of past injury, or simply an area of special interest to you. When you discover that area let me know where it is. [I pause for the Traveler to discover this area of the body.] Now take a moment and be in touch with whatever feelings, thoughts, or qualities seem most related to that area. When you've discovered them, you needn't tell me, just nod your head and let me know.

Again this process does not rely on the Guide knowing the details of the Traveler's issues. The focus of this method is physical sensation, not emotions. When an area of the body is selected and the Traveler has made his or her connections to the emotional/psychological content the process can continue.

4. Lightly touch this area and instruct the Traveler to follow his or her awareness of physical sensation.

You may need to ask for permission to touch this area of the Traveler's body first. Touch the area gently and provide the Traveler with instructions similar to these:

I'll be gently touching this area of your body and I'd like you just to pay attention to the physical sensation here. While you're doing this, thoughts, feelings, images, sounds, colors, or other items may enter your awareness. Note their presence but do not follow them, bring your awareness back to the physical sensation in the area I'm touching. If that physical sensation changes let yourself follow the new sensation that arises. Periodically, check in with me and let me know what sensation you are experiencing.

The Guide is simply asking the Traveler to be aware of physical sensation in the area. The Traveler is also asked to follow any changes that occur in that sensation. Other material will enter the Traveler's consciousness. This material can be important but the Traveler is asked to focus solely on physical sensation.

5. If the Traveler goes too long without checking in.
If the Traveler fails to check in at reasonable intervals during this process, the Guide can simply say: "Check in with me now and let me know what you're experiencing," or "What's your experience in this area of your body like now?"

6. If the Traveler's awareness is diverted from the area of the body he or she began with.
The Traveler's awareness will drift to other sensations in different locations of the body. The Traveler might say, "As I focus on my neck I'm aware of some pain in my lower back." The Traveler's awareness may then shift to the lower back. The Guide should gently intervene by saying:

I understand that you feel some pain in. . . . However, let me invite you to bring your awareness back to the area of your body I'm touching.

One purpose of having the Traveler check in is so the Guide can monitor the Traveler's awareness to see if it is drifting away from the area in question.

7. After a appropriate period of time the Guide should offer the Traveler a way of bringing the process to conclusion.

There is no formula for how long a process like this should last. There are several ways of placing a reasonable time limit on the Traveler. One way is to establish a time before starting. The Guide might say to the Traveler, "We'll spend fifteen minutes exploring this area of your body." Alternatively, the Guide can sense when the Traveler is drawing near conclusion. In either case when the Guide feels it is time to draw the process to conclusion he or she can use an intervention similar to this:

> In the next few minutes would you find a way of bringing this process to conclusion. When you've done that let me know.

8. Guide the Traveler out of relaxation.

You can use the following intervention, or one similar to it:

> Bring your awareness back to your breathing and as you do, carry back with you whatever it is you now know. Take a few minutes to feel how you might use this knowledge in your life now.

> [Pause for a few minutes.]

> Bring your awareness back to your breathing again. When you're ready, take several deep breaths, stretch if you need to, and then open your eyes.

THE BENEFITS OF SIMPLE AWARENESS

After concluding this process the Traveler should be given an opportunity to speak about his or her experience. Once the Traveler has spoken, the Guide can offer his or her impressions of the exercise. This exercise seems extremely simple, but don't underestimate its power. Several subtle currents are moving through this process. First, there is the power of focused awareness. Focusing on physical sensation instead of the underlying emotional issues seems to give these emotional issues space to emerge and be transformed. For example, a Traveler may initially be aware of tightness in the shoulder and anger related to that tightness. When asked to focus on the anger, the Traveler may recall the incident that precipitated those feelings. Reliving that experience may produce more tightness and even more anger. At times this may be just what is desired or needed.

Yet the Traveler's anger may mask even deeper emotion. By asking the Traveler to focus on sensation, the anger may emerge and the Traveler may note its emergence. But the Traveler's awareness is brought back to the pain. Suddenly sadness may emerge where there was anger, and trembling may exist where there was pain. Again, the Traveler is asked to focus on the trembling. Seemingly out of nowhere, loneliness is replaced by sadness as trembling is replaced by coolness. Perhaps the process concludes here. Beneath the anger then was sadness, and beneath the sadness was loneliness. The Traveler may be better served by focusing on the loneliness than the anger. Sometimes the process continues to a remarkable conclusion where both the physical sensation and emotional issues seem to dissolve into each other. I reported such a case in the first chapter. A young man in one of my workshops began by focusing on the pain between his shoulder blades. He reached successively deeper levels of sensation until he was simply aware of the space between the molecules making up his body. At that level the pain disappeared and the related emotional experience resolved of its own accord.

There are several additional benefits to a somatic technique like this. The Guide really does not need to be touching the Traveler. The Traveler alone can focus his or her awareness on physical sensation in an area of the body. With periodic checking in, the Guide can still follow the Traveler's journey and help keep it on course. I recommend a method similar to this for therapists who work with physically or sexually abused clients. Directly touching the body of abuse survivors is not advised. Still the body can be brought into the therapeutic process. Since the Traveler is never asked specifically to talk about underlying emotional issues this technique also works well for somatic

202 . . . DR. CLYDE W. FORD

therapists who feel uncomfortable with verbal therapy. When
working with the body, emotional resolution can take place
even in the absence of specific discussion about emotional issues.

SOMATIC IMAGES AND COUNTERIMAGES

At several points I've discussed the body's ability to image somatically. Ordinarily we associate imaging with vision, although imaging, as I suggested earlier, is merely a way of
organizing information. I've already described how our system
of touch can transform pressure into visual and auditory images. Still we needn't experience an image through sight or
sound for its effect to be felt. Our body works with images of
physical sensation. We can create, change, and explore such
somatic images and physically experience the results.

Imaging and counterimaging is a basic idea behind working
with emotional and psychological issues somatically. For example, when a Traveler informs me he or she experiences pain
as a knot, we might pursue that somatic image further. I might
first find the kind of pressure—depth, direction, and duration—
that would mimic the sensation of the knot. I might even increase that pressure to amplify the experience of the knot. This
in turn provides deeper awareness of the significance of that
physical sensation to other issues for the Traveler. At some
point the Traveler may choose to transform the knot—to loosen
it, remove it, or change it some way. There's always a way to
create the process of change through touching or moving the
body with resulting physical and psychological changes for the
Traveler.

SOMATIC IMAGING AND COUNTERIMAGING

1. Explain the process to the Traveler.

Inform the Traveler that you will be working with an area of his
or her body. First you'll discover how he or she currently expe-

riences this area of the body and then you'll explore how he or she would like to experience this area.

2. Guide the Traveler through relaxation and inner focusing.

Consult the appendix for a sample relaxation and inner focusing script, or create a similar one of your own.

3. Select an area of the Traveler's body to work with.

Consult step three of the previous exercise on simple awareness for some suggested ways of doing this.

4. Use touch to mirror the Traveler's experience of this area of the body.

If you need permission to touch the Traveler obtain that first. Then ask the Traveler how he or she experiences this area of their body. Let the Traveler's answer guide the way you touch this area. For example, if the Traveler says he or she experiences tightness in this area you may need to press and twist. If the Traveler experiences the area as heavy you may need to use deeper pressure. Under no circumstances should your pressure further injure the Traveler. The Traveler should inform you if the discomfort increases and you should stop touching him or her immediately. You should now be mirroring the Traveler's body through your touch. After a while ask the Traveler: "What's it like to have your body touched [or held] in this way?" Allow the Traveler time to describe that experience.

5. Counter the Traveler's experience in this area of the body.

Here's an opportunity for the Guide to be creative. Working with the Traveler, find a way to create a counterimage in this area of the body. If the Traveler's initial experience was tightness, you may need to find a way of gently manipulating this area of the body as though you were loosening a knot. If the Traveler experiences an object like a rock or a knife in this area of their body you may decide to remove it slowly. Remember it's the Traveler's decision what to do. The Guide is there to help make that decision happen.

6. Allow the Traveler to bring the process to conclusion.
Let the Traveler inform you when the image has transformed into the counterimage: "When you feel this process of change has gone as far as it can for now please let me know."

7. Bring the Traveler's awareness back to the area of the body you began with.
Ask the Traveler to bring his or her awareness back to the area of the body you originally began with and discover what it's like there now. You might say: "Bring your awareness back to your [whatever area you began with] and notice what it's like now."

Afterward the Traveler and Guide should talk about this experience. Within this process of imaging and counterimaging are the fundamental steps of healing and recovery. We begin where we are (the image), we have a notion of where we need to be (the counterimage), and we discover how to get from where we are to where we need to be (the transformational process).

MOVEMENT AND HEALING
So far we have primarily discussed the use of touch and body awareness as somatic methods to aid healing and recovery. Movement is important as well. In fact movement is directly related to the process of imaging and counterimaging we just explored. Neuroscientist Karl Pribram has shown that the brain areas governing movement do not store patterns of motion, instead they store "images of achievement." As mentioned earlier, writing your name is a good example of how the brain stores and uses images of achievement. Instead of storing the complex sequence of muscular actions required to write your name, the brain stores the image that needs to be achieved—in this case a

legible signature. If you pick up a pen with your right hand the brain attempts to achieve the image through those muscles. If you pick up a pen with your left hand or your teeth the brain recruits a different set of muscles to achieve the same image. The image governs your movement by organizing your actions. But we store more than just images of achievement. We also store images of experience. These images of experience govern our movement and actions in a similar way. Ordinarily we do not pause to consider the images behind our movement. The following exercises explore these images of experience and achievement. To try them you'll need to clear a space to move in.

GUIDELINES FOR SELF-EXPLORATION THROUGH MOVEMENT

The basic sequence of steps behind all the following movement exercises is:

1. Stand for several minutes with eyes open or closed and relax.
2. While still standing, sense the particular image, issue, or quality you want to explore. You can experience what areas of your body seem most affected, what sounds or sights are related, and anything else that is connected with this image.
3. Spend five or ten minutes moving from the experience of this image. For example, if you were feeling sad you would move as though your entire body expressed this sadness through its movement. You may walk, sway, take up a position on the floor, stretch, or move your body in any way that seems appropriate.
4. After moving, stand quietly for a few moments and feel the impact of your movement throughout your body.

Let me now suggest a sequence of images you can embody and move from.

MOVING WITH THE IMAGE AND COUNTERIMAGE

1. As you stand, allow yourself to be in touch with the most predominant emotion, issue, or quality expressing itself in your life right now. When you are ready, follow the guidelines given previously and move from this emotion, issue, or quality. If you have a paper and pen handy you may wish to write down what your experience of movement was like.
2. While still standing, allow yourself to be aware of how you would like this predominant emotion, issue, or quality to be expressed in your life. Now move from this new awareness. When you're through, note what this movement was like.
3. Compare both movements observing what was different or meaningful about each. Now stand silently again, allowing yourself to be aware of how you would like to change the way you ordinarily move based on what you now know. When you're ready, move around in this new way.
4. When you've done this exercise, take a moment to reflect on the physical and emotional impact of the movement.

I'm certain you can see why this is related to image/counterimage. First you moved from your present experience (the image), then you moved from your sense of how things should be (the counterimage), and finally you discovered what you need to incorporate into your ordinary movement based on that experience (the transformational process).

Movement is a wonderful way of exploring relationships—the relationship we have with our self and the ones we form with others. The following exercise explores how our relationship with others governs the way we move in life.

MOVING INTO RELATIONSHIP

1. In your mind, select a person with whom you are in, or have had a significant relationship. Check in with yourself that this

is a safe relationship to explore. If this person feels unsafe then select someone else.

2. Stand for a moment, relax, and let yourself sense how this other person moves within his or her body. When you're ready, move as you imagine how this other person moves. Afterward note what that experience was like.

3. Stand quietly again. This time be aware of how you ordinarily move in the presence of this other person. Move around in this way. How is it different from your normal way of movement? Why do you feel you move in this different way?

4. Stand quietly again. Now be aware of how you would like to move in the presence of this person. When you're ready, move around in that way. Stop after a while and note your experience. What's this new movement like? What do you know about yourself and this person? How would you like to incorporate what you now know into this relationship?

Like all somatic methods, movement allows us to communicate and express ourselves beyond sight and sound. Where I live there is a beautiful two-mile trail around a mountain lake. As a homework assignment I often suggest that a Traveler walk around the lake. Instead of merely putting on walking shoes and a sweatshirt, the Traveler is asked to take on whatever image of achievement or experience is needed most. Sometimes these images come directly out of the other therapy we've engaged in. At other times the assignment is to pause before beginning the trail to discover what image should govern their journey.

TOUCHING BEYOND TECHNIQUE

I have no prescription for somatic therapy; no formula that is always successful for working with the body. I have tried to develop a more refined understanding of the role of touch, movement, and body awareness in physical and emotional wellbeing. Out of this understanding have come methods for including the body in healing and recovery. The previous exercises show some of the techniques that emerge from this integrated approach to the body. But technique is the backdrop

208 . . . DR. CLYDE W. FORD

not the foreground of somatic therapy. Technique sets the stage for change, but technique can never make change happen. Technique is the necessary vehicle, but not the required fuel for this journey of healing and recovery. The journey's fuel lies in the healing relationship between a Guide and a Traveler. Technique makes that relationship possible, reaching out beyond technique to touch the human soul allows for healing to occur.

7.

THE COMPASSIONATE JOURNEY

We have not even to risk the adventure alone;
for the heroes of all time have gone before us;
the labyrinth is thoroughly known;
we have only to follow the thread of the hero-path.
—JOSEPH CAMPBELL

Allowing our body to be part of our journey of healing and recovery is an act of compassion. We provide ourselves a larger context within which to address our physical and emotional issues. We come to understand the deep interdependence of body and mind and the fundamental wholeness of our being. But this interdependence of being is not limited to us individually; it is not confined to the walls of our skin. Through our bodies we can also grasp our interdependence with the universe beyond our bodies. What happens in my body is a mirror of what happens in the universe. Consider the sun, suggests the poet–monk Thich Nhat Hanh, which he describes as an "immense heart."

Plants live thanks to the sun. . . . And thanks to plants, we and other animals can live. All of us—people, animals, and plants— "consume" the sun, directly and indirectly. We cannot begin to describe all the effects of the sun, that great heart outside our body.

Nhat Hanh calls this sense of interdependent being, *inter-being*. It is an abiding sense of wholeness expressed not only in the words of poets and mystics but of scientists as well. Physicists who have penetrated the deepest levels of physical reality emerge with a similar conclusion: I and the universe are one. Erwin Schroedinger, physicist and founder of quantum mechanics, spoke eloquently of this interbeing:

> Thus you can throw yourself flat on the ground, stretched out upon Mother Earth, with the certain conviction that you are one with her and she with you. You are as firmly established, as invulnerable as she, indeed a thousand times firmer and more invulnerable. As surely as she will engulf you tomorrow, so surely will she bring you forth anew to new striving and suffering. And not merely "some day": now, today, every day she is bringing you forth, not once but thousands and thousands of times, just as every day she engulfs you a thousand times over.

Our journey of striving and suffering, while it seems so personal and individual to us, is really part of a universal journey. Holding this larger view of ourselves allows us to bring greater meaning and insight to our journey of healing and recovery. In this larger vision I find the essence of spirituality: an abiding sense of wholeness transcending the confines of my individual body and mind. I also find a connection with those who have taken journeys of discovery, adventure, and insight before. We are the travelers beyond safe borders: meeting obstacles and challenges; finding prizes and treasures; returning enlightened and enlivened. Mythology has helped me deepen this sense of connection between my personal healing journey and the journeys of other heroes and heroines.

THE HERO AND HEROINE WITHIN

Mythology provides a rich backdrop for healing and recovery. While the hero or heroine's journey is a mythological venture outward, the journey of healing and recovery is a mythological venture inward. Where the hero or heroine's journey takes place in far-off realms of splendor and excitement, the healing journey takes place in far-in realms of body and mind. The hero's journey has been retold in countless tales throughout human history. Joseph Campbell chronicled and analyzed many of these myths from cultures around the world. He showed the similarity of the tales regardless of cultural origin. Campbell labeled this universal mythological story the "monomyth." It depicted the journey of the quintessential hero or heroine. Campbell was well aware of the relationship between universal and personal mythology. In fact, he used psychological analysis to help break the coded messages contained within cultural myths. He saw the hero's journey split into three main stages—departure, initiation, and return.

ANSWERING THE CALL

The hero or heroine's journey begins with a call to adventure. A herald beckons the protagonist to venture beyond his or her current circumstances in life: a disembodied voice is heard, a strange creature appears, or a vision occurs when least expected. In the life of Buddha, the famous Four Signs called young Prince Gautama to a saintly life.

At birth it was foretold that Prince Gautama's destiny was twofold. He would either become a powerful world ruler or a saint of the highest order. The king, his concerned father, attempted to influence fate and steer his son away from otherworldly pursuits. He sought to protect his son from four realities of life: old age, disease, death, and sainthood. The king had his ministers remove all the elderly, all the diseased, all the dead, and all the priests within a given distance around the castle. In turn his son was supplied with lavish palaces and thousands of beautiful girls for his pleasure.

Eventually Prince Gautama grew tired of these worldly delights. One day he summoned a chariot to travel outside the palace walls. Meanwhile the gods determined to call Prince Gautama to his future path. On his first trip he encountered an old man, placed there by the gods. Shocked by the ravages of old age, he returned to his palace in great agitation. Upon hearing this, the king had all the elderly rounded up at even greater distances from the palace to protect his son.

On the future Buddha's next trip out he encountered a diseased person, so fashioned for him by the gods. Again he was horrified by disease and returned to his palace in great agitation. Again for his protection, his father ordered all diseased persons removed at even greater distances surrounding the palace.

The gods arranged for a dead person to be encountered by Prince Gautama on his next chariot trip. Repulsed by death, he returned to his palace in great agitation. When informed of this, the king responded by removing all the dead at even greater distances beyond the palace.

The prince encountered a monk on his fourth and final trip. Gautama inquired of the monk's nature. He learned the monk had retired from a life of worldly pleasures in pursuit of enlightenment and liberation. This answer pleased Gautama whereupon he embarked on his journey toward sainthood; a journey ending in his enlightenment as the Buddha.

THE FOUR SIGNS

Illness, injury, disease, aging, or the quest for meaning often call us to our journey of healing and recovery. I routinely ask workshop participants, "How many of you are doing what you do today because of facing some physical or psychological problem?" I and nearly everyone else raise our hands. We are often drawn to what we need most.

I am called to the work I do because of personal challenges. I had difficulty contacting my deepest emotions other than through my body. When asked what I felt, I stumbled for words. However, it was relatively easy for me to be aware of what occurred in my body. I compared myself to others who spoke freely about their feelings and I felt inferior.

Eventually I learned to use my body to talk about my feelings. First, I'd check in with what I felt physically—tightness, tingling, warmth, relaxation. Then, I'd describe those physical sensations in emotional terms. For example, "I'm feeling restricted (tightness)"; "I've got some fear around that (tingling)"; "I feel very open right now (warmth)"; or "I'm relieved that we understand each other (relaxation)."

Step one of all Twelve-Step journeys of recovery admits to our call. This first step acknowledges powerlessness over our illness or dysfunctional behavior. It is not, however, hopeless surrender. We have been called to take this journey of healing and recovery. Hope lies in recognizing and answering the call. In fact we are admitting our powerlessness to refuse this call any longer. To do otherwise we would become Gautama ignoring the old man, the diseased man, the dead body, and the monk.

REFUSING THE CALL

Many of the world's tragic myths concern a hero or heroine who does fail to answer the call. The Greek myth of the Minotaur is an example of this. King Minos asked the gods for a prize bull to sacrifice. The bull was sent, but Minos, taken by its beauty, refused to sacrifice the animal. Angered by this refusal, the gods caused his wife to conceive a child by the bull: a half-man, half-bull Minotaur. Minos attempted to deny this disgrace. He hid the Minotaur at the center of a labyrinth so complex that any who entered were hopelessly lost. But the Minotaur was demanding. Every seven years Minos had to sacrifice young men and women by sending them into the labyrinth. Minos's obsession with the Minotaur eventually became his undoing.

Symbolically this is a tale about the problems created by attempting to hide disgrace behind the walls of denial. We become trapped in a Minoan labyrinth—blocked and confounded at every turn. A similar fate awaits those who fail to answer the call to healing and recovery. We say these individuals are in denial. A chemically addicted person will vehemently and convincingly deny the addiction. A codependent individual will continue to engage in unhealthy, dysfunctional relationships. A person with a life-threatening medical diagnosis will simply say, "It can't be happening to me." These are the makings of a tragically premature end to a healing journey—a journey that never really begins.

I am reminded of Mary Ann, a woman in her late fifties with rheumatoid arthritis and high blood pressure. The arthritis had gotten progressively worse over the years, leading to disfiguring joint changes and severe pain. Her blood pressure could not be controlled without medication. Both conditions were metaphors of Mary Ann's underlying, unresolved emotional issues.

Rheumatoid arthritis results when a malfunctioning immune system fails to distinguish normal body cells from foreign organisms. This inability to distinguish "self" from "other" leads the body to attack itself. Joints are usually the center of this self-destructive assault. They become malformed, appear partially eaten away, and develop inflammation, swelling, and pain.

Rheumatoid arthritis implies a failed self-identity. In particular, Mary Ann had struggled many years to find her separate identity apart from a domineering mother and a dysfunctional family. The condition also symbolizes rejection: one part of the self rejecting another part. Mary Ann had experienced such rejection from her father. Since her childhood, he was emotionally unavailable and at times had been physically abusive to her.

Mary Ann, who had been a lawyer for nearly forty years, was recently married for the fourth time. Out of loneliness she married a blue-collar laborer who derided her desire to resume a legal career. Instead, he wanted her to stay home to pursue domestic activities like cooking and cleaning. Mary Ann sacrificed, and thereby rejected, this professional part of herself for the sake of her marriage. Deep down she was unhappy and very angry, but she was also very skillful at hiding these feelings from herself and others. Her blood pressure, however, was symptomatic of this underlying emotional turmoil. Mary Ann had been through a number of years of psychotherapy but was never able to directly experience or express her deepest emotions.

She was quite aware of many aspects of her psychological and physical problems. Instead of tackling these issues directly, Mary Ann worked hard at developing another side of herself.

She became a deeply spiritual person and, thereby, found great salvation from her inner strife. Tragically Mary Ann only partially answered the call to healing and recovery: her spiritual side flowered while her personal side floundered. She never addressed the deeper emotional issues expressed symptomatically in her body. They persisted and proved to be her undoing. As the pressure from these underlying conflicts continued to mount, so did her blood pressure. She made a few abortive attempts to confront her parents with the anger she held since childhood, but her efforts were too little and too late. She came home one day, sat down to meditate, had a heart attack instead, and died.

SUPERNATURAL AID

Upon answering the call to adventure, the hero or heroine frequently receives aid from supernatural sources. A fairy godmother, angel, wizard, hermit, shepherd, or special animal may appear. The hero or heroine receives an amulet, special instructions, or a map of the kingdom he or she is about to enter. This supernatural aid guides the hero or heroine on the journey, providing protection and warning against the hazards to come. At times the guide may seem to disappear, leaving a traveler to his or her own devices. Then, just in the nick of time, the guide appears and helps the protagonist avert certain doom.

It is the Guide, in the form of a therapist or concerned other, who helps the Traveler on the journey of healing and recovery. While there may be no magical amulets to give for this journey, the Guide's wisdom and compassion can direct the journey's course. The Guide can be with the Traveler as a silent companion or an active coach. The Guide can suggest, cajole, beckon, warn, or encourage the Traveler. Through the body, the Guide can touch and move with the Traveler as well.

CROSSING THE THRESHOLD

For those who have not refused the call, adventure awaits. Our hero or heroine proceeds unscathed until reaching what Campbell called the "threshold guardian." Cast as an ogre or devilish figure, this threshold guardian protects the doorway to the world the hero must enter. This creature must be met and overcome. Beyond the threshold lies the dark kingdom: an unknown realm of danger filled with demons, monsters, dragons, and untold obstacles. This threshold separates a protected zone from an imperiled zone. Most mythological tales begin in the safety of familiar surroundings—family, society, or a well-fortified castle. But the hero or heroine must leave these comforts and travel deep into unsafe and fearful lands.

So it is on the journey of healing and recovery as well. In somatoemotional therapy, however, the body becomes the threshold guardian. Our protected zone is the world we have lived in until hearing the call to healing and recovery. Addictive behavior, abusive behavior, dysfunctional relationships, unresolved emotions, and chronic physical pain create a world that is comfortable only because it is familiar.

The Safety and Familiarity of Dysfunction

If we learned as children to take care of an alcoholic parent the caretaker role is familiar and easily assumed. This role is frequently accompanied by poor emotional and psychological boundaries and an inability to express one's needs. The bodies of caretakers will reflect these difficulties as well. We examined some of these body patterns when discussing the Lost Satellite and the Submerged Self. Chronic muscular tightness and spasm, for example, serve the body's effort to replace unavailable emotional boundaries with more tangible physical ones. The caretaker's emotional and physical stance may be unhealthy, but it is easily assumed.

Thus armored, the body will guard against access to deeper emotional issues. Travelers who have not crossed this threshold describe feelings of "stiffening up" in the presence of uncomfortable emotions, "shrinking back" instead of "standing up," "holding in" rather than "letting out," or "turning away" from issues instead of "facing them head on." Evidence of the body as threshold guardian is obvious in these statements.

Stifling a cry is an example of the body as threshold guardian. We exert a tremendous amount of muscular effort to hold back a cry. Not only do we close our eyes tightly but muscles in our face, neck, and throughout our body tighten to guard against this emotional outburst. Stiffening when faced with unpleasant emotions is another example. Can you remember the last time someone told you, "I have something to say that you may not like." A typical response to anticipated unpleasant feelings is to stiffen the body, thereby bracing oneself against potential emotional upheaval.

Our bodies are guarding against access to the dark kingdom within—our inner landscape of dragons and demons, tricksters and temptresses. The dark kingdom symbolizes our unconscious mind—that safety deposit box for the forces within us that are untapped and unknown. This is our Pandora's box. This is our imperiled zone. This is the land of our wounded child. But our hero or heroine must venture into the heart of this dark land. Dragons and demons must be slain. Tricksters and temptresses must be conquered. The forces of good must be harnessed. The forces of evil must be reckoned with. Our inner child must be reclaimed and healed.

GAINING ACCESS THROUGH THE BODY

As a threshold guardian our body serves double duty. It not only guards against this unconscious realm but also gives us access to it. This is the basis of the somatoemotional approach to healing and recovery. Through touch, movement, and body awareness the threshold guardian steps aside, allowing our hero or heroine to enter the forbidden zone. This access can be swift, and often surprising.

One typically encounters such rapid entry in the initial somatoemotional therapy session. Here the Guide's use of touch, for example, may challenge the "body as threshold guardian" in unaccustomed ways. There may be little resistance as the

Traveler is suddenly thrust into the depths of the unconscious self, coming face to face with long buried feelings, images, and thoughts. When this happens, I envision a hero or heroine encountering a threshold guardian. The hero or heroine is determined to prevail and comes closer and closer to this menacing figure. It looks certain that he or she will be pushed back, only to meet with some terrible fate. Miraculously, soft ground appears: A hole opens into a funnel and the hero or heroine rides wildly into the depths of the earth to be dumped off in a strange, new land. The journey now begins.

After a session like this a Traveler often expresses astonishment. "Where'd we go?" "How did we get there?" "I had no idea all this was there." "All that was in me?" These are the common refrains. Now the first dragons appear. Astonishment often turns into fear as our hero or heroine begins to realize what threshold has been crossed. It may be the first time our heroine has faced her history of sexual abuse, or the first time our hero admits the depths of his addictive behavior. Once the threshold is crossed, the Traveler's options are few. Going on may be difficult, but retreat is less comforting than staying the journey's course.

Slaying the Dragons

The threshold crossed, our mythic traveler now enters an enchanted land. Immediately there are heroic trials to face. Hercules labored at his twelve tasks. Psyche toiled at the unrelenting requests of Venus. Throughout recorded history the hero–adventurer, in this middle portion of the journey, has encountered the impossible: a never-sleeping dragon to slay; a jewel to reclaim from the jaws of a beast; a maiden to rescue from the hands of an evil prince; a treacherous mountain to climb; a forbidding ocean to navigate; a dark forest to trek; a clever creature to outwit; a well-armed foe to conquer. Through physical prowess, sharp wit, and sometimes with supernatural assistance, our hero or heroine meets and masters each required task.

But the mythological journey, lest we forget, is nothing but the outer manifestation of our inner healing journey. Once we have crossed this threshold within, we too venture on enchanted ground. Our trials are none the less real than those of lore, though not given by a god or goddess. Rather we face the realm of our unconscious. The monsters, dragons, and demons are just as real, the forests just as dark, the summits just as high, the oceans just as forbidding, the creatures just as clever, and the foes just as well armed. We too need strength of body and mind. We too need occasional assistance from sources we cannot fathom. We too need the inner hero or heroine to meet and master each required task.

The human body is fertile ground for this stage of the journey. Travelers report impressions of the body in mythological terms. "My pelvis is like a dark cave, I dare not enter for fear of what's in there," said one adult survivor of childhood sexual abuse. "A voice in my legs told me to run, but I couldn't," lamented another.

"The flesh in my buttocks feels as if its being ripped off," said a Traveler describing sciatic pain after his children were removed from his custody in a divorce proceeding. "This pain in my middle back reminds me of being stabbed over and over again," reported a gentleman only beginning to come to terms with a marriage that had ended five years earlier.

"My heart feels imprisoned in my rib cage," noted a Traveler describing pain in her upper chest and back. "My shoulders are so burdened from believing I was responsible for everyone else," sighed a woman describing shoulder pain related to years of caretaking in codependent relationships. "It stopped being a part of me years ago," said a Traveler about an area of her body involved in sexual abuse. "I wonder if I can find and reclaim it now?"

"When I focus on my neck it feels as if I'm walking alone in a vast, arid desert," said another Traveler, "I've got to keep walking but I don't see water anywhere." When asked to be aware of her abdomen, a female Traveler reported, "It's like falling into the belly of a whale."

"It feels as if a wolf keeps eating my intestines," said a Traveler about his abdominal pain, "each time they grow back only to be eaten again." "That arm is quite angry," said another, "it's screaming 'go away, go away, leave me alone.'"

A Traveler complaining of chest pain had the impression of a small coin pouch with its drawstring pulled tight. Relaxing the muscles around her collar bone was like loosening the drawstring. She then reached into the purse and one by one pulled out a coin. Each coin was inscribed with one emotion. I asked yet another Traveler to find that part of herself that remained unscathed throughout her years of abuse. She pointed to a place near her heart and said, "There's a small spark here but it's covered up by so much dirt. I'd like to remove that dirt and rekindle the flame."

Dragons and demons live in our hearts and minds—and in our bodies as well. The hero's or heroine's task is to slay them wherever they are found. For a dragon left untouched lives on only to rise up again and terrorize the land it roams. However, not just dragons and demons roam this land. Here we also find angels and champion spirits, the benevolent forces aiding our heroes or heroines in overcoming the obstacles they confront.

When I asked one Traveler about the tightness in her throat, she responded, "This area has a lot of fear. It's afraid to allow my creativity to be expressed. It's afraid to let out who I really am."

"Close your eyes and scan your body from head to toe," I suggested. "Can you find an area where that creativity resides?"

"Yes," she said, "in my pelvis."

"If your pelvis had a voice," I continued, "what would it say to you right now?"

"It says that it is tired of being held back and held down," the Traveler offered. "It's tired of not being allowed to express itself."

"What's it like for your throat to hear your pelvis say that," I asked.

"My throat says to my pelvis: Be quiet!" she exclaimed. "It's scared and doesn't want to hear that message." This traveler then hosted a dialogue between the two parts of herself expressed in her body, her creative, authentic self (represented by her pelvis), and a part fearful of that creativity and authenticity (represented by her tight throat). She also had a history of sexual abuse. Consequently, her pelvis—the seat of her biological creativity—felt unsafe and vulnerable. Through this dialogue she discovered the neck tightness to be a displaced attempt to protect her pelvis.

"It doesn't feel safe for me to express my creativity," she said, "that's why my throat is so tight. It's been protecting me all this time. If I create a safe place for my pelvis, my throat says it will then relax."

A Journey Through the Body

Judith, a woman thirty-five years old, actually embarked on a journey through her body. She was very distraught the day I saw her. "I'm very confused," she lamented, "nothing seems to be working in my life."

I asked her if there was an area of her body that expressed the confusion and chaos she felt in her life. "Yes," she said after mentally scrutinizing her body, "it's an area under my right shoulder blade."

I gently touched that area and asked her to be aware of the sensations she had there. "It's tight, painful, and in spasm," she noted, "just the way I feel right now."

I continued by asking her, "Can you find an area of your body that feels the way you would feel in the absence of this tightness, pain, and confusion?" Judith located this second area in her upper abdomen just below her rib cage. "What's it like there?" I inquired. "Relaxed, warm and peaceful," she replied.

"Now find a path between your shoulder blade and stomach," I requested. "What route would that follow?" She said this path would go down her back and follow the bottom of her rib cage across and around to her stomach. I invited her to take this journey from shoulder blade to stomach with me.

Slowly and gently, I kneaded Judith's muscles and skin in the direction she had laid out. Our only agreement was that at any time if she felt I was moving too quickly, she could ask me to stop. Likewise if I felt we were moving too quickly, I could ask her to stop.

I continually monitored the tension in her body as I kneaded her soft tissue. At times I could feel an area of her body tighten under my hands. "We need to stop here for a moment," I'd let her know. "What's going on under my hand, Judith?"

Judith would then tell me what she experienced physically: tension, pain, burning, itching, or some other sensation. She also focused on the emotions related to those physical sensations: anger, grief, fear, or shame, for example. I would lightly hold this area, while she stayed with the feelings there. Eventually the feeling would dissolve and I could sense her body soften and relax under my hand. I'd give the go-ahead to continue the journey. We did this all the way from her shoulder to her upper abdomen. At the conclusion of this journey Judith remarked, "I feel as if I've made a huge transition from a confused and chaotic part of myself to a much clearer and calmer part."

AN AGE-OLD DRAMA
The script is ready and the actors present on the stage of this mythological drama. Malevolent forces are blocking the advance of our heroine or hero, and benevolent forces are impelling our protagonist toward victory and reward. These mythological forces symbolize the unconscious forces within our bodies and minds. In every mythic battle fought by a hero or heroine across time are echoes of the internal struggles we face on our journey of healing and recovery.

RECLAIMING THE INNER CHILD
Conquering the fearsome creatures of this realm by no means ends the journey. Overcoming these obstacles merely prepares the Traveler for receiving the journey's first reward: reclamation of the wounded inner child. Traditional mythology has no single representation of the wounded inner child. Although this is a modern-day notion, it is rooted in our mythological past.

In fact, the wounded inner child is a myth we have created for our journey of healing and recovery. But mythology is not fiction. Mythology is the outer display of the inner human drama. The mythological wounded inner child represents that part of ourself—body, mind, and soul—that unfolded in a corrupt and incomplete manner during our earliest formative years. While the phrase may reflect modern thinking, the drama of the inner child is as ancient as human history. All men and women are born of human flesh. All have had to negotiate the stormy waters from birth to becoming an independent, separate self. None have emerged from this journey without scars and trauma. So the mythological journey sets aside a separate phase for rediscovering this wounded inner child and making it whole again.

The Mythology of the Inner Child

Parental figures are the main actors in the drama of the inner child. On the mythological journey our hero or heroine must ultimately face symbolic representation of Mother and Father. Unlike the dragons and demons of the previous phase, these figures are not to be slain or conquered. Campbell describes this as "meeting with the Goddess" and "atonement with Father." Rather than overcoming these forces, our hero or heroine must come to terms with them, for they have shaped, and continue to shape, our adventurer's destiny.

The Great Goddess or Universal Mother often appears first as a repulsive hag categorically rejected by all but the hero. Somehow he is able to look beyond her external appearance. Then upon giving her a kiss, she is magically transformed into a beautiful princess. Enraptured, they wed and travel off together. This basic theme—with many different mythological manifestations—symbolizes an important inner milestone for a child: the ability to wed or integrate conflicting aspects of Mother.

In a previous chapter we explored the world of the newborn, a world encompassed by a central mothering figure. Mother was, and we needed her to be, the consummate seductress—all-beautiful, all-good, all-young, all-nurturing, all-pervasive. Time banishes this image to the deeper recesses of our unconscious mind, where it lingers in suspended animation. Not long after struggling to separate from mother physically in birth, we struggle to separate from her psychologically in self. We've already seen that during this psychological birth our inner child receives its wings and its wounds.

In mythological terms we must reckon with the beautiful seductress—the one in whose presence personal boundaries and sense of self melt away. We must also reckon with the hag—who hampers, forbids, punishes, and even abuses. Successfully integrating this split image is an important step toward the emergence of our separate self and healthy inner child. When unsuccessful, we may need to return to this period later in life, retracing, and reworking the steps we missed. This is the mythological significance of the hero or heroine "meeting with the Goddess."

ATONEMENT WITH THE FATHER

Atonement with the Father finds the hero or heroine passing through the realm of the Good and Evil Witches (conflicting mother images) to the threshold of a grand kingdom. There the hero or heroine undergoes the trials and fires of initiation. For the image of the Father is also twofold: the sun-god and the storm-god. While one god brings forth light and life represented by the sun, the other rains down terror and fear as thunder and lighting. One aspect challenges, the other aspect accepts the existence of the hero or heroine. Often the initiatory challenge must be weathered before the life-giving acceptance is found.

In the Navaho tale of Spider Woman and the Twin Brothers, the father image is the Sun. The Twin Brothers, heroes of this journey, venture through many hardships to reach the house of the Sun, their father. When he returns, the Sun denies his paternity and subjects the two to many dangerous ordeals. With the help of animals, natural forces, and amulets given them by Spider Woman (here the Good Mother), they withstand these challenges. Finally they are accepted by a proud Sun who asks, "Now, my children what is it you want from me? Why do you seek me?"

Here is the reflected struggle of our inner child: while separating from Mother is crucial, so too is meeting the challenge and gaining acceptance of Father. The challenge is an opportunity for the child to assert itself in the larger world beyond Mother, a world symbolically represented in the Father. Acceptance says to the child, "Who you are in this world is all right." It is a message of comfort, support, and hope. Unfortunately, we frequently receive just the opposite message as children. This nonacceptance, often punctuated by abuse and neglect, adds to our inner child's wounds. Mythology provides a way to capture this challenge and acceptance of oneself in the world. And this is a healing gift we must also give our wounded inner child.

Each stage of the mythological journey is preparation for the next stage. Atonement with the Father readies the hero or heroine for crossing the journey's final threshold, the border between human and spiritual experience. To do this the hero or heroine must come to know the material world as it really is. Mother is symbolic of the material world. Father is symbolic of intimate and ultimate knowledge of that world.

The material world is polarized—good and bad, dark and light, love and hate, rich and poor. While the image of the Universal Mother symbolizes this split world personally, the Universal Father symbolizes these dualities globally. There is the interesting statue of the Hindu god Siva dancing the dance of the world symbolic of the Universal Father. While one hand holds the gesture of "fear not," the other hand holds the fire of destruction. One foot stands on the demon of ignorance, the other foot is lifted, transforming ignorance to awareness and bliss. In one ear is a man's earring, in the other a woman's. In Siva's hair is the skull of death as well as the crescent moon of birth and bounty. Siva's gaze is complacent and serene in the midst of this chaos and turmoil.

EMBODYING FORGIVENESS

The world our hero or heroine inherits is often unfair and unjust—a world of tumult and turmoil. Our protagonist has struggled long and hard, and is soon to find a new, deeper insight into this world. The hero or heroine is about to take on Siva's gaze: serenity in the face of strife, tranquility in the face of turmoil. Atonement with the father means *at-one-ment* with the world as it is.

This is also the point of forgiveness on our personal journey of healing and recovery. It is the point at which we can give thanks that our personal situation in life, however dark and bleak, called us to begin the journey itself. It is a point at which we can look back and let go of hard struggles faced and won. Forgiveness is not a point we simply leap to—there are no detours on the hero's or heroine's journey.

I often ask Travelers to embody this phase of their healing journey through movement. I suggested that one group of workshop participants stand silently while imaging what it would be like to inhabit their mother's body. They were then given fifteen or twenty minutes to move around the room. Then they visualized their father's body, and moved around the room again. Finally they moved around as their ideal selves free to incorporate as much or as little of either parental image. Afterward we talked about the experience as a group.

"For the first time I really felt how much pain and anger my mother carried around," said one woman. "I know why I feared my father so much. His body was heavy with anger and guilt," said one man. "I'm amazed at how much of my mother's fearfulness and timidity I carry in my body," another participant noted. "I walk more like her then I ever knew." "My dad was a proud man," someone else added. "He carried himself with dignity. I like that. I began to incorporate his stride and it felt good."

Patterns of behavior run through families, generation after generation. We benefit from the positive, healthy family patterns and struggle against the dysfunctional, unhealthy ones. As we reach within to reclaim and heal our wounded inner child, we encounter the effects of these family dynamics. To heal our inner child on this journey, we must meet the Goddess and the Father in body as well as mind.

Apotheosis: The Final Gift

The final conquest of the hero or heroine is often symbolized by the discovery and retrieval of an object or a person: a rescued princess; the recaptured and sacred sword; repossession of the Holy Grail; the lost jewel that is found; the stolen treasure that is recovered; finding and drinking the magical elixir. Like all elements of myth, however, these are symbolic references to a much larger truth. The ultimate conquest, the journey's final gift, is neither person nor object. Instead it is a gift of spirit. This is not a spiritual gift in the ordinary sense; not a religious doctrine or dogma that the hero finds. This gift of spirit allows the mythic traveler to see beyond the immediate reality of the journey. Thus the hero or heroine is enlightened through revelation of the ultimate meaning and purpose in the trials and obstacles encountered along the way. Campbell called this final gift *apotheosis,* which mythologically means the exaltation of a mortal to the ranks of the gods.

Mythologically this final stage is often represented as the union of male and female form and energy. In Hindu mythology enlightenment is represented by the union of Siva (universal male form and energy) and Shakti (universal female form and energy). In Buddhism it is the union of Yang (male) and Yin (female). In certain African traditions it is represented by a hermaphroditic figure with a male face, a female upper body, and male genitals. In Christianity it is represented by ringing the bell at Mass along with the verse, "And the Word was made flesh."

Why this motif? The hero or heroine has moved beyond the previous phase of the journey, beyond meeting with the Goddess and atonement with the Father. Our traveler is now set to receive the final gift: the experience and knowledge that Goddess and Father are one. Symbolically, this is the sought-after goal of the great religious and spiritual traditions, a vision of God as the unity beyond duality, the wholeness beneath fragmentation, and the sacred union of worldly opposites. This is the experience of enlightenment, the "peace that surpasseth all

228 . . . DR. CLYDE W. FORD

peace" in Christianity, the "Supreme Bliss" of Hinduism, and the Buddhist state of "Nirvana."

On the journey of healing and recovery this is the enlightened step beyond forgiveness—the emergence of compassion for oneself and for others. It is the compassion we spoke of earlier, which finds wholeness beneath pain and suffering. It is a point at which we look back over our journey and realize the work we've done is about more than just getting well. It's about more than expressing deeply held emotions. It's about more than healing our wounded inner child. It's about more than forgiveness. All of this is the important work of recovery. But beyond recovery is the light, hope, and gift of compassion.

Compassion is the peace we've gained after weathering the storms of our journey. Compassion is the discovery of our connectedness to all we have encountered along the way—those who have helped us and those who may have harmed us as well. It is compassion that allows for a victim to be at one with the perpetrator or for one actor in a dysfunctional relationship to be at one with all the other actors in that relationship. Compassion is the realization that everyone is on this journey of healing and recovery, albeit at different stages. Some have just begun to awaken to their journey's call, while many have crossed the first threshold and are well along the way. Others are in denial and have yet to answer their journey's call.

Compassion is knowing that the journey of healing and recovery comes to no abrupt end. There will always be calls to answer, thresholds to cross, challenges to face, victories to win, and gifts of healing and recovery to claim. Compassion is knowing that we can answer the next call of our next journey. Compassion is all this, and more. It is an attitude of grace toward self and others that emerges from working with body and mind. Compassion cannot be reasoned out. It is not a philosophical or intellectual position that can be adopted or accepted. It is a living experience gained by meeting and passing the challenges and trials of the journey of healing and recovery. With this compassion comes the final empowerment of the hero or heroine. For the few Travelers I have been with at this stage of their healing and recovery the experience is riveting and powerful. In the previous chapter on sexual abuse I told the story of one Traveler, named Charlene, who reached this place of compassion and empowerment through her body.

CLAIMING THE JOURNEY'S VICTORY

With the receipt of this final gift the summit has been reached. The hero or heroine's task takes on a different quality. The dilemma then becomes when, and if, and how to travel back down the mountain, and whether to return to the ordinary surroundings left so long ago. It is a problem many of us know if we have spent long periods in prayer or meditation, or in an intensive time of insight, introspection, and growth. As we re-enter our ordinary world, we feel ourselves cloaked again in layer upon layer of mundane experience. These layers are the thresholds through which the hero or heroine must return.

In some myths the heroine returns to enlighten the community from which she departed. In other myths the hero cannot bear to leave the land of exaltation discovered at the journey's end. In either case the hero or heroine becomes the beacon by which others are inspired to answer the call. So this journey of the spirit renews itself again and again.

The mythological journey of the hero or heroine is a universal tale that parallels our personal journey of healing and recovery. Set against this world mythology our personal healing journey takes on new meaning. We are not alone, for on this path of recovery and healing we walk with the heroes and heroines of all time. We are summoned by them to tell our story, to fashion our journey into a heroic tale rather than a victim's lament. World mythology becomes personal mythology as the power of the myth empowers our life. This is our call to a compassionate journey of healing and recovery.

Appendix I. Body Assessment Form

Front   Back

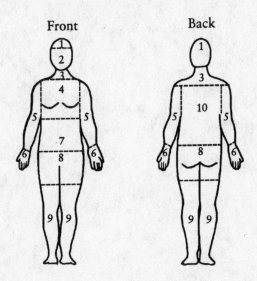

BODY AREA	ASSESSMENT/OBSERVATIONS/COMMENTS
1. Head/Forehead	
2. Face	
3. Neck Shoulders	
4. Upper Torso/Chest	
5. Arms	
6. Hands	
7. Lower Torso/Abdomen	
8. Pelvis/Buttocks/Thigh	
9. Legs	
10.Back	

APPENDIX 2. A SAMPLE RELAXATION SCRIPT

This sample relaxation script can be used as it is written or modified to suit individual tastes. It begins by observation of one's breath, then incorporates one's body and mind in the relaxation, and finally mobilizes one's inner awareness symbolized by a light. If you are using this relaxation as the Guide, then slowly pace yourself as you read it to the Traveler. Allow the Traveler time to incorporate each suggested step of the relaxation before continuing.

A GUIDED RELAXATION

Bring your awareness to your breathing and just observe your breath. Try not to control your breathing, just allow it to deepen naturally. With each exhalation imagine that you are breathing out stress, tension, and discomfort. With each inhalation imagine that you are breathing in a gentle wave of relaxation that crests at your head and flows softly down your body to your feet. Feel your relaxed body as it sinks into the surface you are resting upon.

Now, allow your mind to follow your body into relaxation. Feel that your mind is a leaf falling from the branch of a tree into a pond below. Watch the leaf as it gently floats through the air and comes to rest on the surface of this calm, quiet, clear pond. Let your mind find a similar calm, quiet, clear place to rest.

As your body and mind relax and let go, allow your awareness to be drawn deeper within. Imagine you could travel to the center of your being. Your center could be located in the middle of your chest, in your abdomen, in the space between your eyes, or in some other part of you. Wherever you feel this center, draw your attention there. From this center, notice a dim light that grows stronger and brighter. Watch this light as it grows to illuminate the entire inside of your body—from head to toes. Feel this light illuminate your mind and your thoughts, your heart and your emotions, your entire being. Once you are filled with this light, allow it to radiate out from you into the world around you.

REFERENCES

An annotated reference for the sources cited in the text follows. This reference guide is organized on a chapter-by-chapter basis. It includes bibliographic information, suggested additional reading, and comments about the source material.

Chapter 1. The Embodiment of Healing and Recovery

For additional information on touch, emotions, and the body, see *Where Healing Waters Meet: Touching Mind and Emotion Through the Body* by Clyde Ford (Barrytown, NY: Station Hill, 1989). Also see *Touching: Body Therapy and Depth Psychology* by D. A. McNeely (Toronto: Inner City Books, 1987) and *Touching: The Human Significance of the Skin* by Ashley Montagu (New York: Harper & Row, 1984). For a review of the work of William James, psychiatrist Donald Nathanson, and Silvan Tomkins on the body, biology, and emotions see *Brain/Mind Bulletin*, vol. 16. nos. 4–7. For source material from these

236 . . . DR. CLYDE W. FORD

authors, see *Principles of Psychology* by William James (New York: Holt, Rinehart & Winston, 1890); the three-volume set entitled *Affect Imagery Consciousness* by Silvan Tomkins (New York: Springer Publishing, 1962, 1963, 1991); "The Project for the Study of Emotions" by Donald L. Nathanson, M.D., in *Pleasure Beyond the Pleasure Principle,* eds. Robert A. Glick and Stanley Bone (New Haven: Yale University, 1990). Very enjoyable, nontechnical reading about neurological disorders can be found in all of Oliver Sacks's books. The account of Tourette's syndrome was taken from Sacks's book *The Man Who Mistook His Wife for a Hat* (New York: Harper & Row, 1985).

A good overview of the role of the body in psychotherapy is given by Thomas Pruzinsky, "Somatopsychic Approaches to Psychotherapy and Personal Growth" in *Body Images: Development, Deviance and Change* (New York: Guilford, 1990). You'll also find useful information on this topic in Carl Roger's works: *On Personal Power* (New York: Delacorte, 1977); *On Becoming a Person* (Boston: Houghton-Mifflin, 1961); *Client-Centered Therapy* (Boston: Houghton-Mifflin, 1965). Little has been written about the body's role in healing from sexual abuse; see the references for Chapter 5.

There is a growing body of work in the general field of somatics, which encompasses body-based analysis of a wide range of human endeavors from religion to politics. For an overview of the field, see Morris Berman's *Coming to Our Senses: Body and Spirit in the Hidden History of the West* (New York: Bantam, 1990).

On compassion, the writing of Vietnamese scholar–monk Thich Nhat Hanh is recommended: *The Miracle of Mindfulness* (Boston: Beacon, 1987); and *The Sun My Heart* (Berkeley: Parallax, 1988). Buddhist teachings about compassion and emotion are described by U Silananda in *The Four Foundations of Mindfulness* (Boston: Wisdom, 1990) and William Hart's *Vipasana Meditation in the Style of the S. N. Goenka* (New York: Harper & Row, 1976).

Chapter 2. The Neurobiology of Compassionate Touch

Cartesian dualism is discussed in any text on Western philosophy. For a particularly readable account see T. Z. Lavine's *From Socrates to Sartre: The Philosophic Quest* (New York: Bantam, 1984). Ken Wilber explores the implications of Cartesian philosophy in *No Boundary* (Boston: Shambhala, 1981).

Basmajian's paper "Control and Training of Individual Motor Units" appeared in *Mind/Body Integration,* eds. Peper, Ancoli, and Quinn (New York: Plenum, 1979). This is a good reference collection on biofeedback. Also see Elymer and Alyce Green's classic work *Beyond Biofeedback* (New York: Delacorte, 1979) and *Supermind* by Barbara Brown (New York: Harper & Row, 1980).

On imagery and healing see J. Achterberg's *Imagery in Healing* (Boston: Shambhala, 1985); *Imagery and Disease* (Champaign, IL: Institute for Personality and Ability Testing, 1984); and C. O. and S. M. Simonton's *Getting Well Again* (Los Angeles: J. P. Tarcher, 1978).

There is a growing body of literature on psychoneuroimmunology. For an overview see "Mind, Molecules and Emotions" in *Smithsonian Magazine,* December 1987. Other sources: D. M. Levin and G. F. Solomon, "The Discursive Formation of the Body in the History of Medicine" in *Journal of Medicine and Philosophy,* vol. 15, 1990; *Psychoneuroimmunology,* ed. Robert Ader (New York: Academic Press, 1981); *Foundations of Psychoneuroimmunology,* eds. Locke et al. (Hawthorne, NY: Aldine Publishing Company, 1985); *Journal of Neuroscience Research,* vol. 18, no. 1, 1986; "A Brief Tour of Psychoneuroimmunology" by D. Darko, in *Annals of Allergy,* vol. 57, no. 4, 1986, pp. 233–38; and Candace Pert's synopsis of her early work in this field, "The Wisdom of the Receptors: Neuropeptides, the Emotions, and the Bodymind" in *Advances,* vol. 3, no.3, 1986, pp. 8–16.

Karl Pribram's contribution to the neurosciences is vast and impressive. He has been called the "Magellan of brain research." An overview of his research on the amygdala appears in *Languages of the Brain* (Englewood Cliffs, NJ: Prentice-Hall, 1971) and *Brain and Perception* (Hillsdale, NJ: Lawrence Erlbaum, 1991). Pribram is best known for his holographic hypothesis of brain function. The exercise about writing one's name with different parts of the body comes from his discussions on holographic function. For additional information on holography and the brain see his two books previously mentioned. Two nontechnical and thoroughly readable accounts on the same subject are "A New Perspective on Reality" in *Brain/Mind Bulletin*, vol. 2, no. 26, 1977, and "Holographic Memory" in *Psychology Today*, February 1979.

On the body's role in repression see Michael Washburn's *Ego and the Dynamic Ground* (Albany: SUNY, 1988). Bachy-Rita's experiments with the blind are described in his book *Brain Mechanisms in Sensory Substitution* (New York: Academic Press, 1972) and "Tactile Vision Substitution: Past and Present" in *International Journal of Neuroscience,* vol. 19, 1983, pp. 29–36. M. A. Clements, et al. report their work with tactile substitution for the deaf in "Tactile Communication of Speech: Comparison of Two Computer-based Displays" in *Journal of Rehabilitation Research and Development,* vol. 25, no. 4, 1988, pp. 25–44. For Békésy's experiments on the skin see *Sensory Inhibition* (Princeton: Princeton University Press, 1967). His research also helped Karl Pribram develop a holographic theory of brain function. Also see D. Krieger's *Therapeutic Touch* (Englewood Cliffs, NJ: Prentice-Hall, 1979). John Zimmerman's results with the magnetic fields of healers and subjects were reported by personal communication. For a review of his work see "New Technologies Detect Effects of Healing Hands" in *Brain/Mind Bulletin,* vol. 10, no. 16, 1985.

Chapter 3. The Body Crucible

Margaret Mahler's *The Psychological Birth of the Human Infant* (New York: Basic Books, 1975) is still the classic work on the subject of psychological development. Perhaps the largest caution to this field is its cultural dependence. While many of the same phases of development occur cross-culturally, a decidedly different emphasis is given. Jean Liedloff in *The Contin-uum Concept* (Harmondsworth, England: Penguin Books, 1986) reports on the role of being held in the psychological development of the Yequana Indians of Brazil. Among these indigenous people an infant is literally held by someone twenty-four hours a day for the first two years of life. The gap between body and mind, self and other so endemic to the Western psyche does not exist in this culture.

Recent research in this field disputes the actual times of when each developmental phase is achieved. For example, some say the period of initial bonding of the infant and mother is much earlier than Mahler believed. In utero, and right after birth, newborns are sensitive to a variety of different stimuli, which some researchers say show a greater degree of individu-ation than Mahler accepted. However, the basic sequence of psychological development proposed by Mahler is documented in her work and the work of others.

Mahler's quoted material comes from *The Psychological Birth of the Human Infant*. For additional material see Mahler and McDevitt, "Thoughts on the Emergence of the Sense of Self with Particular Emphasis on the Body Self" in *Journal of the American Psychoanalytic Association,* vol. 30, no. 4, 1982, p. 837; Morris Berman's *Coming to Our Senses* (New York: Ban-tam, 1990), especially the first chapter; Ken Wilber's chapters in *Transformations of Consciousness* (Boston: Shambhala, 1986) place Mahler's work in the context of consciousness research. The work of Ashley Montagu is also invaluable for understand-ing the importance of touch on the life of the newly born infant. See his classic work *Touching: The Human Significance of the Skin* (New York: Harper & Row, 1984). The sequence by which a mother first touches her child was reported by Montagu in this book. H. Stephen Glenn's anecdote was recorded at one of his workshops; also see his book *Raising Self-Reliant Children in a Self-Indulgent World* (Rocklin, CA: Prima, 1989).

Several theories of personality disorders are based around the work of Mahler and the school of psychological develop-mentalists. James F. Masterson's *The Search for the Real Self: Unmasking the Personality Disorders of Our Age* (New York:

Macmillan, 1988) is a highly readable account of borderline and narcissistic personality disorders (the Lost Satellite and the Submerged Self) by a leader in the treatment of these problems. Also see *Borderline Conditions and Pathological Narcissism* by O. *Kernberg* (New York: Jason Aronson, 1975); H. Kohut's *The Restoration of the Self* (New York: International Universities Press, 1977); *Borderline Psychopathology and Its Treatment* by G. Adler (New York: Jason Aronson, 1985).

The remarks on the body as the sage within the temple come from the writings of Thich Nhat Hanh, *The Sun My Heart* (Berkeley: Parallax, 1988).

Chapter 4. Touching the Child Within

Charles L. Whitfield's popular book, *Healing the Child Within: Discovery and Recovery for Adult Children of Dysfunctional Families* (Deerfield Beach, FL: Health Communications, 1987) is a good starting point for material on the inner child. Other sources: two books by Claudia Black, *It Will Never Happen to Me* (New York: Ballantine, 1987) and *Double Duty* (New York: Ballantine, 1990); John Bradshaw's *Bradshaw on the Family: A Revolutionary Way of Self-Discovery* (Deerfield Beach, FL: Health Communications, 1988); Melody Beattie's *Beyond Codependency* (Center City, MN: Hazelden, 1989); Jacqui Bishop and Mary Grunte's *How To Love Yourself When You Don't Know How: Healing All Your Inner Children* (Barrytown, NY: Station Hill Press, 1992); *Beyond Codependency: And Getting Better All the Time* by Melody Beattie (New York: Prentice Hall, 1990).

For William Condon's work with micromotion analysis of movement, see "Multiple Response to Sound in Dysfunctional Children" in *Journal of Autism and Childhood Schizophrenia*, vol. 5, no. 1, 1975, pp. 37–56.

Chapter 5. Safe Touch: The Somatic Reality of Sexual Abuse and Recovery

There is little written specifically on the subject of using touch to work with survivors of sexual abuse. Most enlightened therapists recognize the need for somatic work with survivors, but some still oppose any use of touch in therapy. On the general subject of sexual abuse: Ellen Bass and Laura Davis wrote the comprehensive guide *The Courage to Heal: A Guide for Women Survivors of Child Sexual Abuse* (New York: Harper & Row, 1988); see also Laura Davis's *The Courage to Heal Workbook* (New York: Harper & Row, 1988); Eliana Gil's two books, *Outgrowing the Pain* (New York: Dell, 1988) and *Treatment of Adult Survivors of Childhood Abuse* (Walnut Creek, CA: Launch Press, 1990); and Claudia Black's two books, *Double Duty* and *It Will Never Happen to Me* (see the references for Chapter 4). The SAFE TOUCH protocol is available as a poster from ISTAR, P.O. Box 3056, Bellingham, WA 98227. Pribram's research with the amygdala is reviewed in *Languages of the Brain and Brain and Perception* (see the references for Chapter 2).

Chapter 6. The Art of Compassionate Touch

For information on orientation, habituation, and related neurophysiology see the two books by Karl Pribram mentioned in the references for Chapter 2. Manfred Clyne's work appears in his book *Sentics: The Touch of Emotions* (Garden City, NY: Avery, 1989). Joseph Weiss's study of psychotherapy appeared in *Scientific American,* March 1990.

For scientific studies on intention, see William A. Tiller's, "A Gas Discharge Device for Investigating Focused Human Attention" in *Journal of Scientific Exploration,* vol. 4, no. 5, 1990, pp. 255–71; a review of Nash's work with bacteria, which appeared in *Brain/Mind Bulletin,* vol. 9, no. 15, 1984; and Braud's work with electrodermal activity (EDA), which was reviewed in *Brain/Mind Bulletin,* vol. 9, no. 16, 1984.

On the Einstein–Podolsky–Rosen paradox, see Gary Zukav's *The Dancing Wu Li Masters* (New York: Bantam, 1980); *Space, Time and Medicine* by Larry Dossey (Boston: Shambhala, 1981); *In Search of Reality* by Bernard d'Espagnat (New York: Springer-Verlag, 1983).

Chapter 7. The Compassionate Journey

Joseph Campbell's extensive writings on mythology were the source for most of this chapter; see especially *A Hero With a Thousand Faces* (Princeton: Princeton University Press, 1972) and *The Power of the Myth* (New York: Bantam, 1988). Thich Nhat Hanh's quote comes from *The Sun My Heart,* for this and additional sources on compassion see the references for Chapter 1. Erwin Schroedinger's quote is from his book *My View of the World* (London: Cambridge University Press, 1962).

INDEX

Braud, William, 183
Breathing, 70
Buddhism, 43, 174, 196–97, 211–212, 227, 228

Call
  answering of, 211–12
  refusing of, 213–15
Campbell, Joseph, 209, 211, 223, 227
Caretaking, 111–12
Cells
  glial, 54–55
  skin, 177–78
  in visual system, 177, 178
Change, readiness for, 181–82
Checking in, by Traveler, 199
Child within, *see* Inner child
Cholecystokinin (CCK), 53–54
Christianity, 227, 228
Claiming journey's victory, 229
Clements, M. A., 63
Client session, transcript of, 161–166
  see also Traveler(s)
Clinging, 89–90
Clues, within body, 35–37
Clynes, Manfred, 179–80
Codependency, 111–12
Communication, through skin, 63–65
Compassion
  in ancient wisdom and modern thought, 43–44
  attitude of, 44–45
  and healing, 41–42
  nature of, 228–29
  path of, 42
Compassionate journey, 209–29
Compassionate touch, 39–40, 44
  art of, 173–208
  neurobiology of, 47–72
Conditioned response, 51–52
Condon, William S., 126–27
Containment, emotional, 120–22
Controlling physical and psychological boundaries, 60–61
Controversy, in recovery, 25–26

Coping, with abuse, by turning off body, 141–42
Countering, 178, 179
Countertransference, 27
Crack in the egg, 77–78
Crossing the threshold, 215–16
Crucible, body, 21–23, 73–106
  exploring of, 99
Curaceptive reflex, 48

Dance of life, 74–75, 76–77, 83, 88–98
  steps of, 80
Denial, of separateness, 90
Depth
  of pain, 40–41
  of touch, 176–77
Descartes, René, 49
Description of events, by inner child, 108
The Diagnostic and Statistical Manual of Mental Disorders (DSM-III-R), 134–35
Dialogue, with image of inner child, 108
Dissociation, 118–20, 134–35, 136
  Safe Touch for assessment of, 154, 164–66
Dorsal horn, 55
Dragons, slaying of, 218–21
Drama, age-old, 222
Duration, of touch, 178
Dysfunction
  safety and familiarity of, 216–217
  two studies in, 97–98
Dysfunctional behavior, body's role in, 98–99
Dysfunctional emotional cycles, 117–23
Dysfunctional relationships, 29
  embodiment of, 126–32

Einstein, Albert, 43, 183–85
Einstein–Podolsky–Rosen (EPR) paradox, 183–85
Electrical activity of skin (EDA), 183

Tactile Visual Substitution System, 63
Talking, about feelings, by client, 108
Talking hands, 69–71
Tapes, 108
Technique, touching beyond, 207–8
Technique maze, 174–76
Telling about feelings, by inner child, 108
Temple, sage within, 106
Therapeutic rapport, Safe Touch for building, 154–55
Therapeutic Touch, 67
Therapist(s)
feelings of, about abuse, 149
Safe Touch and, 156–57
see also Guide(s)
Therapy
audiovisual (AV), 108
somatic, see Somatic therapy
somatoemotional, 24
verbal, moving beyond, 20
see also Interventions; Treatment
Thigmotaxis, 47
Thigmotropism, 47
Things, realm of, 49
Thought(s)
modern, compassion in, 43–44
realm of, 49
Three generations, bodies of, 127–32
Threshold, crossing of, 215–16
Tiller, William, 182
Touch
compassionate, see Compassionate touch
conveying meaning through, 178–79
depth of, 176–77
duration of, 178
and emotional recall, 27
and healing, as instinctual human capacity, 48–49
language of, 176–78
right of bonding through or separating through avoidance of, 113–14

role of, in recovery, 25–26
safe place to, 100–102
safe, see Safe touch
self-, 29
simple, 101–3
influence of, 105–6
Touching: The Human Significance of the Skin, 77
Touching
beyond technique, 207–8
of child within, 107–32
of mind and emotion, through body, 29–31
Tourette's syndrome, 35, 36
Traditional proverb, 73
Transcript, of client session, 161–166
Transference, 27
Trauma, body in, 81–82
Traveler(s), 37–39, 42, 43, 44–45, 99–106, 151–52, 154, 172, 178–79, 181, 185–94, 197–204, 207, 208, 215, 216, 218, 219–20, 226, 228–29
see also Client session
Treatment
of abuse, somatic process in, 160–61
of sexual abuse, integration of body and mind in, 136–37
see also Interventions; Therapeutic entries
Trust, Safe Touch for creation of, 155
Turning off body, coping with abuse by, 141–42
Twelve-Step programs, 93, 213
Twin Brothers, 224

Unconditional positive regard, 44
Universal Father, 225
Universal Mother, 223, 225
University of Colorado, 67

Validation, in creation of body map, 192–93
Verbal therapy, moving beyond, 20

Safe touch protocol 147 ...
            practice
- Cat 49